PLAYING FOR TIME

PLAYING FOR TIME

Guido Schmidt and the
Struggle for Austria

Richard Bassett

Anthony Eyre
MOUNT ORLEANS PRESS

Published in Great Britain in 2022
by Anthony Eyre, Mount Orleans Press
23 High Street, Cricklade sn6 6ap
www.anthonyeyre.com

© Richard Bassett 2022

Richard Bassett has asserted his right to be
identified as the author of this work in accordance with
the Copyright, Designs and Patents Act 1988.

isbn 978-1-912945-37-5

A CIP record for this book is available
from the British Library

Printed in the uk by
Short Run Press

Contents

Acknowledgements

THIS, THE FIRST study of Austria's last Foreign Minister in the run-up to the Second World War, could never have been possible without the support of Guido Schmidt's descendants, notably his daughter-in-law Stephanie Schmidt-Chiari. Her generous hospitality in Vienna and St Anton made the rather daunting task of examining hundreds of documents a much more agreeable challenge. As often with long neglected family papers, the element of serendipity was never far distant from the task in hand and I can only attempt to describe here a fraction of the surprise and delight which accompanied our unwrapping of a bundle of newspapers from the 1930s which had long gathered dust in a St Anton attic, but in between whose pages had been carefully concealed the verbatim record of the initial 1945 interrogation of Guido Schmidt by the Allied prosecutors. *Meine Verantwortung* as this unique folder was entitled was only one of scores of fascinating documents which show the *Anschluss* of 1938 from a singularly illuminating perspective. In addition, there were cartons of private correspondence between 1935 and 1955, many bureaucratic and official memoranda and an extensive archive (uncatalogued) of political documentation.

In the interpretation of these documents, I have been immensely helped by my Austrian colleagues who shared their intellectual rigour and knowledge with a "foreigner." I am especially grateful to Professor Gerald Stourzh and Dr Erwin Schmidl. These two experts on the dramatic events in Austria of 1938 showed great patience with my questions as did Professor T.G. Otte who kindly read the early draft of this text and made invaluable suggestions for its improvement. I am also grateful to Wolfgang Neugebauer, Austria's expert on the indigenous resistance to the Nazis.

I am immensely in the debt of many other scholars who have guided my research. At Churchill College, Katharine Thomson demonstrated her encyclopaedic knowledge of the archives there, in particular the Vansittart papers, which throw a fascinating light on the intimacy of the Anglo-Austrian diplomatic relationship as personified by Sir Robert Vansittart's at times rather controversial and even mischievous interaction with Dr Schmidt. The National Archives in Kew were as always of invaluable help but I should have found much of the annotation of Foreign Office papers puzzling had I not also enjoyed the guidance and forensic interpreting skills of Professor David Dilks, who on more than one occasion identified the author of some half illegible scrawl on a dispatch. Notwithstanding the near impenetrability of the handwriting, these "short sharp" comments often revealed the direction of debate within the Foreign Office more vividly than the actual document itself.

The Rothschild archives, despite certain significant gaps, proved that Guido Schmidt played absolutely no known role in the negotiations with the Austrian branch of the family in collaboration with attempts by Göring to requisition the Witkowitz steel works between 1938 and 1939. My thanks go to Lionel de Rothschild and Melanie Aspey and her team for their prompt and committed support for my research.

At Cambridge, I also benefited from the advice of my colleagues in the Forum for Geopolitics, notably Professor Brendan Simms and my friends in the history faculty, William O'Reilly and Helen Pfeiffer. I owe thanks also to John Jolliffe whose kinsman, Sir Michael Palairet, was the last British minister in Vienna before the German annexation. I am also grateful to Christopher Brennan, and my very longstanding friend Nella Gawrońska whose father was Polish ambassador in Vienna in 1938 and who witnessed the *Anschluss* as it occurred in Vienna. I am also tremendously grateful to Wenzel Meran-Kirpicsenko, Karl Eugen Czernin, John Nicholson and Kathleen Taylor.

In this context I should also perhaps mention Father Anthony Meredith SJ who over the years has given me perhaps a greater appreciation than anyone else of what a Jesuit education should aspire to. To him and the late Father Tony Barrett SJ, the late Father Ignatius St Lawrence SJ and the late Father Dick Randolph SJ I owe the benefits of their "well-furnished minds."

Although I was spared the rigours of the Cambridge history faculty as an undergraduate, my time there coincided with the late Professor Norman Stone who shared and encouraged in the 1970s my emerging enthusiasm for *Mitteleuropa*. I have also enjoyed many insights into the diplomacy of this period from the late Professor Owen Chadwick, the late Professor Anthony Blunt and the late Professor Ernst Gombrich.

A particular debt of thanks is due to my former horn and music teacher Dr W.H. Salaman who brought his considerable intellect and forensic editing skills to bear on the early drafts of this book. The entire text was checked with his usual scrupulous attention to detail by Sebastian Wormell before going to Anthony Eyre at the Mount Orleans Press who made an interesting book into a beautiful one.

Finally, it is my pleasure to thank the Master and Fellows of Christ's College for tolerating my disappearance for more or less two years while I immersed myself in the research required to do justice to the complex and intriguing Dr Guido Schmidt. My wife, Emma-Louise, and the rest of my family coped well with these protracted absences but of course without their unstinting support the task of writing this book would have proved utterly impossible.

Christ's College Cambridge, 1st October 2021

Abbreviations

Amery	Private papers of Leo Amery, Churchill College Cambridge.
GSN	Guido Schmidt *Nachlass* (private family and state papers in the possession of the Schmidt-Chiari family in Vienna and St Anton).
RA	Rothschild Archive, London.
DöW	Dokumentationsarchiv des österreichischen Widerstandes.
NA	National Archives (formerly Public Records Office) Kew, London.
FO	Foreign Office London (National Archives).
Avon	Private papers of Anthony Eden (National Archives).
Henderson	Private papers of Sir Nevile Henderson (National Archives).
HVPGGS	*Hochverratsprozess gegen Dr Guido Schmidt vor dem Wiener Volksgericht* (Proceedings of the Vienna People's Court, 1947).
SIS	Secret Intelligence Service Assessments (Vansittart Papers, Churchill College Cambridge).
HHStA	Haus-, Hof- und Staatsarchiv (Österreichisches Staatsarchiv, Vienna).
DBFP	*Documents on British Foreign Policy*.
SEL	Private papers of Sir Walford Selby (Oxford, Bodleian Libraries).
SHA	Service Historique de l'Armée de Terre, Vincennes.
PAL	Private correspondence of Sir Michael Palairet (Cambridge University Library).
IMT	International Military Tribunal (Nuremberg).
VNST	Papers of Sir Robert Vansittart (Churchill College Cambridge).

Guido Schmidt's career: Timeline

1901	Born Bludenz, Vorarlberg, Austria.
1911–18	Stella Matutina Jesuit College in Feldkirch, Vorarlberg.
1918	Collapse and dissolution of the Austrian (Austro-Hungarian) Empire. First Republic proclaimed in Vienna.
1918–24	Law studies in Vienna (at the same time parallel commercial training); visits London, Berlin, Paris and Florence.
1924	Graduates *cum laude* with a doctorate in law from the University of Vienna. Passes out top of the *Konsularakademie* exams.
1925	Enrols in the Austrian Diplomatic Service; posted as junior voluntary *attaché* to Paris.
1927	Appointed to President Miklas's office (on the recommendation of Alfred Grünberger, Secretary for Foreign Affairs in Ignaz Seipel's government).
1928	Deputy Director of Presidential Cabinet.
1930	Head of Presidential Cabinet (*Chef du Cabinet*).
1931	Marries Maria Annunziata Chiari in Vienna (service conducted by Monsignor Ignaz Seipel, former Chancellor of Austria).
1933	Hitler seizes power in Germany. Schmidt joins the Fatherland Front of Chancellor Dollfuss.
1934	February: workers' uprising against the Dollfuss government in Vienna crushed by the Austrian army within a week. July: Chancellor Dollfuss assassinated by Austrian Nazis. Kurt Schuschnigg replaces him after a brief interlude.
1936	Schmidt plays a leading role in conclusion of the Austro-German Agreement of 11th July. Schmidt appointed State Secretary for Foreign Affairs. Travels with Schuschnigg to Budapest for the Funeral of Hungarian Prime

Minister Gömbös and meets Hermann Göring. A visit to Berlin and a secret correspondence between the two men ensue.

1937	Schmidt visits Venice with Chancellor Schuschnigg to meet with Ciano and Mussolini in the context of the "Rome Protocols."
	Schmidt visits London for the celebrations around the Coronation of George VI and meets again Sir Robert Vansittart whom he has first encountered in Geneva.
	Offers "Van" confidential confirmation concerning major security breach at British embassy in Rome.
1938	February: accompanies Chancellor Schuschnigg to Berchtesgaden for summit with Adolf Hitler.
	February: appointed Austrian Foreign Minister.
	March: Austrian Nazis seize power in Austria, Germany's troops cross into Austria, Hitler declares the *Anschluss*. Many of Schmidt's colleagues including the former Chancellor Schuschnigg are arrested or forced to commit suicide. The new Austrian Nazi Chancellor Seyss-Inquart offers Schmidt his old job back but Schmidt citing "honour and loyalty" refuses. Göring rescues Schmidt from certain arrest and offers him various state and diplomatic positions which Schmidt refuses.
	After failing to find any commercial employment in Austria, Schmidt approaches Göring again.
	April: Schmidt joins the Hermann Göring Works (HGW) as Director, responsible for shipping and mining.
1942	January: Schmidt is forced to make way for Göring's appointee and sets up a small consultancy trade business dealing in the export of white goods to neutral countries.
1944	February: returns to the HGW briefly to take over running of shipping division of Hermann Göring Works.
1945–46	Gives himself up to the French military authorities on their arrival in Vorarlberg. Transferred to US military forces who interrogate him and deploy him as a witness at the Nuremberg trials.
1947	Indicted for high treason by the People's Court of Vienna. Acquitted after a three month trial.
1950	Employed as director of the partly American-owned Austrian Semperit tyre company.
1957	5th December: death in Vorarlberg (aged 56).

The Guido Schmidt Papers

T HE ENGLISH HISTORIAN, even one with all the advantages of a background in the "old Austria," treads with trepidation into the most explosive chapter of Austria's twentieth century history, the so-called *Anschluss*. So much has been written about the events of March 1938 the reader might well ask what could there possibly be new to say? Enormous amounts of research into the subject line the shelves of every university history faculty library (and bookshop) in the world. Yet, despite the extensive coverage of the 1938 crisis and exhaustive analysis of Austria's foreign policy between 1936 and 1938, there are compelling reasons for renewed study. Many key documents in the British files were only released in 1989, after most of the protagonists in the dramas of Schuschnigg's government had died. These documents alone cast new light on the numerous post factum apologia of the Austrian Chancellor, Kurt Schuschnigg, his colleagues, including Guido Schmidt, and their international counterparts. As far as I have found, very few of these insights have been systematically examined by historians in either Britain or Austria. The British historian is traditionally sceptical of Austria and the Austrian historian rightly immersed in the archival detail sometimes fails to gauge fully the nuances of the British position. Yet a study of Guido Schmidt shows that London alone held the key to Austria's survival and only an examination of that dynamic can bring us closer to the truth of what motivated the Chancellor and his State Secretary of Foreign Affairs. Perhaps a *mischling* half-Austrian, half-British historian can succeed in highlighting some of these aspects so far overlooked, or undiscovered. The family papers of Guido Schmidt cover the period in exhaustive detail from a personal but also political perspective. There are many copies of state documents which include correspondence between members of the Schuschigg government and Schmidt. Among the many private papers are several state memoranda which display the workings of Schmidt's mind and his pivotal role in the events leading up to the *Anschluss*.

Dr Guido Schmidt's personality is therefore a significant factor in any understanding of the European drama of 1936–38. Yet one looks in vain for any serious work on his character and motivation outside the enormous documentation connected with his trial for high treason in 1947. Historians have long used this vast, now rather faded, green-bound text to fill in many of the gaps in the standard narrative of the events leading up to the *Anschluss*, the seizure of power by the Austrian Nazis and the annexation of Austria by Nazi Germany. Few have questioned the testimony despite the obvious distortions and economy with the *actualité* which marked nearly every contribution to this extraordinary show-trial. It was not only Nazis such as von Papen and Göring who lied in their evidence. A host of anti-Nazi characters such as Theodor Hornbostel and Johannes Schwarzenberg veered, understandably, on the side of "discretion" when they took the witness stand. As Alexander Lassner has written, "the failure of many scholars to see the enormous degree of deceit present in the European diplomatic record in general is but one stumbling block to our understanding."[1]

The British Foreign Office followed the trial minutely but no British diplomat was called upon to testify at the trial. Even when Schmidt was questioned on all the diplomats with whom he came into contact, he avoided mention of the British minister in Vienna in 1938, Michael Palairet, a diplomat who greatly distrusted Schmidt. Yet, as we shall see, the Austro-British relationship was crucial to Vienna's decision-making in March 1938. A good two weeks before Chancellor Schuschnigg revealed to his colleagues on 7th March his plan to call a referendum in a gamble to secure an overwhelming vote in favour of an independent Austria, it had

---

1   Alexander Lassner, "Peace at Hitler's price: Austria, the Great Powers and the *Anschluss* 1932–38," PhD thesis Ohio State University, 2001.

been debated at length by the mandarins of the Foreign Office on 23rd February in London. Then, the Austrians had apparently "ruled the idea completely out as unrealistic" but within a few days all that had changed. One mandarin in particular chose to throw his weight behind the idea and not for the first time did Sir Robert Vansittart ("Van") help shape the destiny of Austria, for better or ill. He had already moved Sir Walford Selby, the passionately pro-Austrian British minister, out of Vienna a few months before the crisis in order to replace him with the more pliant Palairet. The papers show that the idea which generally forms the standard historical narrative that Schuschnigg decided "spontaneously" to hold the referendum without external influence needs, at the very least, revisiting.

It is a moot point whether, but for the referendum, Hitler would have mobilised in March against Austria and whether the game of preserving Austria's independence might have continued for a few more months if there had been no referendum. The papers in the Schmidt *Nachlass* show that Schmidt was against the referendum idea and against Schuschnigg's rousing speech at Innsbruck in early March 1938. Schmidt shared Mussolini's well-known remark to the Austrian military *attaché* in Rome, Colonel Liebitsky, that the referendum was "*un errore,*" a "grenade" which would go off in Schuschnigg's and Austria's hand. Given the strength of the British support for the referendum such a point of view brought Schmidt into even greater conflict with the British minister in Vienna. Nevertheless, for all his personal reservations about the referendum, Schmidt loyally and effectively defended it up to the last moment in the face of increasing Nazi German pressure to cancel it or change its terms of reference.

The relationship between Vansittart and Schmidt is an intriguing one and sheds much light on how a small powerless European state is in times of crisis painfully dependent on the machinations of more powerful players in the European drama. Britain, Italy, Germany and France all had differing but significant interests at play in watching how the Austrian game unfolded. Ultimately Germany prevailed because the other states failed to coordinate effectively a policy which could preserve Austria's independence. But this failure should not be confused with neglect. A year before the *Anschluss* Schmidt had demonstrated that he was part of Vansittart's "informal intelligence gathering network," to use Ian Colvin's phrase. Schmidt had deliberately revealed to "Van" the Italian source of the most serious known breach of security at the Foreign Office in the entire run-up and prosecution of the war.[2] Given that Schmidt was supposedly faithful to the Rome Protocols which allied Austria to Italy and Hungary at the time, this was an indiscretion or "favour" which the official papers can only hint at.

Robert Vansittart's papers extensively catalogued by Churchill College Cambridge offer one line into the thorny issues of the "Austrian Question" as seen from the British perspective. The Guido Schmidt *Nachlass* offers much that illuminates the other side of this dynamic. Vansittart pursued a personal interest in Austria which suppressed the British minister in Vienna Walford Selby's advice and all his warnings concerning Austria. Selby was convinced that only a British guarantee of Austria's independence could save Austria from Germany and prevent Mussolini falling into the arms of Hitler, but for Van this was anathema to his own views which always saw the dialogue with Germany as the key. Therefore, he viewed Austria as a vehicle for more complex manoeuvres which could advance the Anglo-German understanding. This led to multiple misunderstandings in Vienna.

For Schmidt and Schuschnigg the theory that Britain could eventually create a system of informal guarantees for Austrian independence was persuasive. It was actively encouraged by Van. Other British diplomats and politicians took up the theme to the exclusion of other solutions. Vansittart, in Walford Selby's phrase, "paralysed the Foreign Office by his belief in his own infallibility." The Schmidt papers reflect this all too well.

The value of the Guido Schmidt *Nachlass* also stems from the fact that it seems by inference that some sensitive material concerning Britain, Germany and Austria was not written down in the Austrian state documents in late 1937 and early 1938 on account of the risk of Nazi espionage. It is clear that at least one member of Schmidt's staff was a Nazi sympathiser and informer.[3] After Berchtesgaden, the British Legation in

---

2　See Chapter 7 and Ian Colvin, *Vansittart in Office: The origins of World War II* (London, 1965).

3　Otto Peter-Pirkham, who accompanied Schmidt to Berchtesgaden and was a distant relative of the notorious Nazi Reinhard Spitzy is perhaps the most likely candidate

Vienna shared in these precautions, warning in a dispatch to London that "because of leakage no direct communication is possible with the Austrian government."[4]

On a more personal level, some of the *Nachlass* papers reveal views both Schmidt and Schuschnigg were understandably at pains to keep from the Nazis. For example, one letter from the Chancellor to his State Secretary makes a reference (just before Berchtesgaden) to Hitler as a man who "as Bismarck once remarked of the Bavarians, is something which is halfway between humanity and an Austrian."[5]

The late Nico Schmidt-Chiari, Guido's son and the former chairman of CreditAnstalt Bank, then Austria's foremost financial institution, assembled many documents which cast light on his father's career. It was Nico's wish that the material should receive serious scholarly treatment and that a narrative which, above all, sought to explain his father would emerge from this research. Unfortunately, he is no longer alive to pass judgement on the modest efforts here but I hope he would have approved of its results, even though he might not have agreed entirely with all my conclusions concerning his father's conduct.

The material is of significant value to future historians of the *Anschluss*. It casts a new light on certain aspects of the 1938 crisis and it throws Dr Schmidt into the sharpest of reliefs. Undoubtedly there will be those among his detractors who will find yet more evidence of his egotism, ambition, "duplicity" and "double-dealing'. Rather than blindly join the stampede towards the swelled ranks of his critics—their number far exceeds today (as it did in 1938 and 1947) his supporters—I have tried to avoid the intellectually lazy blanket condemnation which attributes only at best venality and at worst treachery to his character. Rather I have tried to explain Guido Schmidt and his motivation. The reader can decide whether despite acquittal in 1947 for lack of evidence he remains morally condemned for his behaviour before and after the *Anschluss* or whether, like millions of other Austrians, he simply sought survival as best he could with the cards dealt him.

---

and most easily identifiable. See Chapter 13.

4   See Chapter 12.

5   GSN: Schuschnigg to Schmidt, 10 Feb. 1938.

INTRODUCTION

Guido Schmidt

IN THE RANKS of the numerous and colourful supporting cast who took the European stage in the run-up to the 1939–45 war, the personality of Guido Schmidt, Austria's last foreign minister before the *Anschluss*, has so far escaped any rigorous and detailed examination by historians. Those Austrian scholars who have tried to get to grips with him have rarely penetrated the surface of his complicated and rather highly strung personality. They have mostly preferred to join in the unquestioned drive towards opprobrium and denunciation. In this they are only expressing the conclusion which the post war Austrian media, the Soviet occupation forces and a surprisingly large number of Schmidt's former colleagues in the Austrian Foreign Ministry, as well as most Austrian Socialists, Austrian Legitimists, and even many British, Italian and French diplomats, believed well merited the accusation of high treason.

This remarkably broad consensus view holds that pre-war Austria's last Foreign Minister paved the way for the *Anschluss*, collaborated with high-ranking Nazis and sold his Chancellor and country down the river. When in 1947, Schmidt was put on trial precisely for that in Vienna, outside observers thought the entire pre-war Schuschnigg/Dollfuss system which had governed Austria in the 1930s was also under investigation. His acquittal after the three-month trial aroused a storm of controversy which continues in milder after-shocks among Austrian historians even to this day.

Schmidt was at the epicentre of Austro-German dialogue, and of Austria's relations with her other neighbours and the western powers, for barely two years, 1936–1938. Nevertheless, his influence over Austrian foreign policy during that short but critical period was immense. As he was one of the very few members of the Schuschnigg government to have avoided the concentration camps after the Nazi takeover, thanks to the personal intervention of Göring, the post-war accusations of his betraying not only his Chancellor but also his country were inevitable. But it did not help that Schmidt, even by the standards of those febrile times, made enemies in every political camp. Statesmen and diplomats who could rarely agree on anything of political or strategic substance were almost unanimous in condemning Guido Schmidt.

Nevile Henderson, the passionately pro-German British Ambassador to Berlin, thought Schmidt had "long been the Nazi spy in Schuschnigg's camp all the time… Talk of Judas. He… lost no time in coming for his thirty pieces of silver."[6] For G.E.R. Gedye, the *Daily Telegraph* correspondent in Vienna and a stern critic of Henderson's, Schmidt was the man who brought Schuschnigg to the sacrificial altar of Berchtesgaden, betrayed Austria, his chief and "in reality was just pro-Guido Schmidt."

For Otto von Habsburg, the pretender to the Austrian throne and someone who also could never have agreed with Henderson on anything to do with Austria, Schmidt was "the only Austrian politician I refused point-blank to ever meet with during the run-up to the crisis."[7] For the Italian Foreign Minister, Galeazzo Ciano, Schmidt was the "man who betrayed us all."[8] The American ambassador in Vienna, George Messersmith, made no secret of his belief that Schmidt was a "crypto-Nazi" laying "all the ground work for the German invasion."[9] Most scathing of all perhaps was the British minister in Vienna in the weeks before the *Anschluss*, Michael Palairet. He wrote in a private letter to the Head of the Foreign Office, Sir Alexander Cadogan: "Should we not warn the (Austrian) Chancellor that his Foreign Minister is double-dealing."[10]

---

6   Henderson to Cadogan 16/3/39 FO800/269 Henderson papers.

7   Otto von Habsburg to author, 17 Oct. 1984. See also Egon and Heinrich Berger Waldenegg, *Biographie im Spiegel: die Memoiren zweier Generationen* (Vienna, 1998).

8   *Ciano's Diary 1937–1943* (London, 1947), p. 70 *et seq.* Ciano was commenting to Berger Waldenegg just after the *Anschluss*.

9   Messersmith dispatches: see Peter Broucek (ed.): *Feldmarschalleutnant Alfred Jansa: ein österreichischer General gegen Hitler, Erinnerungen* (Vienna, 2011), p. 554.

10   Palairet to Cadogan FO *DBFP* 2 516/XIX, pp. 895 *et seq.*

Palairet's aversion was personal: "I think he (Schmidt) has begun to realise his charm has had no effect on my distrust of him… he is von Papen's willing accomplice and I use the words deliberately." Palairet was in close contact with his French counterpart, Puaux, who shared his negative view of Schmidt as "totally untrustworthy."[11] Even the Polish ambassador, Jan Gawroński, widely regarded as a crypto-Nazi himself and markedly pro-German, noted in his memoirs that he had "never in a long diplomatic career heard such a great stream of lies and untruths than I heard from Guido Schmidt briefing me after Berchtesgaden."[12] Many of Schmidt's colleagues from the Austrian Foreign Ministry were just as critical. Schmidt's predecessor as Foreign Minister, the later ambassador to Rome, Berger Waldenegg, was almost violent in his denunciation to Ciano of Schmidt's "treachery," promising Ciano "proof of his betrayal."[13]

The head of the Austrian Foreign Ministry's press department, Eduard Ludwig, even produced evidence that Guido Schmidt had been in direct contact with Austrian Nazis from the time long before his appointment to the Austrian Foreign Ministry, bringing the sober proceedings of the Vienna 1947 trial to a standstill with his shouting match with Schmidt across the court room.[14] Other Austrian contemporaries were no less dismissive. Prince Starhemberg, the leader of the right wing *Heimwehr* made no secret of his contempt for Schmidt and his, as he characterised it with typical aloofness, "*als Vorstadt passend chic*" (suburban chic).[15]

There were moments in early 1938 when only Schuschnigg's seemingly unquestioning endorsement of his State Secretary for Foreign Affairs seemed to save Schmidt from imminent dismissal. But though,

11 For Puaux's hostile view of Schmidt's policies since 1936 see Erika Weinzierl: "Die französischösterreichischen Beziehungen Jänner–März nach den Berichten der österreichischen Botschaft in Paris" in Fritz Kreissler (ed.), *Fünfzig Jahre danach: Der Anschluss von Innen und Aussen gesehen* (Vienna, 1988). Also Puaux's memoirs: *Mort et transfiguration en Autriche* (Paris, 1964).

12 Jan Gawroński, *Moja misja w Wiedniu* (Warsaw, 1954), pp. 32–38.

13 *Ciano's Diary*, p. 70.

14 GSN: Evidence presented by Ludwig in interrogation of Guido Schmidt by Dr Sucher, Dec. 1945.

15 See *Between Hitler and Mussolini: memoirs of Ernst Rüdiger Prince Starhemberg* (London, 1942).

after the war, the former Austrian Chancellor, Schuschnigg, and a number
of diplomats, mostly Austrian, came to Schmidt's defence, pointing out
inter alia that he had never joined the Nazi party and had always been
on the Gestapo's list of political enemies, most later Austrian historians,
irrespective of their political alignment have endorsed the verdict of
Schmidt's critics. Peter Broucek, Knight of Malta and a well-known conservative and an outstanding Austrian military historian is scathing about
the damage Schmidt inflicted as "a complete military ignoramus" in the
critical days before the *Anschluss*. He presents documents which imply
that Schmidt plotted to have the anti-Nazi chief of the Austrian general
staff, Alfred Jansa, removed in order to facilitate a military exchange
programme and more intense cooperation between the Austrian and
German officer corps.[16]

For Oliver Rathkolb, the doyen of modern Austrian left-wing historians and not an obvious stablemate of Broucek's, the case against Guido
Schmidt seems almost to possess the intensity of a personal vendetta.
Writing on the fiftieth anniversary of the *Anschluss*, Rathkolb noted that
even though the People's Court had tried Guido Schmidt for three months
and found him not guilty of high treason, they should have focussed on
his role as a senior manager "assisting the German war machine" in his
capacity as a *Generaldirektor* at the Hermann Göring Works during the
war.[17] In fact the Schmidt *Nachlass* shows that the Austrian Ministry of
the Interior exhaustively conducted just such an investigation into this
"complaint" in 1947 only to find Schmidt's defence and the witnesses'
evidence sufficiently convincing to drop the case.[18]

It is not the intention of this study to replay in full the 1947 trial of
Guido Schmidt for high treason. Whatever the shortcomings of the actual
indictment or the charges against the former Foreign Minister, or the mis-
representations of the witnesses, the trial and its accompanying documentation remain a formidable corpus of evidence. Even Schmidt's sternest

---

16 Broucek, *Jansa*, p. 99.
17 Oliver Rathkolb, "Liquidierung des Bundeskanzleramtes, Auswärtige Angelegen-
    heiten durch die 'Dienststelle des Auswärtigen Amtes in Wien' im März 1938" in
    Kreissler, *Fünfzig Jahre danach*, p. 175.
18 See Chapter 16.

critics largely concede this.[19] But I have not hesitated to point out where the material in the *Nachlass* appears to contradict the trial evidence.

The story of Guido Schmidt is *par excellence* the story of Austria's struggle with her larger more powerful neighbour to find a *modus vivendi*. The collapse of the Habsburg empire in 1918 created many a dilemma for the draftsmen and statesmen who sought to redraw the map of Europe in the months afterwards. The empire had been thought of in T.G. Masaryk's words as a counterpoise to Germany, a necessary organisation of small peoples "and odds and ends of peoples and as a safeguard against Balkanisation."[20] The wishes of the nationalities of the component nations of the former empire combined with the political strategy of the Allies to bring the succession states into being but no such wish—to form an Austrian *Nationalstaat*—had ever been formulated by German Austrians. Their new nationality was forced upon them; their state was in Clemenceau's memorable phrase, "that which was left over" (*L'Autriche c'est ce qui reste*).

Perhaps the eternally challenging dynamic which always exists and always will exist between Austria and Germany is best character-ised by a study of Guido Schmidt's career.[21] The question obsessed many Austrian politicians and in particular his mentor, Ignaz Seipel, Chancellor of Austria in the 1920s. In the First Republic, few Austrians could be indifferent to the issue. Thanks to his upbringing and educa-tion Schmidt was undoubtedly *grossdeutsch gesinnt* but in an "Austrian" rather than "German" sense.[22] At the Jesuit school of Stella Matutina

19 See Magdalena Neumüller, "Diskursanalyse des Hochverratsprozesses gegen Dr Guido Schmidt," Diplomarbeit, University of Vienna, January 2012.

20 See Karl Stadler, *Austria* (London, 1971), pp. 100–127.

21 For the issues surrounding the impact of geography on identity in Austria see Gerald Stourzh, *Vom Reich zur Republik: Studien zum Österreichbewusstsein im 20. Jahrhundert* (Vienna, 1998).

22 The English reader especially must be patient with this seemingly semantic formu-lation: for the Germans, especially von Papen, *grossdeutsch* meant Austria's seamless incorporation into Germany. For Austrians like Schmidt, *grossdeutsch* meant Austria's playing a role within the German-speaking space but as "a second German state" enjoying autonomy. For the recurring view that the Austrians were "the better Ger-mans" see Lothar Höbelt, *Die Heimwehren und die österreichische Politik 1927–1936* (Graz, 2017).

he had learnt to see "German culture as a whole," an entity in which the Austrian was distinctive, autonomous and independent but nonetheless, not least through shared language and history, a participatory member of the entirety.[23]

These views were shared by his chief, Kurt Schuschnigg, the Austrian Chancellor, another product of and contemporary at the same Jesuit school. In 1915, the two teenagers took part in a school theatre production. The relationship and bonds forged on a college stage in Feldkirch would endure until 12th March 1938. The *Nachlass* shows that it did not survive much beyond then. The documents reveal a more complex friendship than is generally supposed but they largely dispel the idea, prevalent in many narratives of 1938, that the Chancellor was unduly influenced by his former school colleague. Rather, both men were convinced that without a satisfactory relationship with her larger and more powerful neighbour Austria was doomed. Unlike many of his colleagues in the Foreign Ministry, Schmidt was no *Preussenfresser* ("Prussian eater"). Nor was he a Legitimist. These attitudes together with his formation in a school which had always regarded "Germany" as an indivisible concept made Schmidt the ideal man to carry out Schuschnigg's policy, but like his chief, Schmidt was fiercely patriotic and determined to preserve Austria's autonomy. This did not prevent differences emerging between the two men on the pace and depth of the agreed policy. The British minister in Vienna until October 1937, Walford Selby noted that the Austrian Chancellor had complained to him that "Schmidt had gone too far" during his visit to Berlin.[24]

Despite Broucek's criticisms of Schmidt's limited military expertise, the documents suggest that Schmidt took the question of Austria's military independence with some seriousness, even though, as he confessed, he was "not at all versed in military affairs."[25] By examining the interaction between Guido Schmidt and the Austrian Chief of the General

---

23 See Chapter 1.

24 SEL Oxford, Bodleian Libraries MS Eng.c.6588 *Vienna Legation Registry* (of telegrams). The summary only is available as the actual dispatch did not survive PRO "weeding."

25 For accusations of Schmidt's "frivolity" in military affairs see Broucek, *Jansa*, p. 676.

Staff, Alfred Jansa, there is an opportunity to revisit the arguments for and against a more robust Austrian military policy and to debate whether an armed resistance to the German invasion of March 1938, "a second Königgrätz" in Chancellor Schuschnigg's phrase, was credible or possible.

Any study of Guido Schmidt cannot limit itself to the Austro-German dimension of the years between 1936 and 1938. An analysis of the *Ständestaat's* last Foreign Minister's career would be rather one dimensional without exploring the other avenues of European diplomacy upon which he was engaged. Schmidt's activities shine a powerful light onto the relations between Austria and her other neighbours, Italy, Yugoslavia, Hungary and Czechoslovakia. They also offer, as mentioned above, unique insights into the policy-making decisions of the western powers. Above all, the lines of communication with London where Schmidt attended the coronation celebrations in 1937, show that he had an important, if at times opaque and complicated, relationship with London. Schmidt's insights brought Van many benefits, not least the intelligence that a major breach of security was occurring in the British embassy in Rome.[26] Conversely the relationship between Schmidt and Van brought only muddle and confusion to the Austrian who relied for far too long on Van's vague indications of theoretical support, indications which were never backed by any practical steps.

This unsatisfactory but at the same time intimate relationship with London was reinforced by Vansittart's and Schmidt's familiarity with the detail of the industrial and financial interests in central Europe of the Vienna, London and Paris based Rothschild family.[27] Although a trained diplomat, Schmidt had an unusual capacity for business understanding, and he was at ease in the world of balance sheets and accounts. He had received a commercial training alongside his legal studies, and this stood him in good stead as State Secretary for Foreign Affairs. Although today there is barely any sign of the Rothschild family's enormously important role in the Austrian First Republic's financial affairs, pre-war Austria's

---

26 See Chapter 12.

27 See RA (Rothschild Archive London) 38/39/51. Correspondence between Lionel de Rothschild and Sir Robert Vansittart, 24 Nov. 1936. See also GSN 1941 Wolzt/Borstett correspondence, 14 Feb. 1941.

banking system was undoubtedly dominated by the Austrian branch of the family which owned a controlling interest in the CreditAnstalt Bank until the crash of 1929 and which was hugely influential in securing for Austria loans from the City of London with the help of the British branch of the family.[28] Schmidt was directly involved in this thanks to his participation in the negotiations with London for favourable amendments to the City's loans to Austria during the mid-1930s. Austria depended on these following the Bank of England's governor, Montague Norman's, dramatic decision to intervene decisively to save the Austrian government of Otto Ender from impending bankruptcy in early 1931 by (in a brief evening telephone call) granting the Austrian First Republic the largest loan in her history.[29]

To attempt to influence British policy positively towards Austria was undoubtedly Schmidt and Schuschnigg's priority. But at best British policy towards Austria was benignly incoherent, another example of the Foreign Office's predisposition towards "creative ambiguity."[30] Such policy led to sharp disagreements within the Foreign Office, notably between Van and Walford Selby.

Increasingly, as we shall see, Van undermined Selby, his philo-Austrian envoy in Vienna, eventually succeeding in "digging him out" in October 1937, replacing him with the more compliant Palairet. Selby neither forgave nor forgot: writing after the crisis, he insisted: Van was "more implicated than anyone else in the major blunder which sold us out into the arms of Hitler."[31]

Ironically, Schmidt's career shows that this was a perfectly compatible

---

28 The relationship between the Austrian Rothschild family headed by Louis von Rothschild and the British Royal Family were sufficiently close for the former Edward VIII to head to one of their properties, Schloss Enzesfeld, in Austria shortly after his abdication in 1936.

29 See Peter Melichar, *Otto Ender* (Vienna, 2018).

30 Readers may recall that it was just this "quality" of British policy making which muddied the waters in the July Crisis of 1914 causing Edward Grey agonies of self-reproach until the day of his death. See A. F. Pribram *Austria–Hungary and Great Britain 1908–1914* (Oxford, 1951), p. 82 and p. 161.

31 SEL: Selby Papers as British minister in Vienna, 1932–1941, Oxford, Bodleian Libraries MS Eng. c. 6587–6589.

counterpoint to his and his Chancellor's own policy of seeking an understanding with Germany but it was never his most desirable outcome.
It would have been preferable if Britain, joining with Italy and France,
could be persuaded to offer some, however soft, form of guarantee of
Austria's independence. Thus would Austria's sovereignty be preserved.
This was the realignment of European diplomacy which Schmidt and
Schuschnigg desperately hoped for. It was the realignment Van appears
to have promised with one hand while resisting with the other. British
policy was unlikely to comply in any practical way with the Austrians'
request, although it made many sympathetic noises. Increasingly,
Vansittart's view that supporting Austria was backing "a losing horse"
became the received wisdom. The "winning horse," as a memorandum
from Allen Leeper at the Foreign Office to Selby made clear as early as
1934, was without doubt "for the Austrian Nazis, Hitler." Van's final fling
at interfering with Austria in February 1938 to promote the referendum
which had such disastrous consequences for the country's independence
takes on an unhelpful note when viewed in this context, especially as
Selby remained convinced to the end of his life that Van had told the
Sudetenland German leader Konrad Henlein that London would be
indifferent to Hitler's seizure of Austria, a view Henlein quickly passed
to Hitler.[32]

Vansittart himself appears to have played a strange game in his vacil-
lating attitude towards Austria, On several occasions Van's instructions to
his minister in Vienna had to be ignored by the Legation. Selby recalled,
"I had received instructions from Van in the Autumn of 1935 which I had
no intention of carrying out. Van proposed to make Austria the scapegoat
for the Stresa blunder."[33]

By the time of the March 1938 crisis, Selby had finally been removed
and Van could rest assured his instructions to Vienna were carried
out, even though he too had been "dug out" and replaced in London.
Nevertheless, Van intervened directly to stiffen Austrian resolve during
the crisis, if not inspiring certainly throwing his support massively behind

32 SEL 6857, 1–219, Leeper, 27 Sept. 1933 to Selby: "Most Austrians look at the Nazis
   as likely to come out on top...."
33 SEL 6587 "Stresa blunder...."

Schuschnigg's ill-fated decision to call a plebiscite, the *casus foederis* for the German military operation which followed the political extinguishing of Austria's independence. Yet this privately expressed support was increasingly remote from the practical reality. Van only backed down in the wake of realities and a blazing row with his successor as Permanent Under-Secretary, Alexander Cadogan.[34]

An examination of this context which the present study of Guido Schmidt affords can only add to our understanding of the tragic days of 1938 when the "lynchpin of Europe," to use Leo Amery's phrase,[35] the "key position of Vienna for our security" was destroyed by a convergence of geopolitical factors which were unlikely to spare the fate of any of the other smaller countries in central Europe. Whether Guido Schmidt could have saved Austria from this, as many of the hostile witnesses at his trial in 1947 seemed to imply, is something which the reader more than eighty years after the *Anschluss* may find easier to judge than those who confronted those events at first hand. In any event, this book will have succeeded in its purpose if it demonstrates that those operating at the highest levels of the machinery of government in Vienna possessed no easy options in the months before March 1938, however powerful their sense of Austrian patriotism and however strong their belief in an independent and free Austria, and however sympathetic the advice emanating from Paris and London.

It did not help that the domestic Austrian landscape was so philo-Nazi. It is often forgotten that Austrian National Socialism was an indigenous Austrian political movement with a long tradition of its own. It was not, as is sometimes thought, especially by British historians, a simple offshoot of the German party but rather an independent movement with a party which was only partly (and never completely until 1938) "controlled" by Germany. Schmidt was attempting always to navigate a way through this "enemy within" but this enemy was no ordinary fifth column; it was

---

34 See *The Diaries of Sir Alexander Cadogan: 1938–1945* (ed. Dilks) (London, 1971), 11 Mar. 1938, p. 60.

35 See *The Empire at Bay: The Leo Amery Diaries 1929–1945* (London, 1988), and Richard Bassett, *Last Imperialist: A portrait of Julian Amery.* (Settrington: Stone Trough, 2015). Also SEL 6588.

everywhere. There can be no doubt that both Schuschnigg and Schmidt believed Austria's independence could only be bought with a compromise agreement with Nazi Germany. The 1936 Austro-German agreement of 30th July was an attempt to secure precisely that. But informed outside observers were highly sceptical that such an agreement could "buy" Austria much time. The Austrian lawyers advising the Rothschild family in Vienna saw the 1936 agreement as a spur to accelerate their plans to transfer the most important holdings of the Austrian Rothschilds to London.[36] "Nazi influence was bound to come" was their verdict.

Thus, while the state of Austria was indeed a victim in 1938 (as were many individual Austrians: Jews and Roma, political dissidents, Monarchists, Legitimists, Marxists and the mentally and physically handicapped) the "Austrian People" were not. By 1943, more than 700,000 Austrians were members of the Nazi party, a membership which compares easily with that of one of the major parties in Austria after the war. Austria was not an "occupied country" like France or Norway. Given the strength of Austria's indigenous National Socialism, "collaboration" is also not quite the right word in the sense of cooperation with the forces of an occupying power. Yet Austria was not just another part of the German Reich like Bavaria or Saxony. The cultural differences were too great. As has been pointed out, Austria's ambiguity was in part the result of her national identity being in a state of transition during the First Republic. The process of forging an autonomous Austrian nation would be accelerated by the Nazi experience but German nationalism remained a potent force in Austria well after the war.[37]

Guido Schmidt never joined the Nazi party and studiously avoided ever giving the Hitler salute but Schmidt's conduct after the *Anschluss* (unlike his behaviour as Foreign Minister) was less than heroic. His acceptance of a highly paid post in the Hermann Göring Works while

---

36 RA 38/39/51 Memorandum re Witkowitz advising: "much more strongly their [Louis von Rothschild and others] advice now since the German–Austrian entente of the end of last week." (4 Aug. 1936). Ibid: Leonard Keesing and Louis de Rothschild, 16 October 1935: "Nazi influence in Austria was bound to come ...".

37 See Wolfgang Neugebauer, *The Austrian Resistance 1938–1945*, tr. John Nicholson (Vienna, 2014), pp. 23–25.

his former colleagues rotted, at best, in concentration camps and prison reveals an opportunism and egotism which is undoubtedly, if not difficult to explain, far from easy to forgive. But unlike millions of Austrians, he never identified with the Nazi cause or, like tens of thousands of Austrians, from the expropriation of Jewish property. He intervened many times, at some personal risk, to try to secure the release of those with whom he had worked and in that alone he could rightly claim to have "improved" on the average Austrian's conduct, rightly described by the French air *attaché* in Vienna, Salland, during the dark days of March 1938 as "spineless."[38]

Undoubtedly, had Göring not personally intervened to rescue him, Schmidt would have been arrested and dispatched to a concentration camp. This no doubt would have spared him much reputational damage after the war. But a short spell in a camp was unlikely to be an option for Schmidt. His bitter, tenacious and consistently hostile stance towards the Austrian Nazis had made him far too many enemies for such "half-solutions." Kaltenbrunner, most egregious of the Austrian Nazis, a man whose large rough hands filled the Head of the *Abwehr*, Admiral Canaris, with dread, vowed to shoot Schmidt on many occasions.[39] If Schmidt had unilaterally surrendered Göring's protection his days might well have been numbered.

Of course, it should not be forgotten that there were many Austrians who were prepared to face execution rather than cooperate with the Nazis[40]—at one extreme there are the Catholic martyrs, Franz Jägerstätter and others, but the comparison is perhaps flawed; none of these men had quite the same opportunities to save themselves that were presented to Guido Schmidt. The reader can determine whether in these circumstances one can expect martyrdom to fall easily to men, cursed or blessed by their exalted station in life, for surely rare is the man who would willingly embrace the guillotine.

---

38 Salland quoted by Erwin Schmidl in *März 1938: Der deutsche Einmarsch in Österreich* (Vienna, 1987).

39 Canaris remarked: "Look: those are the hands of a killer." See Richard Bassett, *Hitler's Spy Chief* (London, 2005), p. 288.

40 Franz Jägerstätter to name but one of the better known. See Neugebauer, *Austrian Resistance*, pp. 136–137.

CHAPTER 1

A Vorarlberg upbringing

IN MAY 2019, a survey conducted by the Austrian newspaper, the *Vorarlberger Nachrichten*[41] claimed that of 4,000 people in the province of Vorarlberg in western Austria who were questioned as to whether they would wish to join neighbouring Switzerland, more than 65% of them replied in the affirmative. *Wir sind anders* (We are different) was the common response to Viennese journalists questioning of this separatist sentiment.[42] One after another of those interviewed stressed the similarities with their Swiss neighbours in *Kultur* and language. Older inhabitants even recalled the words of their grandparents who had lamented when the spectacular Arlberg railway had linked the province through a long tunnel more effectively to the rest of Austria: "What God had divided man should not link." The veteran British correspondent of Austria before the war wrote in 1955:

> "Vorarlberg is the least typically Austrian province (along with Hungarian-like Burgenland). Other Austrians call it the Ländle which is the Swiss not the Austrian diminutive of 'Land' or province... the exceeding neatness and trimness of Swiss architecture, the meticulous Swiss cleanliness, the Schwitzer-Deutsch dialect continue here well over the frontier and give the keynote to Vorarlberg civilisation."[43]

---

41   See *Die Presse*, 12 May 2019.
42   See *Profil* 42, 13 Oct. 2019.
43   See G. E. R. Gedye: *Introducing Austria*: (London, 1955).

They also give the keynote to much of Guido Schmidt's personality. This was the land of his birth and he inherited every one of these traits.

"We have always looked west; towards Switzerland and Germany; Stuttgart and Bavaria," is a frequently encountered opinion while local businessmen are keen to point out that Vorarlberg is very different from Tyrol which is in their view "more agricultural and less industrial."[44] In Vorarlberg "you are respected for what you have achieved through your hard work and efforts."

These views are nothing new. A hundred years earlier, after the collapse of the Habsburg Empire, the population of Vorarlberg had even conducted a referendum on whether they wished to be united with the adjoining Swiss canton of St Gallen. Nearly 29,000 people, more than half of the province's population at that time, had voted in favour. But even if the victorious allied powers had permitted such a move, and the Treaty of Saint-Germain in 1919 expressly ruled against such frontier changes, the Swiss were most unwilling to contemplate such an aggrandisement of their territory. *Wir kaufen uns ein Armutshaus ein* (We are buying a poorhouse) was the reaction of the Swiss Calvinist politicians, determined not to increase the population of their own country's Catholics with thousands of destitute Austrians. Strategically, too, the Swiss saw only disadvantages in a "correction" of a border which would compromise their own geographical frontier along the principality of Liechtenstein.

Austrian politicians, including those from the region, such as the later Austrian Chancellor, Otto Ender, were against the movement but 86% of their Vorarlberg constituency were in favour. Geopolitically speaking there was much to be said for the Vorarlbergers to become a new "27th Swiss canton." Vorarlberg was intersected then as now by eleven border crossings with Switzerland. Indeed, a third of Vorarlberg's borders were with Switzerland and more than a fifth of its industry was in Swiss hands. Inhabiting an area which also bordered on Germany, they had long been used to working in the towns of their more prosperous neighbours. Every summer the so-called "Schwabenkinder" would leave their families and walk across the frontier to seek work in the mills and factories

---

of nearby Swabia. This annual six-month exodus—the children returned in time for Christmas—expressed more vividly than anything else the austerity and poverty of the region.[45] When the idea of unification with Switzerland faltered, the alternative of linking with neighbouring Bavaria and Baden-Württemberg to form a new province of Weimar Germany, "Schwabenland," was also briefly mooted only to be dismissed again by the Treaty of Saint-Germain's clauses prohibiting any part of Austria uniting with Germany. The Treaty of Versailles contained the same clauses.

The Austrians of this most westerly province were thus of a very different mentality from the Viennese, whose urban and sophisticated manners were heavily influenced by their Czech and Hungarian neighbours and a large indigenous Jewish population whose numbers swelled the ranks of the large *Bildungsbürgertum*. Nor did they share the Slavic cultural and temperamental impulses of the Styrians and Carinthians to the south and east. Moreover, the opulent clerical legacy of the former Prince Archbishoprics of Salzburg (still faintly apparent to this day) was also alien to the Vorarlbergers. Although nominally Catholic, they were powerfully influenced by the Protestant work ethic of their immediate neighbours. *Schlichtheit, Fleiss, Nüchternheit* (modesty, hard work and sobriety) were the watchwords of the region's populace, qualities that Guido Schmidt would epitomise.[46] Indeed at his trial for high treason in 1947, he opened his defence with a recognition of these attributes: "The Vorarlberger is on average a practical and spare person, a man of careful consideration and a realist. These were qualities which I inherited. The great ideas of Peace, Religion, Christianity present us with realities; they were firmly anchored in my personal thoughts."[47]

Born on 15th January 1901 in Bludenz, an important if small industrial town of the Vorarlberg, situated in the valley of a tributary of the Rhine, Guido was the last of six children born to Josef and Maria Schmidt. The Schmidts were modest businessmen with a strong local following. One of

---

45 For the *Schwabenkinder* see the exhibition documentation *Schwabenkinder am Weg* (Museum St Anton am Arlberg, 2018).

46 *Profil* 42, 13 Oct. 2019.

47 *HVPGGS*, p. 24.

Guido's elder brothers, Josef, known as Beppo, would become mayor of
Bludenz. His nearest sibling, Sofie, would become a nun, taking the name
of Sister Borgia and, although the family was probably less clerically
minded than Austrians in more southern and eastern parts of Austria,
a committed Catholic piety certainly permeated the family. This acted
as a solid bulwark against the pagan Nazi ideology. In the run-up to the
Anschluss the family's business premises would be regularly vandalised by
Nazi followers.

In Guido's case it would be powerfully reinforced by his formal education. His parents and siblings had not received the benefits of higher
education but the Austrian school system before 1914 was excellent
and a general high standard of literacy and numeracy was widespread.
Nevertheless, Guido's mother, decided to send him, alone of the children,
but inspired by his obvious intelligence, to an elite Jesuit college. He
was already considered very bright as an infant and because he was the
youngest and no more children were expected, the decision to send him
to the prestigious Stella Matutina college in Feldkirch was taken easily.[48]

This college, comparable perhaps to Stonyhurst in England, enjoyed
international prestige. Indeed, in the nineteenth century its reputation
had even spread as far as England and the Conan Doyles had sent their
son Arthur there. The soon to be famous author of Sherlock Holmes,
found his alpine sensibility much reinforced by the experience, while it is
no exaggeration to say that the education Guido received at the hands of
the Jesuits in Feldkirch would change the course of his life dramatically,
setting him on a path which would take him far from the world of his
family and the provincial milieu of Bludenz.

As a secret Nazi memorandum composed in the months preceding
the projected invasion of Britain in 1940 reported enthusiastically, the
English considered the public school system to be one of the foundations
of entry into the higher echelons of political and financial life.[49] The
British system was considered unique in Europe but a brief perusal of the

---

48 *Stella Matutina* ("Morning Star"), not to be confused with the Rosicrucian construct
    of the same name.
49 See Walther Schellenberg, *Informationsheft Grossbritannien* (Berlin, 1940), original
    copy in archives of Imperial War Museum, London.

Stella Matutina's alumni shows, in addition to Schmidt, two chancellors of Austria and a host of other figures important in Austria's later political and financial life were among his near contemporaries. Jesuit education was considered then even by non-Catholics to be the finest intellectual and character training in the world. "Give me the child and I shall show you the man" was only one of the more widely attributed aspects of the formation. Another was the oft-repeated mantra that any child exposed to the Jesuits by the age of eight would be a loyal Catholic for the rest of his life.

Even Robert Vansittart, one of the most influential mandarins of his generation at the Foreign Office in the 1930s, could wax lyrical on the Austrian products of the Jesuits' education. Writing in his memoirs, *The Mist Procession*, he could well have had Guido Schmidt in mind—after all he came to know him quite well—when he notes the plight of every Etonian, himself included, coming into contact with the product of Jesuitical formation:

> "My classical education made me seem ignorant. Caesar's wars were of no use among those who knew the nineteenth century and got on with it. Young Englishmen abroad used to suffer from a sense of immaturity because the products of Jesuit schools had more to put in the shop window and professed more. They made me wonder whether I really knew anything...."[50]

That all certainly might have applied to Guido Schmidt.

The rigour of the religious education Guido Schmidt received at Stella Matutina cannot be doubted. The school had been founded in 1649 and had supplied many distinguished Catholic theologians and princes of the Church. As well as fluency in Latin and Greek, Schmidt was grounded in Mathematics, German Literature and Astronomy. He was also given a thorough knowledge of Theology, History and Philosophy. Compared to most schools in England at the time this was an academic training of the highest quality. The Jesuits kept their pupils hard at work through the whole school year with only the shortest of breaks for Easter and Christmas. Fencing, riding and swimming were all encouraged even if the

---

50   See Robert Vansittart, *The Mist Procession* (London, 1958), p. 34.

team sports so beloved of the English were rather neglected. A form of football played on stilts was briefly popular before the violence that accompanied it forced the Jesuits to ban it. Music and theatre were important, particularly the former which meant that many of the pupils, especially those from aristocratic families, were given a musical training which "went far beyond that of the average amateur."[51] The pupils were divided into social divisions—the *Hochadel* (high aristocracy: count, prince, margrave) from the *Kleinadel* (baron, freiherr, edler *etc*.) and bourgeois families. This distinction would also play a part in Schmidt's formation. The lazy drawl of the *Hochadel*, born of generations of unquestioned privilege and a tradition of the situation always being "hopeless but not serious," did not appeal to his instincts. This class apartheid was enforced with great rigour in the school; the different groups of pupils had separate tutors, dormitories and even recreational spaces. The only time the entire school came together was to pray, or for the annual school play.

In the school magazine of 1915, there is a description of the play performed that winter: Schiller's *Wallenstein's Death*. The fourteen-year-old Schmidt played Count Terzky, the faithful lieutenant of Wallenstein who is murdered with him. Wallenstein was played by an older boy, one who would make much use of Schmidt as a faithful lieutenant in real life. Kurt Schuschnigg was four years older than Schmidt and as he was leaving to enlist as an officer in the war, he was given the leading role.[52] It is hard not to imagine the close bond of friendship between these two men, which would be so fateful for Austria, being sealed in the excitement and drama of this greatest of Schiller's works. The 14-year-old Schmidt as the loyal aide of the 18-year-old Schuschnigg in one of the most fateful dramas of the German stage was, prophetically, a blueprint for much that would follow. Life would imitate Art in 1938: did the words of Schmidt's Terzky ring in Schuschnigg's ears at Berchtesgaden: 'We are betrayed… but I shall not desert you !'[53] Perhaps the words were recalled with bitter irony a few months later. Unlike Count Terzky, Schmidt, controversially, would not share his master's fate in 1938.

---

51 See R. K. Sheridan, *Kurt von Schuschnigg* (London, 1942), p.13.
52 GSN: Stella Matutina programme, 15 Feb. 1915.
53 Schiller, *Wallensteins Tod*, Act III scene 5.

There was an important difference between Stella Matutina and other Austrian Jesuit schools which reflected the peculiarity of Stella Matutina's geographical situation in Feldkirch, not far from the Swiss and German borders. Many of the pupils at Stella Matutina were from Germany and from the roof of the buildings there flew not just the Black and Gold imperial flag but also the Black, Red and White colours of imperial Germany. Thus, from an early age, Guido Schmidt was living in what might be termed a pan-German environment where sympathy, understanding and cooperation between Austrians and Germans were unquestioned parts of everyday life. To add to the Austro-German concord several of the Jesuits teaching at Stella Matutina were also from Germany. Reflecting this cross-border mix of staff and pupils was the celebration of both countries' sovereigns' birthdays and other national holidays.

Hans Jung, an intimate friend of Guido Schmidt's from their time at the Stella, noted that eight years at the college left a profound impression on all the pupils with regard to their views of German culture: "We both learnt to see German culture as a single entity (*die deutsche Kultur als ganzes zu sehen*)."[54] This was helped by the fact that there were almost as many *Reichsdeutsche* as Austrian pupils in the school. Of the 400 in the college only half were from Austria. Friendships barred by class distinctions knew no equivalent geographical inhibitions.

This sympathy and understanding for Germans across the frontier carried on beyond the College when Schmidt, like most of the graduates of the Stella, later joined the CV (Cartellverband), the Union of Catholic German Student Fraternities. This organisation was set up in Germany at the time of Bismarck as a response to the Prussian Chancellor's *Kulturkampf* against the Catholic church. These student organisations were, unlike their Protestant equivalents, non-duelling. Eventually, as part of the general anti-Catholic policies of the Nazis which gathered increasing intensity in the run-up to the war, they would be closed down as politically unreliable. The Fraternity Schmidt and Schuschnigg belonged to was appropriately enough called "Austria" and had been founded in 1876.

---

54   GSN: Letter Hans Jung to GS, 2 Feb. 1947.

Guido Schmidt's involvement with the CV would bring him once again into contact with his fellow pupil of the Stella, Kurt Schuschnigg. The good relationship the Austrian CV fraternities enjoyed with their equivalents in Germany contributed again to pan-German sentiments. But as Jung noted in a letter, "This understanding for the great connexion (*grossen Zusammenhang*) did not prevent either Dr Schmidt or myself from feeling ourselves to be Austrians (*hat weder Dr Schmidt noch mich jemals gehindert sich als Österreicher zu fühlen*) ."

If Guido Schmidt absorbed these ideas at the Stella and the CV, he was at the same time powerfully jolted into an environment where he was surrounded by the offspring of socially superior families. The Austria of the Habsburgs was an unashamedly class-based society, as the rigid division into two distinctive social groups at Stella Matutina demonstrated. Ironically perhaps, this was particularly noticeable to upper-class English observers who were amazed at the "stiffness" of Austrian society. As Vansittart noted on arriving in Vienna before the First World War to learn German: "Mankind begins with the rank of Baron."[55] His successor, another Etonian, Alec Cadogan, was then a junior secretary at the embassy in Vienna, and observed with astonishment how low that form of life was, seeing the Counts and Princes at a ball turning their backs when a "mere Baron" entered the room.[56]

Guido Schmidt would have felt all the anxieties and social insecurities of someone coming from a minor lower-middle-class trade background confronted with contemporaries the majority of whom were minor aristocracy and members of a caste which despised trade and were not often accustomed to either hard work or austerity. In addition Vorarlberg was on account of its proximity to Switzerland the only part of Austria to have virtually no large aristocratic estates. The province was in the hands of middle-class industrialists rather than counts.

The Stella's aristocratic pupils posed an immediate challenge. Only his formidable intellectual and academic abilities would keep him afloat in such a challenging social milieu. To these were added another attribute which the Jesuit priests in their reports were quick to pick up on:

---

55 Vansittart, *Mist Procession*, p. 34.
56 *Cadogan Diaries 1938–1945*, p. 4.

ambition. Undoubtedly Guido Schmidt was determined not just to do his work well but, as the Jesuits instructed, "to the greater glory of God" (*Ad Maiorem Dei Gloriam*). He fully accepted that to do a thing well was not enough and that the regular, daily, strict examination of conscience which was an integral part of his Jesuitical formation demanded relentlessly and mercilessly an answer to the simple question: Have you done this to the very best of your ability? Mediocrity for the gifted was therefore never acceptable. Sloth was the deadliest of sins.

The eight years at the Stella thus nurtured a first-class intellect, self-confidence and an overweening ambition to succeed in all spheres, together with a ruthless intolerance of anything and anyone who failed to match these exacting standards. It was a recipe guaranteed to lead to professional achievement, but it was not a formula for winning friends.

From the quiet, cloistered world of Feldkirch, Guido resolved to study law in Vienna. His time at school had encompassed dramatic changes. Like the future Austrian Chancellor, Kurt Schuschnigg, Schmidt was present in June 1914 in the refectory at the Stella when one of the college servants rushed into the dining hall and gasped out the news that the Austrian heir apparent, the Archduke Franz Ferdinand, had been assassinated at Sarajevo. Schmidt, thanks to the accident of his birth, would just avoid active service. Had the First World War which subsequently broke out a month later gone on another year he would have been called up but, as it turned out, he would endure the four years of war as a schoolboy. His graduation coincided with the disintegration of the Habsburg Empire.

The Austria Guido Schmidt found himself in on leaving school was unrecognisable from the Imperial and Royal empire in which he had grown up, but he faced it with boldness and excitement. Unlike the circumstances facing the aristocracy with which he had been educated and whose estates were often compromised by the new succession states of Czechoslovakia, Yugoslavia and Romania, life for the Schmidts did not change too dramatically. The new economic conditions were appalling but for a meritocrat gifted with dynamism and intellect, this new world was a challenge to be grasped. Unlike the scions of the aristocracy, he saw little point in dreaming of a Habsburg restoration. For Schmidt the post-1918 world of central Europe was just a new phase in the history of the continent to be faced squarely and realistically. It was a sign of Schmidt's "progressive" outlook that he never ever voiced any nostalgia for the multi-national, multi-confessional Habsburg empire. He had made more close friends at school with Germans than Austrians and he was never touched by the languor mingled with social insularity which were characteristics of the often effete Austrian aristocracy. How these characteristics would mould his development was now to be put to the test in the challenging terrain of the wider world. The Stella had given him a "Rolls-Royce" of an education and as one of their most hard-working pupils, the burden of expectation on him was considerable. Taking the Consular Academy exams aged 24, he passed out with the highest marks in the history of the institution. For someone of such ability, the provincial world of Vorarlberg was far too small a chessboard on which to act out his next moves. As for many other intelligent Austrians leaving their colleges in the provinces, the magnetic draw of the capital Vienna would prove irresistible. This was especially the case for a young man interested in foreign affairs and someone who had absorbed the international flavour of a Jesuit education. It is not clear whether Guido Schmidt had determined on a career in the Austrian state service by the time he had left the Stella but, by choosing to study law, then a *sine qua non* for the Austrian diplomatic service, he left open the possibility of pursuing a course which would well prepare him for serving any future Austrian government.[57]

---

57 As late as 1958, entry to the Austrian diplomatic service was limited to those holding doctorates in law. See Max Thurn, *Erinnerungen meines Lebens*, ed. Ines Felder (Vienna, 1996).

CHAPTER 2

The "Revolver Capital": Vienna in the 1920s

I N ADDITION TO his studies in Vienna, Schmidt also decided to spend a semester in Berlin but while much was made of this early 'evidence' of pro-German sentiment by Schmidt's later critics, it was very common for Austrian students in the 1920s and even 1930s to study in the German capital. No less a patriotic Austrian than Otto von Habsburg was studying in Berlin when Adolf Hitler came to power.

Moreover, Schmidt had family connexions through the marriage of one of his future wife's sisters to a German accountant by the name of Breitenfeld. He formed a close friendship with Hubert von Breitenfeld which would prove of immense help during the war, not least when the Nazi authorities began questioning Schmidt's tax returns.[58] But overall, the Berlin experience was far less influential than his studies in Vienna. He also spent a term in Bologna, learning Italian but more significantly than this Italian interlude, he supplemented his legal studies with courses in business at the Vienna Trade College.

There, thanks to his membership of the Austria CV, he soon reconnected with other pupils of the Stella, notably another law student, his fellow thespian of 1915, Kurt Schuschnigg, who after leaving the Stella had fought on the Italian front in the First World War. When the war

---

58   See Chapter 14.

ended, Schuschnigg had also studied law in Vienna. This professional and educational network was of immense value to Schmidt given the climate of the early years of the First Republic. In the 1920s Austria faced challenging times. To the disruption of an empire whose structures collapsed virtually overnight was added the economic dislocation which brought starvation, unemployment and disease. In 1920, a thousand people a day were dying from hunger in the Vienna streets. Many gave up the struggle to earn a living. Young men who had fought in the last years of the war emerged with little hope and few illusions. Many families emigrated to find poorly paid work; at least the artificial silk and starch factories of France offered wages and survival. Hardship was the norm and few from any strata of Austrian society were immune from it. For those young Austrians who remained there was little heating, scant food and *ersatz* clothing made from nettles and other weeds. The Catholic Church offered a spiritual bedrock against more revolutionary elements but it could offer little more in the way of practical sustenance. Anti-clericalism was rife, especially among socialists and German nationalists.

The political situation reflected all this: strong currents of Austro-Marxism jostled for power with the main great party of state, the Christian-Socials. This party had begun in the 1880s as a Catholic reformist party. In 1907, they had fused with their right-wing rivals, the Catholic People's party and turned increasingly to the peasants of the country rather than the craftsmen of the towns for votes. Thus developed the cleft between "Red" Vienna, already by 1911 a socialist stronghold, and the "Black" (Catholic) provinces. By 1918, the two groupings were diametrically opposed. Stormy events in neighbouring Munich and Budapest where political unrest also was endemic only polarised the Austrian political situation more.

Both groupings sought help from outside. For the Socialists, support was sought from the Second International and especially the Social Democratic Party of Germany. For the Christian-Socials, the support of Rome for a more Catholic "corporative" state implied by Mussolini's fascism became a source of inspiration. In this sharpest of political divides, the alumni of Stella Matutina could only support one side and the papal encyclical *Quadregesimo Anno* issued by Pope Pius XI ten years later in 1931, and powerfully influenced by German Jesuits, some of whom had taught at the Stella made it very clear which side that was. While condemning the excesses of capitalism, the encyclical maintained the imperative of preserving the social order. The "virus" of communism was starkly rejected.

Another feature of the chaos and unrest which followed the establishment of the successor states in late October and Austria–Hungary's armistice of 3rd November 1918 was the establishment already in early November of local armed forces, recruited partly from the former Imperial and Royal army, and partly from local groups, workers' forces and other, often highly politicised elements. In some areas, especially in the Tyrol, these ad hoc units supported the weak police force to maintain order when often embittered demobilised troops passed through. For political reasons, and to prevent a continuity from the "monarchist" era, the Social Democrats deliberately had the old army demobilised, establishing a new volunteer army, the *Volkswehr* (People's Defence Force). In contested areas such as southern Styria and Carinthia with its mixed German and Slovene populations, these *Volkswehr* units together with local volunteer units fought successfully against Slovene/Yugoslav forces in Carinthia, although with less success in Styria. Even less successful were German–Austrian attempts to hold onto the mainly German-speaking areas of new Czechoslovakia.

Even when the situation became more stable, and the *Volkswehr* in 1920 gave way to the new *Bundesheer*, the professional army of the new Republic of Austria permitted by the Saint-Germain Treaty, these local groups continued to exist and came increasingly under the influence of radically anti-democratic party politics. When the Social Democrats left the government in 1920, they responded by establishing their own paramilitary group, the *Schutzbund* (Protection League). Both "reactionary" and "Marxist" paramilitary forces easily outnumbered the *Bundesheer*, the latter being limited to 30,000 soldiers, although not even reaching this number because of lack of finance.

With political tensions between these political groups from Left and Right increasing, a third element gained importance with the rise of the Austrian Nazis. The German Workers' Party had originated in the

Austrian mixed German–Czech areas of Bohemia before the First World War, and soon found followers both in Austria and in Germany. With Austrian-born Adolf Hitler's rise in the National Socialist Workers' Party in Germany in the 1920s, the German Nazis soon became the focus for most of the Austrian Nazis.

The Austrian politician who had to cope with this kaleidoscope of political unrest was a man of stature and considerable wisdom. But Monsignor Ignaz Seipel, who had served in the last Imperial government, was widely seen as an arch-conservative and his policies as Austrian Chancellor between 1922 and 1924, and then between 1926 and 1929, reflected a philosophical outlook which placed the state on a higher level than the nation.[59] An interesting correspondence which came to light after the Second World War, however, shows that Seipel was not completely averse to some form of *Anschluss* (union) between the two "German" states.[60] The correspondence is remarkable in that although it was filed away as a quasi-official document, it is a personal letter which enabled Seipel to ventilate his views without fear of being quoted in the following days' newspapers. It is thus perhaps the most accurate record of Seipel's views on Austria's relationship with Germany and her future role in Europe. As Seipel was a strong formative influence on Schmidt's political views, the correspondence repays a closer examination.

Towards the end of July 1928, Seipel received a letter, dated 24th July, from an official working for the Austrian federal railways in Paris. Dr W. Bauer had only met Seipel once and then fleetingly as a child, yet, reflecting the high levels of education then prevalent among the Austrian official class, he felt able to engage with the Austrian Chancellor in an intellectual debate on the advantages and disadvantages of an *Anschluss* with Germany. Bauer expressed his concern that many Austrians appeared to want such a union with Germany despite the fact that "no economic, cultural or any other sort of consideration can obviate the fact that a still greater Germany is a still greater threat to peace because of the unfortunate character of the Reich-Germans which is quite alien to

---

59 See I. Seipel, *Nation und Staat* (Vienna, 1916).

60 See Paul Sweet, "'Seipel's views on *Anschluss* in 1928: an unpublished exchange of letters'", *Journal of Modern History*, Vol. 19 number 4 (1947), pp. 370–323.

us Austrians." This was in Bauer's phrase an undisputable "psychologi-cal–historical fact." In words which today sound penetratingly prophetic, Bauer argued that it was far better for Austria to be a "small neutral state" because "*Anschluss* will sooner or later cost the blood of hundreds of thousands." To avoid this fate it was vital for the systematic education of Austrians to guide them towards a "new Austrian patriotism."

Seipel replied that the "real reason" against *Anschluss* was altogether rather more prosaic. The "character of the Austrian people," he wrote, was not very energetic and "they do not like selfdiscipline." This is a valid if curious argument especially as Seipel went on to say that such a passive character was always waiting for "some external *deus ex machina*." Ten years later in 1938, these arguments would be made to explain and even justify why the Austrians so enthusiastically embraced the Nazi invasion.

The Austrian Germans, Seipel continued, had had an historical mission but had botched it. It was that rather than the ultimatum of 1914 and the subsequent declaration of war against Serbia which arraigned them in the dock of the courts of history. They might yet redeem them-selves by embracing a wider German, European or pan-German task. The Austrians were "a big state people." Some "third way" of attempting to become a Switzerland or Belgium was simply a "wrong policy." Worse it was a "Czech or French idea" not an Austrian or German one. "Just to cultivate our garden and show it to foreigners to make money is no proper task for the heirs of the Carolingian Ostmark and the great victo-ries over the Ottoman empire."[61]

In an astonishing paragraph which demonstrated Seipel's geo-strate-gic naivety, he went on to write that there was nothing to suggest that an *Anschluss* was "a threat to peace." It was not a violation of any peace treaty, as the Treaty of Saint-Germain had "predicted" the *Anschluss* by containing a clause stipulating that an *Anschluss* was possible follow-ing a unanimous vote of the League of Nations. This clause far from prohibiting an *Anschluss*, actually foresaw its inevitability according to

---

61 The term *Ostmark* which Hitler used to designate Austria after the *Anschluss* can be seen here to have a less abysmal pedigree. Originally coined for the Bavarian bor-derlands ruled by the Babenbergs it was hijacked and inaccurately expanded by the Nazis to counter the Habsburg connotations of the term Austria.

Seipel. "If no greater mission falls to Austria then there still remains important tasks to carry out in cooperation with the rest of Germany. This is the argument for *Anschluss*."[62] Seipel completely rejected Bauer's argument that differences between the Prussian and Austrian character should impede developments of far greater European significance. This personal openness towards possible future union with Germany, something Seipel could not articulate in public where Austria's weak economic situation required total subservience to the western powers insistence on no greater Germany, was significant. He must have expressed these views to his favourite *protégés*, including Guido Schmidt. The effect would have undoubtedly led Schmidt to keep at the very least an open mind with regard to the question of *Anschluss* although his idea of such an event would be very different from the eventual reality.[63] Given the intimacy of the relationship between Seipel and Schmidt—the former would conduct the marriage service for the latter when he married Maria Chiari in 1931—Seipel's ideas are far from irrelevant to Schmidt's own thinking. He undoubtedly incorporated some of them into his own outlook and deployed them to his own advantage when dealing with the German Nazis. Seipel's arguments if repeated by Schmidt in Berlin to Göring or even discreetly in Vienna to von Papen would have been enough to make Hitler's acolytes sit up.

Whatever Seipel's personal views; he was compelled to renounce in public the desire of Austrians to unite with Germany. By doing so the Monsignor paved the way for international loans which alone could stabilise the Austrian economy. As a priest he saw history in terms of centuries rather than just months. Long term trends were matters he could view with some detachment. This did not inhibit him believing in the need for a strong temporal arm to guard the spiritual values of his faith. Whether he saw in the private armies of the right-wing movements, as one journalist wrote, "the ragged conscripts of God" is probably an exaggeration.[64] In any event he had no monopoly over these forces.

---

62 The original correspondence is to be found in the Austrian State Archives: HHStA PA I 465 Geheimliassen Deutschland.
63 See Chapter 13.
64 See Gordon Shepherd, *The Austrian Odyssey* (London, 1957), pp. 88–90.

The Austrian Marxists had been the first to organise themselves, aided and abetted by the Socialist government of 1920 which sought to erase all trace of the old imperial army and its traditions through new uniforms and drill.[65] They even tried to sow mistrust between the rank and file and the old imperial officer corps (the embodiment of the old Austria) to facilitate a "socialist cooperation" with the new German Republic.

When right-wing forces followed their example and amalgamated their provincial groups into one "federal" organisation, known as the *Heimwehr* in 1927, it was clear that the rival paramilitary fronts had atrophied into determinedly opposed extremes. At the head of the *Heimatschutz* or *Heimwehr* stood one of the most forceful and colourful figures of twentieth century Austrian history. Prince Ernst Rüdiger Starhemberg was the descendant of the commander of Vienna in 1683 who had seen off the great Turkish siege. An unashamed scion of one of Austria's oldest families he had exhibited an Olympian disdain for the demands of the post imperial world when told by a distraught servant that the Austrian Republic had banned all titles and forbidden the use of the noble prefix, *von.* "What a pity," the Prince had languidly drawled after a pause, "for the likes of Herr von Müller." For those governing Austria, the presence of such a figure showed all too well the innate polarisation of their country's politics, ridden by class-prejudice. Astute observers noted even then how rapidly reactionary forces could be mobilised.[66]

This was well summed up by the British minister in Vienna a few years later in 1934, Sir Walford Selby:

> "When in the rout and demoralisation of 1919, the Socialist party triumphed in Vienna and seemed for a while to be sweeping away the old order in the country districts of Austria, the landed gentry and local leaders created... the *Heimatschutz*... which have now, after fifteen years of bitter hatred, succeeded with the help of the Government... in outlawing socialism in Austria."[67]

But in 1928 that was still to come. For the moment, more moderate

---

65 The success of this policy can be widely experienced even in modern Austria, two generations later.

66 See Erik von Kühnelt-Leddihn, *Kirche contra Zeitgeist* (Graz, 1997).

67 Selby to Simon 37 (R1259/37/3) 17 Feb. 1934.

but still conservative forces held sway. If uncompromising in his private views, Seipel possessed a considerable following. He was the leading clerical intellectual of his time and he sought to share his views with the upcoming generation of Austria's Catholic intelligentsia.

By chance, Seipel attended a lecture of Schmidt's on authority and freedom in the modern state. Schmidt had been asked at the last moment to stand in for a Vienna university friend but he had, as always, done his homework and prepared his presentation carefully. He changed the title, calling it *Der Mensch und der Staat* (The Person and the State) and introduced his own narrative. The lecture which he developed and repeated in other contexts in later years was an intellectual tour de force. The manuscript has survived and shows not only a firm grasp of political theory but also a deep understanding of theology and ethics.[68] As it is one of the few surviving documents which encapsulates Schmidt's view on abstract Austrian political themes within the broader context of ethics and religion it is worth examining in some detail. Schmidt began by asking the question he maintained every simple Austrian had the right to ask, namely "What does the State mean for the people and what does it demand of us—and what do we in return demand of it?" Before answering these questions, he argued in words which would have pleased his future mentor, it was important to recall that "the basis of the relationship between the Austrian state and its people was Christianity." Schmidt went on to quote St Paul's letter to the Romans (chapter XIII), Machiavelli, Hegel, John Locke, Adam Smith and Humboldt in a spirited defence of the rights of the individual in the face of the "ever louder demands for a strong man and a strong state." "Even if such a state was to appear in Austria, rising like a throne over the clouds, it would only be the means to an end." This was a thinly veiled attack on fascism, especially as it was developing in Italy.

Schmidt confronted the concepts of authority in the state head on but struck an Austrian patriotic note observing that the Austrian had his own specific thought patterns and inheritance (*Gedankengut*). These included a love of his homeland, a recognition of the qualities of German culture

---

68   See GSN: Vortrag, *Der Mensch und der Staat*.

and his faith. "The man of the Alps is not a man of the masses. He is made of a lively interchange between authority and freedom and in this way a state is created from a homeland." The foundations of all Schmidt's future public speeches can be traced back to this lecture although, later versions took into account his own burgeoning interest in politics and the challenges of Nazi Germany.

Unsurprisingly, Seipel was impressed and went up to Schmidt at the end of the lecture and asked what career he was interested in pursuing. When Schmidt replied "Foreign Service for the Austrian government," the Monsignor asked Schmidt to visit him and pledged his interest and support. In the small Austrian world of professional *Protektion* such a gesture was invaluable. Then, as today, merit alone was unlikely to succeed and the old Jesuit mantra *nihil sine nepos* (nothing without nepotism) was widely observed.[69] Nevertheless, merit was clearly an abundant quality for Schmidt. His performance in the Consular academy exams was proof enough of that. Seipel would quickly have grasped that the examining board had been unanimous in saying Schmidt's work was the best they had ever witnessed.[70]

Seipel made it clear to Schmidt that he would be expected to have perfected his English and French if he was to have a successful career as a diplomat. The young man took the hint and he broadened his horizons by spending a few months improving his English in London and his French in Paris. By this stage determined to join the fledgling Austrian republic's foreign service, a branch of the Austrian state which was then still dominated by members of the aristocracy, he threw himself into these linguistic studies with great energy. Although the expected entrée did not immediately appear, he remained always optimistic and practical. "If it becomes too difficult here in Vienna for me, I shall pack my bags and go to Paris," he later wrote to his brother.[71] After a nine-month wait, he was eventually accepted into the Foreign Ministry and posted as a junior *attaché* to Paris. The city suited him in every way and he was always fond of recalling that his native Bludenz was the same distance from Paris as it was from Vienna.

69   Dick Randolph SJ, *Wardour and Tisbury Newsletter*, June 1997.
70   GSN: Verhör, p. 32.
71   GSN: Letter GS to Josef Schmidt, 9 Jan. 1930.

Here he was able to renew his acquaintance with Seipel when the latter visited Paris and needed an interpreter for a lecture he was giving at the Sorbonne. The lecture was memorable not only for the skill of Schmidt's interpreting but also on account of the content. As Schmidt later recalled, it was the first time he had encountered the concept of Austria as a "second German state."[72] This was a term which he would resort to using on many occasions with his German interlocutors. It had a useful ambiguity: a second German state could be autonomous and independent while still acknowledging its belonging to a bigger entity. The phrase well represented the *Weltanschauung* of the Stella.

The rapport between the two men grew and Seipel arranged for Schmidt to be transferred to the office of the recently appointed Austrian Republic's President, Wilhelm Miklas, another member incidentally of the CV *Austria*. It was a move Schmidt at first resisted—he was enjoying the life of bachelor *attaché* in the French capital. Schmidt later recalled that it was in Paris that he got to know the 'real Austria'" for the first time by encountering Austrian exiles such as Rilke, Faistauer, Hofmannsthal and Stefan Zweig. Like the Englishman abroad who could argue, "What do they know of England that only England know?"[73] Schmidt was in these formative years of his twenties brought into contact with men for whom "hinterland" was critical. These men's background in the old Austria was a defining characteristic and a significant advantage.[74]

But Schmidt soon realised that unhesitating obedience was not just expected of Jesuits. Seipel indicated that he did not expect Schmidt to either question or resist his new appointment. The Monsignor threatened expulsion from the service if Schmidt did not obey.

Before his transfer, Schmidt gave another well-received lecture, this time on the 'The Cultural and Political Mission of Austria'. The lecture aimed to disabuse the French of their prejudices towards the Austrians to whom they often referred as the 'Austro-boche'. Schmidt gave a spirited account of how Austrians could be distinguished from the Germans. In

---

72 *HVPGGS*, p. 24.
73 Rudyard Kipling, "The English Flag" (1881).
74 Even today: see Eric Hobsbawm's observation on the "huge advantages of a background in the old Austria" in *Interesting Times* (London, 2002), p. 8 *et seq.*

this lecture, Schmidt referred to the concept of Austria as the 'Second German State' but he argued forcefully *la difference* with phrases which underlined Austria's special character in contrast to Germany. Seipel when sent a copy of this speech at first criticised it but acknowledged that Schmidt had brought the idea of specifically 'Austrian thought' to public attention for the first time.[75]

Established in the President's office, Schmidt began his duties with overseeing the international correspondence of the Austrian Head of State. This job brought him into contact with ambassadors, senior civil servants and, beyond them, the entire machinery of the Viennese bureaucracy. It was hard work and a steep learning curve but he threw himself into it wholeheartedly. In a letter to his brother, written a few years later, he noted that he was 'now unrecognisable from earlier days' and had lost weight, had given up smoking and drinking. "*Ich lebe jetzt ziemlich brav*' and was now utterly devoted to the challenges of his profession.[76] Already by early 1931, he became sufficiently confident of his prospects to court the beautiful, elegant and socially superior Maria Annunziata Freiin von Chiari. The two had first met in Paris but had plighted their troth in the mountains of Vorarlberg where, to Schmidt's consternation, the courageous aristocratic lady had demonstrated a superior skill at skiing to his own. This was humiliation on the most intense of scales. A Bohemian aristocrat, and a woman to boot was a better skier than a man in the flush of youth who had grown up in the mountains? Never one to fail to rise to the competitive challenge, Schmidt began to take lessons with the great skier Rudi Matt in an attempt to match his female companion's technique.[77]

This was only the first of many hurdles that needed to be negotiated. The young Vorarlberg diplomat had prospects but he was not out of "the same draw" as Maria Chiari. The von Chiaris may not have been able to use their noble prefix in Republican Austria but they were of a cosmopolitan old Austrian stamp. Maria had been born in Trieste; her parents had substantial interests in Moravia, and from the earliest of

75 GSN: *The Cultural and Political Mission of Austria*, with Guido Schmidt's annotations.
76 GSN: Letter 19 Jan.1935, GS to Josef Schmidt; "Liebe Beppo…"
77 Rudi Matt 1936 world champion slalom skier. Fled the Nazis to America in 1938.

ages she had been used to socialising with her Moravian neighbours, the princely Liechtensteins and the aristocratic Arcos. Unsurprisingly, her parents felt she could do better than become engaged to "some little Herr Schmidt from Bludenz." But Schmidt was nothing if not energetic in his devotion and the attractive, well-connected but above all cheerful Maria Chiari soon fell under his charm. She would prove to be a no less devoted companion and wife.[78]

In the years before Hitler came to power in Germany, the atmosphere of the President's office in which Schmidt found himself was calm despite the upheavals and increasing polarisation of Austria's domestic politics. Austrian democracy was moving from the reign of parties to the reign of blocs. When on 13th September 1931, a *Heimwehr* leader from Styria, Walter Pfrimer seized control of Graz for a few hours, he was quickly disarmed and neutralised, becoming a figure of ridicule, known as the "half-day dictator." Hitler's emissaries however continued to make contact with these right-wing Austrian elements in the hope of engineering a full-blown merger between the Nazis in Germany and their Austrian *confrères*.

In May 1931, there were other shocks to the system. That month saw an explosion in the Austrian financial world whose effects, as is so often the case with financial explosions, became only increasingly apparent during the following weeks. The CreditAnstalt Bank, the most prestigious bank in the old Austrian empire, partly owned by the Rothschilds, went bust, triggering a banking crisis which soon developed into the world depression.[79] Austria's economic woes, which had just begun to settle down, erupted in a new and spectacular form. The ensuing deflation caused a quarter of a million unemployed (from a population of just over six million) and once again young Austrians sought work abroad, but as the crisis spread this became more and more difficult. The recruiting ground for Austrian Nazis became more fertile overnight.

Partly to combat this, the new leader of the Christian-Socials,

78 I am grateful to Guido Schmidt's daughter, Monica Pott, for this information. M.P. to the author, 22 Apr. 2020.

79 A good example of George Bernard Shaw's dictum that the "bad news from Vienna is always the most important bad news in the world," *Arms and the Man*, Act 1, scene 2.

Engelbert Dollfuss, a former officer in the Tyrolese elite mountain troops *Kaiserschützen*, adopted an increasingly authoritarian course of action, first as a minister and then as the new Chancellor of Austria from May 1932. The career of Dollfuss still divides Austria to this day. On the one hand the man the Nazis murdered in 1934 was without doubt a factor in the establishing of an Austrian as opposed to a greater or lesser German consciousness in post-Habsburg Austria. On the other hand, ruling with a majority of only one, Dollfuss had little time for a fractious Austrian parliament which became increasingly incapable of facilitating any government policy, either with regard to important international loans to prop up the country or domestic social legislation. Committed to an anti-Marxist pact which ruled out any deal with the Socialists, Dollfuss committed the act for which the Left has ever afterwards condemned him: he shut down the Austrian Parliament. True the institution had rather dug its own grave. On 4th March 1933, the Speaker and both his deputies laid down their offices in a chaotic debate over a railway strike and voted themselves into suspension. Dollfuss, presented with a political vacuum which the best planned putsch could never have equalled, struck accordingly. When the confused deputies tried to re-enter Parliament the next day, they found their way barred by the police. The seeds of the Austrian corporative state, to be established in May 1934 and dubbed by socialists as "Austro-fascism" was born.[80]

The structure of a corporative, or corporatist state as it is sometimes called, with strong authoritarian tendencies had long fascinated Seipel. This interest had grown in the months before his death and we have seen that Guido Schmidt had also in his lecture as a student evaluated and analysed the relationship between state and liberty, authority and the individual. The product of the Jesuits could, like any other intellectually trained Catholic, argue that the Catholic Church was the common link between the various elements of society just as the ordered societies of medieval empires had depended in turn on the protection they had offered to the Catholic Church. For Dollfuss, belief in a God-given

---

80   The term, like that of "clerical fascism" divides Austrians to this day. Supporters of Dollfuss argue that his regime was authoritarian but not fascist. See Max Thurn, *Erinnerungen.ed.(Vienna,).*

mission led him towards one fateful step after another. The "corporatist state" (*Ständestaat*) envisaged society divided into seven groupings: professional services, agricultural and forestry workers, finance and insurance *etc.* Yet this vision left no room for Austrian Marxists, Socialists and a substantial part of the city and town populations. Ironically, it did leave space for some Catholics on the left to embrace aspects of the Nazi ideology later. [81]

That this was about to become increasingly important was shown the day after the Austrian Parliament was eliminated as a factor in Austrian politics. On 5th March 1933 the Nazi party in Germany triumphed in elections. From being a fringe delinquent camp based in Munich, the Nazis became the authorised power in the German state with a population of seventy million behind it.

For Dollfuss and his lieutenants, notably his successor Schuschnigg, the challenge was to invest Austrian politics with a patriotic force which could resist the pull of the new Germany. A new bourgeois Catholic movement, "The Fatherland Front," authoritarian enough to dispense with Parliament, was founded on the anniversary of the great Turkish Siege of Vienna in 1683. Step by step, Dollfuss banned all political parties including the Nazis and orientated his foreign policy sharply towards Mussolini's fascist Italy. But the whole experiment of Austrian authoritarianism could only have survived by finding a broad basis of popular support. The Fatherland Front remained in essence the old Christian-Social Party under a more resounding name.

These developments made Schmidt's impulses towards stronger engagement in politics unavoidable. Dollfuss, of poor peasant stock, excessively vain and physically tiny, although dubbed the "milli-Metternich" was, despite his undoubted charisma, unable to cope with the various pressures that now began to build up. For Schmidt, the *Ständestaat* was imbued not only with an intellectual belief shored up by the precepts of the Catholic Church but also a sense of the need to preserve Austria's identity in an increasingly hostile world. He recalled during his trial that

---

81   For those wishing to unravel the intricacies of the corporatist state there is no better guide than the *Gore Booth memorandum* of 22 November 1937 in PRO 8213. As a mandarin minuted: "exhaustive and explanatory."

his interest in politics was at first rather peripheral. But from the moment he felt Austria to be threatened by a struggle for survival (*Existenzkampf*), he became more and more politicised and above all "a hundred per cent Austrian." As he later pointed out, this was at a time when many (Austrians) maintained quite a distance from that position.[82]

Above all it was interaction with his former school-friend, Kurt Schuschnigg which gave him his political outlook. Schuschnigg, trusted by Dollfuss and seen as his successor cemented his friendship in these days with his contemporary. It would have been difficult to imagine the older boy's experience and views not rubbing off on the younger former pupil of the Stella. Schuschnigg himself had imbibed his political philosophy through Dollfuss and, like him, he recognised the mortal threat to his country which the Nazi government in Germany now posed.

Dollfuss's options were limited and as opposition grew towards his policies, the political temperature rose dramatically. He had to face an uncooperative working class which in Vienna was understandably not prepared to see its political rights extinguished by a lackey of Mussolini's, as they dubbed Dollfuss. When Dollfuss, under pressure from Mussolini in early 1934, ordered his Vice-Chancellor, Major Emil Fey, to proceed with force to drive the "Marxists" from their urban strongholds, the prestigious tenement blocks which had made "Red Vienna" a byword for progress and enlightenment throughout the world, the workers distributed arms and prepared to resist.

It was a heroic gesture of defiance but after four days of fighting, public order was restored by the army acting together with the police and the *Heimwehr*. Of the rebels 196 had been killed, several thousand were incarcerated and several of the ringleaders were executed. Thus was Social Democracy as a political force in Austria extinguished.[83] This would prove an enduring weakness for the government in dealing with the Nazis. Dollfuss and indeed later Schuschnigg would be unable to draw

---

82 *HVPGGS*, p. 25.

83 The experience converted many visiting Englishmen (Kim Philby among others) to a life-long commitment to communism. See also Kurt Bauer, *Der Februaraufstand 1934: Fakten und Mythen* (Vienna, 2019) for a recent survey of the uprising with much useful data hitherto distorted by political polemics.

upon the support of the workers, many of whom in their disillusionment with the regime began to be attracted by the National Socialists' propaganda and its unremitting hostility to Dollfuss. Even some Jewish Social Democrats felt drawn to a concept of *Anschluss* which was, they naively imagined at that stage *grossdeutsch* (greater German) but not *alldeutsch* (totally exclusively German).[84] Unsurprisingly, Dollfuss's next challenge would come from the opposite end of the political spectrum.

When the Vienna SS wing of the Nazis under a thug named Otto Planetta, having plotted for several weeks in the comfortable surroundings of the Café Eiles in Vienna's Josefstadt struck on 25th July 1934, the putsch appeared breathtakingly daring. Calmly walking into the nerve centre of Austrian government on the Ballhausplatz, undeterred by machine guns and armed guards, the assassins, wearing Austrian military uniforms marched up to the first floor where the Chancellor's study was situated and equally unemotionally shot the Chancellor. As he lay bleeding to death in the hours that followed, the chaos and confusion appeared to be total. Until order was restored it had seemed as if the Nazis had succeeded in their *coup de main*. The occupation of the Vienna Chancellery was followed by seizure of the Austrian radio station which broadcast an announcement of the shift of power, immediately sparking unrest in Styria and Carinthia. As the gravestones of Graz's *Zentralfriedhof* even to this day show, there were casualties among those who, as one gravestone still (illegally) reads, "'fell in the struggle for Greater Germany" (*er fiel 1934 im Kampf um Grossdeutschland*). The Austrian army swiftly restored order. Once again, the hangman was at work executing the ringleaders, and Austria's prisons received another few thousand inmates.

Any tangible support from Berlin was always unlikely but had such assistance crystallised it would have been intimidated by Mussolini's prompt action in openly supporting Austria in its moment of crisis. The failure of the Nazi putsch was partly a result of the strong signs of solidarity with the Austrian government which emanated from Rome. Mussolini, determined to demonstrate his support for Dollfuss in as vivid a form as possible, having already mobilised his divisions for an exercise

---

84 See Erin P. Hochman, *Imagining a Greater Germany: Republican Nationalism and the idea of Anschluss* (Ithaca: Cornell UP, 2016).

on the Brenner a few weeks earlier he offered an ensuing demonstration of Italian force. This coincidence had the result of dampening Nazi enthusiasm. At the same time, he put a private plane at the disposal of Prince Starhemberg who was holidaying in Venice so that he could rush back to Vienna and mobilise the *Heimwehr*.

Dollfuss had been the first Austrian statesman of the Republic to see that if Austria was to survive in the modern world it would have to develop an Austrian patriotism. His words "Our country must live even if we must die for it" were a new language for Austrians of all political persuasions and they would be echoed and obeyed by the best of his countrymen in the hard ten years ahead.[85] Some later observers, especially in the years just after the war, saw these sentiments incompatible with pan-Germanism and portrayed Dollfuss as anti-German but, as ever in Austrian politics, the reality was rather more complex. Dollfuss, like his successor Schuschnigg, had also sought an "understanding" with the powerful neighbour to the north.[86]

Schuschnigg was appointed successor to Dollfuss as Chancellor in short order following a brief interim. He had introduced capital punishment a year earlier as minister of justice and he was seen by Marxists and Nazis alike as something of a hardliner. He might have done more to try to heal the wounds and divisions which threatened Austria's very existence, but he was determined to maintain the Catholic pan-German policies of his murdered predecessor. He possessed integrity and patriotism but he had inherited a geo-political hand which was far worse than any of his neighbours in central Europe.

Mussolini enjoyed posing as the protector of Austria, a country which had in every of her wars fought during the previous hundred years defeated and humiliated Italy. This support, even if unacceptable to many older Austrians for whom Italy was always the *Erbfeind* (hereditary enemy) which had stolen Austria's most beautiful province of South Tyrol, was welcomed by the new government. Like Dollfuss, Schuschnigg had fought on the Italian front during the First World War, but both men

---

85　See Shepherd, *Austrian Odyssey*, p. 107. For Mussolini's much exaggerated deployment see Richard Lamb, *Mussolini and the British* (London, 1997) pp. 101–105.

86　Ibid. See also below Chapter 13.

could see in Rome a guardian angel albeit not one they instinctively felt much affection for.

Rome's policy was rooted in geo-political realities. Like France, it was Italy's priority to prevent an Austro-German rapprochement which could dominate central Europe. For Italy, still digesting the former Austrian possessions of South Tyrol, the Trentino and Trieste awarded to her after the First World War, this was a matter of practical common sense. For France, the motives were well established in Paris's long standing, indeed permanent and obsessive aversion to any aggrandisement of German influence.

Austria's other neighbours, Yugoslavia and Hungary had different perspectives. Yugoslavia, ever suspicious, like Hitler, of a planned restoration of the Habsburgs, actively supported the Austrian Nazis, offering them shelter after the failed putsch. Hungary, still nominally a kingdom albeit one which had resisted the last Austrian emperor's attempts to return, was even less supportive of Vienna. A secret memorandum prepared by the Hungarian general staff in early 1934 planned for a full-scale partitioning of Austria among her neighbours including Czechoslovakia and envisaged a Hungarian incursion to reclaim the former Hungarian province of Burgenland ceded to Austria under the terms of the Treaty of Trianon.[87]

It can be seen even from this glance of the diplomatic realities of 1934 that long before Guido Schmidt came to have any influence on Austria's foreign policy, the country was almost totally isolated diplomatically as far as her immediate neighbours were concerned. Except for Italy, no power was prepared to demonstrate in favour of an independent Austria. Only Switzerland was altruistically sympathetic but she was powerless. Well might Ludwig Jedlicka note in his classic study of Austria's modern history, *Vom alten zum neuen Österreich*, that Austria stood in 1934 in "horrific danger" and that the explosive internal situation of Austria was inextricably linked with external dangers.[88]

It was now the turn of Schuschnigg to confront this perilous combination and his training at the Stella left him in no doubt that he would have to proceed with an energy and dynamism that was not a natural

---

87   Lajos Kerekes, *Acta Historica* Vol VII (Budapest, 1960), No. 3–4, p. 359.
88   Ludwig Jedlicka, *Vom alten zum neuen Österreich* (St Pölten, 1975), p. 259.

characteristic for him. He had little of Dollfuss's charm or popular touch. Introspective, shy and increasingly fatalistic, he knew that the political retreat the Nazis had been forced to beat in 1934 was unlikely to last. Italy could only pose as Austria's guardian as long as Germany remained compliant. As the year of 1934 drew to a close all that was about to change.

CHAPTER 3

Power struggles within and without: the Schuschnigg era

FROM THE BEGINNING of his tenure as Chancellor, Schuschnigg faced the intellectual challenge of how he could maintain the Catholic pan-German legacy of his predecessor, to which he entirely subscribed, while initiating policies which could keep Austria's independence and sovereignty intact. Austria was surrounded by deadly enemies at worst and unreliable friends at best. Italy may have helped see off the Nazi threat in 1934 but pressure from Rome to convert Austria into a fully-fledged fascist state had to be resisted. The vital lines of friendship with the western democracies could not be preserved if Austria was absorbed into the fascist bloc.

The diplomatic environment was not without suggestions and advice. Three months before his murder, Dollfuss had signed the "Rome Protocols" in March 1934. This was a tripartite agreement between Hungary, Italy and Austria largely focussed on increasing cooperation in the economic and trading sphere. As the reports of the Hungarian general staff reveal, adherence to these Protocols did not preclude Budapest planning for an eventual partition of Austria. The Protocols may have suggested a new power constellation but in reality it was only a vehicle for Mussolini's foreign policy ambitions with regard to Austria and these, as we shall see, were about to be sacrificed on the altar of higher Italian priorities.

At least, the Protocols officially existed. Two other schemes designed to help Austria find its way in the new post Habsburg world proved to be less capable of reaching fruition. A "Central European Solution" whereby Austria could enter an economic federation with all the succession states of the old empire and thus become politically absorbed into the Little Entente (founded in 1921 by Romania, Czechoslovakia and Yugoslavia as a buffer against Hungarian revanchism or a Habsburg restoration) was favoured by France but was doomed from the outset. The Habsburg card was not one any Austrian conservative politician could easily surrender. The potential for a Habsburg restoration, something Schuschnigg, though not Schmidt, cherished, was for the Chancellor "the last card" he could threaten to play should relations with Germany become too oppressive. But such a restoration could only happen with Hungary's support. Hungary was still nominally a Habsburg kingdom, ruled by a regent.

Attempts by Prague and Vienna to find agreement faltered on Hungary's disapproval. The Hungarian Foreign Minister, Kálmán de Kánya, had been Imperial and Royal ambassador to Mexico in 1913 and his contempt for the arriviste Czechs, a nation of clerks and cooks in his view, was apparent at every meeting he held with the representatives of the newly founded Czechoslovak state.[89] Vienna could hardly relinquish its good relations with Hungary simply to garner favours with Prague.

The Habsburg card seemed to grow stronger in 1935 following a law passed by the Schuschnigg government which restored to members of the Habsburg dynasty their personal property and even permitted them to return to Austria in a private capacity. An earlier law brought back a variant of the elegant old imperial uniforms with their distinctive rank insignia. Support came from Starhemberg, Vice-Chancellor since Dollfuss's time, who now hoisted the imperial black and yellow colours at *Heimwehr* rallies. Perhaps like a Stuart monarch in England secretly espousing Catholicism Schuschnigg could never openly politically embrace the Restoration card, however strong his personal sympathies.

---

89 I am indebted to the late Professor Norman Stone for this characterisation of Kánya. (Conversation with the author, Austrian Embassy Dinner, Budapest, 31 March, 2019). Also GSN: Note on Kánya, quoting his "contempt for the Czechs" as "the easiest of our enemies to despise" (8 Nov. 1936). See page 89

Regular clandestine contacts, however, were maintained with the enlightened, astute and highly intelligent young heir to the throne, the Archduke Otto, but they remained always just that, sporadic secret briefings.

Even though they were doomed from the start by the external diplomatic constellation, these secret encounters nonetheless assumed ever more importance in Schuschnigg's deliberations. It was not only the successor states who were unlikely to be compliant. Above all, Nazi Germany would never tolerate the restoration of a family with claims to power and lands in southeastern Europe. That would threaten Berlin's own perennial interests in Balkan expansion. Irrespective of German hostility, the western powers which between them had created Yugoslavia and Czechoslovakia out of the rubble of the disintegrated Habsburg empire were always hostile to any whiff of a Habsburg restoration. It could only threaten the status quo so painstakingly (if ultimately futilely) constructed by their diplomats at Saint-Germain and Trianon. The response of British statesmen, as Guido Schmidt later discovered all too frequently, was always to stress the desirability and virtues of the Little Entente, a politely coded way of warning the Austrians to avoid the Habsburg route.

In this apparent stalemate of diplomacy, Schuschnigg began to seek some way of unblocking the paralysis which had descended on Austrian policy. The links between domestic stability and external diplomacy appeared ever more intimate. Within a few days of taking up the chancellorship in 1934, Schuschnigg appointed the former Justice Minister Egon Berger-Waldenegg as his new Foreign Minister. Berger-Waldenegg was an ardent monarchist, a landowner and a long-standing member of the *Heimwehr*. Sceptically hostile to Germany, he had served in the Imperial and Royal Foreign Ministry between 1907 and 1918 where he had had ample opportunity to study at close hand Berlin's ambitions towards Austria. He shared most Austrians' distrust for the Italians but saw in Mussolini's Italy, a useful prop not only for Austria but also for Legitimist interests. Rome was the only source of support among Austria's neighbours for the idea of a Habsburg restoration. Berger-Waldenegg's vision of Austria was almost identical to that of Schuschnigg's, with the important exception that he believed, unlike the Chancellor, that it would never be possible to come to an agreement with Hitler which could at the same time preserve Austrian independence. Gradually, the two men's visions of Austria diverged as, partly but not totally by any means under Guido Schmidt's influence, Schuschnigg came to realise that some kind of *modus operandi* with Germany was vital for Austria if she was to win time for a more favourable diplomatic constellation in Europe to emerge.

Certainly, the situation within Austria was worsened significantly by Nazi Germany's hostility towards Austria. The almost complete breakdown in commercial relations between the Reich and Austria was as ruinous for Austrian businesses as the so-called *Tausendmarksperre* was for Austrian tourism. The latter, introduced in May 1933 by Berlin, forced all Germans to pay 1000 Reichmarks (€4,300 in today's money) into the accounts of the German authorities before crossing the Austrian frontier. The specific aim was to destroy Austrian tourism, especially in the alpine regions of Tyrol, Vorarlberg and Salzburg, then, as now, all heavily dependent on German visitors. The move was a clear attempt to bring down the Dollfuss government which had to resort to a cultural propaganda offensive across the rest of Europe. This resulted in many excellent films celebrating Austria which today are classics of European inter-war cinema.[90] But these cultural gestures could not of themselves improve the economic situation which was further aggravated by Austrian Nazi acts of sabotage. Bridges were detonated, railways damaged and public buildings attacked, all part of a deliberate campaign to destroy the country's attractiveness to foreign tourism. Within a few months the critically important timber trade in Austria (some 60,000 wagonloads a year before the conflict) ceased completely. Neither France nor Britain wished to rush to the support of these near-ruined markets. Italy offered no trading alternatives either.

Schuschnigg was also intuitively cynical concerning the enduring value of dependence on Mussolini's Italy being a lasting guarantee of Austrian sovereignty. Within a year of Schuschnigg taking over the reins of government the Italian invasion of Abyssinia in the autumn of 1935 seemed to confirm his worst fears. Overnight, the Italian move brought

90 For example: *Carneval in Vienna* (1935), *Rendezvous in Wien* (1936), *Wiener Mode* (1936) *etc.*

a change in the international temperature. The failure of the British Foreign Secretary to mediate a solution led rapidly to a deterioration in Anglo-Italian relations which Vienna could only observe with increasing alarm. Italy's guarantee as a minor European power not in conflict with the western states of Britain and France was considerably more powerful than any potential actions she might undertake for Austria, diplomatically isolated from those powers. Yet Abyssinia seemed to be a prelude to Rome's ostracism by London and Paris.

The Austrian Chancellor needed no course in international relations to see that an Italy diplomatically isolated from London and Paris, condemned by the League of Nations and embarked on adventures in pursuit of prestige was not a reliable horse to back. Berger-Waldenegg, however, keenly aware that Italy was the only guarantor of Austria's independence (and the only active Habsburg sponsor among the powers in Europe) was keen to continue the Austrian policy unchanged, heavily dependent on the Rome Protocols and Mussolini's personal prestige.

Three months before the Abyssinian crisis drove a horse and cart through Italy's *Salonfähigkeit* as a potential prop for Schuschnigg, another diplomatic development occurred which was to have ominous implications for the Austrian government. In July 1935, Franz-Josef Hermann Michael Maria von Papen, the man largely credited with facilitating Hitler's rise to the chancellorship of Germany, arrived as Berlin's ambassador with a brief to repair Austro-German relations in the wake of the Dollfuss murder. That was the theory but, in practice and at the same time, he was preparing the ground for Austria's eventual absorption in one form or another into the German Reich. Von Papen was, in Guido Schmidt's words, *Ein Herr* (a "Sir"), a man used to command and with an impeccable Catholic aristocratic and cavalry background. He was also devious, sophisticated, Machiavellian and utterly ruthless in pursuing his aims which consisted largely of restoring his own political fortunes through establishing an Austro-German "solution" which preferably could satisfy all parties but, failing that, satisfy his master in Berlin. He reported directly to Hitler and therefore had the exquisite pleasure of interpreting alone the Führer's emotional demands with regard to the country of his birth.

"We all despised von Papen," his cousin through marriage, and later defector to the British in Istanbul in 1944, Erich Vermehren recalled, noting that the emissary had always had an egregious effect on the countries to which he had been posted.[91] Whatever von Papen's moral failings, he had been chosen with some astuteness. He was, in his finely tailored double-breasted pin-stripe suits, well chosen to appeal to a certain type of upper-class Austrian. He was a practising Catholic, as Schmidt and Schuschnigg both were, and he epitomised the voice of reason and understanding which the best Germans were capable of articulating whatever the histrionics of their paladins in Berlin. For Schmidt and Schuschnigg, von Papen did not necessarily convince them that either he or the state he represented was trustworthy but it became clear to Schuschnigg that von Papen was amenable to some kind of compromise which, even if it ultimately would not satisfy Hitler, might give Austria a breathing space until the Abyssinian crisis had blown over and Italy's diplomatic isolation resulting from it ended. It helped that von Papen's wife was a vociferous critic of Hitler, and that von Papen himself was apt to criticise the German Führer and his socially inferior gang of collaborators. Surely as 'gentlemen' the issue of Austro-German relations could be resolved through amicable discussion among such men of *bonne volonté*?

Added to these powerful influences at work in Italy and Germany to encourage better Austro-German relations there were also sympathetic noises from Paris and especially London where Robert Vansittart calculated instinctively that England would have to "choose between Austria and Abyssinia." His colleagues in the Foreign Office, continued to lobby Vienna to repair relations with Berlin as a *sine qua non* of European stability.

Schuschnigg was under no illusions about coming to terms with a man like von Papen whatever the smoothness of the German's charm offensive, but if Austria was to measure foils with Berlin through some high-wire diplomatic engagement, it was clear to the Austrian Chancellor that a man of his Foreign Minister's, Berger-Waldenegg's, monarchist leanings and avowed anti-German views would not be the best person to lead any discussions with the wily von Papen. Schuschnigg after a

---

91   Erich Vermehren to author, Bad Godesberg, 3 June 2003.

long talk with his old school comrade, Guido Schmidt, quickly came to the conclusion that the Vorarlberger was the perfect man to lead such talks. Schmidt was not an ultra-monarchist and, like Schuschnigg, he had grown up in the avowedly pan-German atmosphere of the Stella. He was young, highly intelligent, energetic and undoubtedly just as sophisticated and intellectually impressive as his counterpart. Moreover, his legal and diplomatic training combined with his excellent contacts arising from his job as the Austrian President's cabinet director would give him the necessary authority. He needed no convincing that some attempt had to be made to find a *modus vivendi* with Berlin. As he, later observed ahead of his 1947 interrogation: "Coming as I did from the realistically minded province of Vorarlberg whose economic woes I was fully acquainted with, I was convinced that Austria had only one possibility, namely to attempt to repair the ruinous state of her relations with Germany (*die getrübten Beziehungen zwischen Österreich und dem Deutschen Reich wieder in geordnete Bahnen zu bringen*)."[92] It was time to reprise Act V of Schiller's play with the two actors who had stolen the show in Feldkirch in 1915. Certainly what followed was worthy of the intrigues which had surrounded Wallenstein.

To ditch Berger-Waldenegg would require in theory at least the consent of Schuschnigg's Vice-Chancellor, Prince Starhemberg, the leader of the *Heimwehr* of which Berger-Waldenegg had been a long-standing and important member. While he remained in government, Starhemberg would have to consent to the appointment of Schmidt, a man whom he neither knew nor indeed, from what he had heard of him, cared about. However, relations between Schuschnigg and Starhemberg had in any event been deteriorating for some time. Schuschnigg knew that he was unlikely to engage with the western democracies in any meaningful way as long as he had Mussolini's "fascist henchman," Starhemberg, in a prominent role in his government. With remarkable clarity, Schuschnigg saw, and here he may well have been influenced by Schmidt, that Italy's influence would wane as a consequence of her Abyssinian adventure and that there was now an opportunity to "break" with Starhemberg and his paramilitary forces.

---

92 GSN: Guido Schmidt, *Aufzeichnungen* über *meine Wirksamkeit und meine politische Einstellung in den Jahren 1936–1945*, p. 2.

In his memoirs, hastily composed during the war, Starhemberg recalled the discussion in early 1936 with Schuschnigg about Berger-Waldenegg and a possible replacement. As Starhemberg conceded, Berger-Waldenegg was rather "over-bureaucratic and lacking in initiative." But he found Schuschnigg evasive on who could replace him. As he later found out, the following morning, Schuschnigg had complained to the Austrian president Miklas that he could no longer work with the opinionated prince who always favoured force and fascist methods. Schuschnigg in a stormy scene with Starhemberg insisted that it was time for "psychological propaganda to have its say." By May 1936, Schuschnigg felt confident enough to tell Starhemberg that he was going to sack Berger-Waldenegg and take over the responsibility for foreign affairs himself. When Starhemberg objected that such a combination of portfolios would simply not be possible for practical reasons, Schuschnigg calmed him with the promise that he would soon appoint someone to handle the day-to-day running of the Foreign Ministry. When Starhemberg pointedly asked whom the Chancellor had in mind, Schuschnigg lied, saying he did not know yet but that "I will find someone."[93]

This was blatant deception as Schuschnigg had already agreed with Schmidt that he would become the new State Secretary for Foreign Affairs, a post nominally junior to Berger-Waldenegg to spare his *amour propre* but *de facto* responsible not only for the running of the Foreign Ministry but the formulation and implementation of its policies. The "junior" status of Schmidt's new position disarmed critics of the move— after all how could they criticise the Chancellor who *de jure* was going to be the new foreign minister? Yet as the officials of the Foreign Ministry themselves quickly realised; the new State Secretary was far from being simply some bureaucratic cypher carrying out someone else's instructions. Rather, Guido Schmidt arrived as a hands-on boss with a razor-sharp eye for detail, a quick temper and, always challenging for long established offices of state, an utter inability to suffer fools or incompetents.

Guido Schmidt's ability to make enemies now began to achieve new levels of intensity. The personality-driven system of Austrian diplomacy

---

93   Starhemberg, *Between Hitler and Mussolini*, p. 233 *et seq.*

soon showed that the personal vendettas favoured by the ambassadors and ministers of the old imperial and royal service had not in any way been diminished by the arrival of the First Republic.

One of the first to pass caustic judgement on the young new State Secretary was Starhemberg himself. In his memoir, he left yet another critical picture of Guido Schmidt: "As he came towards me with his mincing steps—he liked to show off his suburban graces (*Vorstadt chic*),"[94] the new minister showered the prince with compliments and flattery—all to no avail. Guido Schmidt would find that while he himself was by no means immune to flattery, others were often more sceptical. Starhemberg's reservations with regard to Schmidt would be shared by many others, notably the later British minister in Vienna, Sir Michael Palairet. For Starhemberg, Schuschnigg's determination to move away from the more outward display of fascist ideology was proof enough that the political sands were shifting in Austria. When the Prince conspicuously congratulated Mussolini on the conquest of Addis Ababa and then publicly criticised the western democracies for imposing sanctions on Italy on account of Abyssinia, Schuschnigg moved swiftly to sack him in May 1936.

This predated only by a few weeks Schmidt's arrival in the Foreign Ministry. While Schmidt settled down to the responsibility of running one of Austria's greatest departments of state, Berger-Waldenegg was shunted off to Rome as ambassador where it was hoped he would keep Mussolini's interest in Austria alive. He would fail to do that signally, later blaming Schmidt roundly for the entire 1938 debacle.[95]

One diplomat who was favourably impressed by Schmidt was the British minister in Vienna, Sir Walford Selby. Selby had had to deal with the fallout of the 1936 abdication crisis when he had arranged with his contacts at court for the former King Edward VIII to "shelter" with the Rothschilds at Enzesfeld near Vienna. This had brought Selby into frequent contact with President Miklas's office and Schmidt had always proved unhesitatingly supportive, so much so that Selby's dispatch to the

---

94 Ibid., p. 245.
95 See *Ciano's Diary*, p. 70: see also p. 148 for Berger's attempts to ingratiate himself with the fascist leadership to secure his own personal advancement.

Foreign Office of 17th August 1936 noted that the new Secretary of State for Foreign Affairs was a "personal friend." With regard to Schmidt's politics, Selby commented: "rather inclined to be black rather than brown" (i.e. Catholic conservative rather than Nazi).[96]

If other members of the older school of Austrian diplomacy who had cut their teeth on imperial foreign policy before the First World War were unimpressed by their young new boss, they had to concede it was a bold move by any stretch of the imagination. Schmidt was barely 35 when Schuschnigg handed him the Austrian Foreign Ministry. Whatever failings Schmidt may have had in his ability to win over Austrians of a certain social stamp, there was at least one other diplomat, apart from Selby, who was open to Schmidt's charms.

At that moment this man was far more important, as far as Schuschnigg was concerned, than either Starhemberg or Berger-Waldenegg. His name was Franz von Papen.

---

96 SEL 6588 extract from Vienna Legation registry.

CHAPTER 4

Enter Guido Schmidt: the Austro-German agreement of 11 July 1936

C ERTAINLY, VON PAPEN was easily charmed by Schmidt whose personal handwritten notes to him were of such a carefully drafted and seductive quality, von Papen even recalled one of them during his trial at Nuremberg. The note was unforgettable on account of the beauty of its language. "I had never read such a beautiful document (*nie ein schöneres Dokument*)."[97]

Von Papen relished his posting to Vienna because it would enable him to implement his theory that Austria could fall into Germany's sphere of influence and eventually become part of the Reich, if only the "right methods" could be applied. These methods did not involve thuggish acts of terrorism such as the Austrian Nazis had spectacularly employed in July 1934 but rather more subtle techniques. Hitler agreed with Papen that the "evolutionary method" demanded the recognition, at least initially, of some form of Austria's autonomy. Already Italy was growing closer to Germany as a result of the Spanish Civil War. Austria would be for Berlin an indispensable part of such a constellation.

Papen was no doubt strengthened in his strategy by the knowledge

---

97 Franz von Papen, *Memoirs* (London, 1952), p. 425. For the most up-to-date study of Papen see Rainer Möckelmann, *Franz von Papen: Hitlers ewiger Vassall* (Darmstadt, 2016).

that the Austrian Chancellor was ready to acknowledge Austria as a "German" state. On the 29th May, Schuschnigg addressed the Austrian political elite with the words: "We have never ceased and we shall never cease to regard ourselves as a German state."[98]

Where Berger-Waldenegg had delayed for three weeks responding to Papen's overtures for talks on some form of Austro-German understanding, and had then only offered a lukewarm reply, it soon became clear to Papen that the Austrian Chancellor did want to explore the chances of such an agreement and that if only Papen was patient the "right man" would be appointed to progress the talks.

Although Guido Schmidt was not formally appointed State Secretary until just after the Austro-German agreement of 11th July 1936 was signed, he was largely held responsible for its negotiation which was a *tour de force* of secret diplomacy. This did not mean, however, that he was the initiator of the agreement. Dollfuss and Schuschnigg had already sought ways of achieving "normalisation" in their relations with Germany. Even so it is clear, that Schmidt's presence injected new dynamism into the attempts and resulted in a document which afforded the basis for that elusive *modus vivendi* between the Reich and Austria. He had already had a positive balancing influence between the Austrian President and the Chancellor, two men who did not get on. He would now deploy his skill and intellect in balancing Austrian and German interests. After extensive discussions with Schuschnigg, the Chancellor instructed Schmidt to sound von Papen out. Both men immediately saw that an agreement would be a feather in their caps and the personal chemistry between the two men pointed to interesting possibilities. [99] The "right man" had arrived.

The agreement, largely forgotten or misrepresented in many modern accounts of pre-*Anschluss* Austria, was an important milestone in the run-up to the tragedy of 1938. It is indispensable in helping us to understand what followed during the next two years culminating in the

98 Quoted in Jürgen Gehl, *Austria, Germany and the Anschluss 1931–38* (London, 1963).

99 It is interesting to recall that von Papen was remembered fondly in Vienna as late as the 1980s by shopkeepers who recalled his charm and dignity (9 Jan. 1985, M. P. von Papen to author).

ill-starred Berchtesgaden meeting of February 1938. It therefore merits analysis.

Schmidt, strongly supported by the political director of the Foreign Ministry, Theodor Hornbostel was *federführend* (in charge—literally: "guiding the pen"), to use a favourite phrase of his, in the negotiations. Hornbostel, the epitome of the old incorruptible Austrian bureaucratic caste and a staunch anti-Nazi, worked well with Schmidt who was open to his advice and experience. The discretion and total secrecy that accompanied its preparation suggest that for most of the negotiations, only Schmidt, Hornbostel, Schuschnigg and von Papen (with his assistant Keppler) were directly involved. When it burst onto the European stage in a joint *communiqué* issued by Berlin and Vienna on 11th July, reactions among the western powers were initially positive. Both the British and the French ministers in Vienna congratulated Schmidt on the agreement.[100] In London, the bold *démarche* was welcomed not least because it implied and reflected British policy towards Austria, ever keen to calm the tension between Vienna and Berlin and entering a phase of improved Anglo-German dynamics.[101] Only the Austrian Rothschilds communicated their concern that it would lead to an inevitable and unwelcome increase in Nazi influence in Austria in a memorandum to their colleagues in London. This accelerated the transfer of ownership of the Witkowitz steel works (jointly owned by the Gutmann and Rothschild families) from Austria to London.[102]

There is a tendency, among some historians to imagine that London's enthusiasm for the *Anschluss* arose rather late in the day with the appointment of Nevile Henderson as British ambassador to Berlin and Lord Halifax as Foreign Secretary upon the resignation of Anthony Eden. In fact, Foreign Office documents reveal a remarkable if regrettable consistency in UK attitudes towards the desirability of Austria's incorporation

---

100 GSN: *Aufzeichnungen*, p. 4.
101 The Anglo-German Naval agreement of 1935 formally initiated the rapprochement which Edward VIII, supported by many leading peers, sought to tighten. See Andrew Roberts, *The Holy Fox: The Life of Lord Halifax* (London, 1992) and William McElwee, *Britain's Locust Years 1918–1940* (London, 1962).
102 RA: Slaughter and May Memorandum, Vienna, 17 July 1936, quoting Louis de Rothschild and Leonard Keesing 57/38 (Witkowitz Folders).

into Nazi Germany. Even Vansittart, around whose name, to quote Alec Douglas-Home, "many myths were woven,"[103] noted as early as 1933 that "we are backing a losing horse in Austria."[104]

Perhaps the most damning document in the Foreign Office archives from this time is the extraordinary and influential paper compiled by the senior diplomat E.H. Carr, who later became a well-known historian (and biographer of Karl Marx). In his study of the "the Austrian problem" of 17th February 1934, which was distributed to all relevant members of the Foreign Office, Carr noted that there was absolutely "no chance of maintaining Austrian independence."[105] Having established from the outset the futility of supporting an independent Austria, Carr then went on, in a series of prejudiced misconceptions which have arguably distorted British intellectual thought with regard to Austria ever since, to argue that "Germany is united to Austria by race, language and traditions of nearly a thousand years."

Although Carr made passing reference to the Austro-Prussian war of 1866, he appeared to be ignorant of the long eighteenth century of violence between Vienna and Berlin and the fact that for two hundred years it had been Berlin's principal foreign policy aim to destroy Austria's influence and power. Nevertheless, Carr continued warming to his theme: "it is difficult to believe that these fundamental impulses (linking Austria to Germany) will not triumph in the end." Carr's paper found support in many quarters with two influential Foreign Office men, O'Malley and Leeper supporting it fulsomely.[106]

This Foreign Office view was echoed in the popular press. On 31st January 1936, the *Daily Mail* carried an article written by Lady Snowden in which she characterised Austria first and foremost as a "land of doubt."[107]

---

103 Alec Douglas-Home (Baron Home of the Hirsel), *Letters to a Grandson* (London, 1983), Chapter 5 *et seq.*

104 R. Vansittart, *Lessons of My Life* (London, 1943), p 11.

105 See E. H. Carr, *The Austrian Problem*, 26 Feb. 1934, R2190/37/3FO 371 18351.

106 Owen O'Malley, Minister to Hungary, later Ambassador to Portugal. His literary wife Anne Bridge adopted a more pro-Austrian position in her best-selling novel, *Illyrian Spring*. Rex Leeper, later head of the powerful political intelligence department, an Australian by birth.

107 *Daily Mail*, 31 Jan. 1936.

The article contained some trivial memories of Graz and Salzburg before continuing in a more serious if subversive vein: "Austria does not want her independence... she is in favour of the *Anschluss* with Germany and the numbers supporting this are growing daily." Taking a swipe at the Catholicism of rural Austria, she continued, "Better unity with Germany than life in a Papal State." Similar views were espoused among the aristocracy and banking clans. Ernest Tennant, a member of the Scottish banking and industrialist family was only one of many pro-Hitler figures in the British establishment. He earned the reputation among bankers at Rothschild of being "the only Englishman Hitler trusts."[108]

The Quai d'Orsay was more sceptical. The *Petit Journal* reported the agreement under the headline "A small diplomatic Sadowa"[109] but even in Paris there was little to indicate more than a faint disquiet over the grim realisation that a cardinal tenet of French policy towards Germany, i.e. to keep it in a state of permanent friction with Austria, had been apparently removed. Even Italy which must have seen that the agreement marked the end of any posturing by Rome as Austria's sole protector loudly welcomed the rapprochement.

Ironically, the most vociferous criticism of the Austro-German agreement came not from the western democracies or Austria's sponsors and neighbours but from Nazis in Germany and Austria who believed the wily Austrians had somehow "pulled a fast one" over the Germans. The arguments were collected and later well-articulated in a book published on the eve of the war by the Austrian Nazi writer Wladimir von Hartlieb.[110] Noting that it was a kind of "gentlemen's agreement" rather than a full-blown written treaty, Hartlieb expressed the verdict of many Nazis when he called it a perfect example of "Jesuitical equivocation" (*jesuitische Verdrehungskünste*) on the part of the Austrians (i.e. Schmidt) "As a result of this really Jesuitical dishonesty (*recht jesuitische Unehrlichkeit*),

---

108 RA (Witkowitz Folders 57/38): Tennant enjoyed a particularly close relationship with Ribbentrop and was the driving force behind the Anglo-German Fellowship.

109 *Petit Journal*, 13 July 1936.

110 Wladimir von Hartlieb, *Parole: Das Reich: eine historische Darstellung der politische Entwicklung in Österreich von März 1933 bis März 1938*. (Vienna, 1939), pp. 422–425.

the pact was doomed from the start."[111] The legacy of the Stella was at the root of all its faults.

The Pact had been negotiated on the German side by von Papen. Writing in his memoirs, the German envoy paid tribute to the close cooperation and goodwill of Guido Schmidt during the challenging days of 1936, noting that he may not have had "much sympathy" or been expressly "Greater German" in his feelings but that he shared von Papen's views that a "joining together of Austria and Germany was in the best interests of joint German and European strategies."[112] Schmidt made, in von Papen's phrase, "my work a lot easier." He also possessed, as von Papen noted, *eine flexible Natur* and nothing illustrated this better than the terms of the Austro-German agreement which are a masterpiece of ambivalent and potentially divergent clauses. Guido Schmidt and Hornbostel drafted a document of considerable sophistication which appeared on the surface to grant the Nazis major concessions while in practice denying them any new rights or privileges.

Clause 1 gave Vienna all it wished as it pledged Germany to accept and respect Austria's *volle Souveränität* ("full sovereignty"). Once this point was yielded by the Nazis, nearly everything else was secondary. But the following clauses showed Schmidt's skill as a negotiator because they extracted further concessions from Berlin under the guise of Austrian compliance. Clause 2 after a slightly pompous preamble about both countries respecting each other's sovereignty, added that the question of the Austrian Nazi party was entirely an internal issue for Austria. Thus the arrest and execution of the Austrian Nazis involved in the murder of Chancellor Dollfuss could no longer be interpreted as a matter of concern for Berlin. But in return for this wide-ranging concession there were further examples of creative ambivalence. Clause 3 conceded something intangible, i.e. that Austria recognised that it was a "German" state and that it would "organise it policies" to reflect this but without prejudice to the existing Rome Protocols overseeing Austria's relations with Italy and Hungary.

Here was a return to Seipel's idea of the two German states. Without

---

111 Hartlieb, *Parole*, p. 424
112 Von Papen, in Hartlieb, *Parole*, p. 425

4: ENTER GUIDO SCHMIDT ❧ 75

doubt this was Schmidt's masterstroke. Hitler and possibly, but probably doubtfully, von Papen, imagined that this would see an alignment in external policy between Berlin and Vienna. But of this dramatic reorientation of Austrian Foreign Policy, there would be under Schmidt, not the slightest sign. Austria, in contrast to Germany which had walked out of the League within nine months of Hitler coming to power, would remain a cooperative member of the League of Nations and she would scrupulously avoid all pressure from Berlin to support Franco's Spain. She would also not introduce racial laws with regard to the civil rights of Vienna's large Jewish population. Moreover, to the extreme annoyance of the Nazis in and outside Austria, there would be no "reorientation" of Austria away from her other neighbours and the western democracies towards Germany. Under Schmidt the Austrian Foreign Ministry would continue to pursue a policy of "a bridge to all nations." Conveniently, the final clause of the agreement noted that "details" would be worked out once the requisite calm and stability had entered into and taken hold of relations between the two countries. Far from making Austria "a mere vassal of Hitler," as the international left claimed,[113] Vienna did not pledge to "subordinate her foreign policy to Germany." Austrian Nazis were understandably sceptical.

In addition to the written document, Schmidt agreed several "verbal terms" which were referenced by an attached protocol. These terms referred to the treatment of Austrian citizens in the Reich, reciprocal cultural relations, press issues, use of titles and national hymns. Somewhere buried amongst these seeming superficialities was the commitment on Berlin's side to abolish the 1000 mark "Sperre" (literally "barrier": the damaging tax levied on all Germans seeking holidays in Austria). Schmidt conceded that there would be an "understanding" that both partners would "discuss foreign policy issues of common interest." But the Austrian characteristically added a clause which diluted German expectations by stressing that Austria would support the foreign policy of the Reich "aimed and striving to achieve peace." There would be "exchanges of opinion" on issues of mutual interest.

Attached to these comments was an unpublished commitment, the

---

113 For example, see Julius Brauntal, *The Tragedy of Austria* (London, 1948), p. 107 *et seq.*

inevitable *zusätzliche Protokoll* (additional protocol), by the Chancellor to permit an extensive amnesty of political prisoners and an undertaking to invite, after a brief elapse of time, members of the "National Opposition" to "participate in the political responsibility" (*zur Mitwirkung an der politischen Verantwortung heranzuziehen*) but this invitation would be extended only to personalities whom the Austrian Chancellor trusted and selected.[114] Despite the suspicions of many Austrian Nazis there were no other secret or verbal protocols.

To intensify the impression that Austria was yielding more than she really was, both Schuschnigg and Schmidt mobilised all the instruments of propaganda at their disposal to beat the drum of *Deutschtum*. Schuschnigg broadcast on 11th July that the agreement was in keeping with the late Chancellor Dollfuss's recognition that something called "Germanness" existed. After all, the Chancellor said, in a phrase which he might have lifted from British Foreign Office thinking, "we are linked by a common language."

Beneath the velvet glove, however, was the proverbial mailed fist and in other speeches, Schuschnigg made it quite clear that as regards the present and the future, there would be no place in Austria for Nazis hostile to Austria's independence. In a line carefully crafted to make sure the Nazis got the message, Schuschnigg reiterated in speech after speech: "Unreconcilable extreme elements will be proceeded against with relentless severity."[115]

In a typical Schmidt/Schuschnigg move to sugar this pill, Schuschnigg brought Glaise-Horstenau, a former imperial officer and Nazi sympathiser, into his cabinet as a minister without portfolio and formally made Schmidt, who, as von Papen noted, appeared committed to both Germany and Austria eventually coming together, the State Secretary for Foreign Affairs. Historians have lazily bracketed Glaise and Schmidt together being Nazis or at least "crypto-Nazis."[116] Both

---

114 GSN: Aufzeichnungen 1936, p. 3. For an excellent recent study of the Pact see Gabriele Volsansky, *Pakt auf Zeit: das deutsch-österreichische Juli Abkommen 1936* (Vienna, 2001).

115 Quoted in Hartlieb, *Parole*, p. 423.

116 See, for example, Peter Neville, *Appeasing Hitler: the diplomacy of Sir Nevile Henderson*

men were very different in their relationship to the Nazi party. Glaise, an urbane and enlightened figure who had worked in the Imperial War Archives was, in Schmidt's phrase *aufgeschlossen* (open minded and approachable).[117] But as a military man he also had a much less flexible temperament than Schmidt. Even though Schmidt had never joined the Nazi party, it suited Schuschnigg in his dealings with the Germans to allow the impression to take hold that his newly appointed State Secretary for Foreign Affairs was sympathetic to the Greater German (and therefore by extension Nazi) cause.

Austrian Nazis, whatever their reservations about the actual drafting, noted that Schmidt's predecessor could never have negotiated such an agreement on account of his monarchist anti-German views. Schmidt on the other hand was seen as "someone with an open mind with regard to the historical significance of National Socialism in Austria" (*mit einen offenen Blick für die Bedeutung der nationalen Bewegung Österreichs*).[118]

Schmidt kept the heir to the Austrian throne out of the loop for as long as possible but Crown Prince Otto could hardly complain; it was even rumoured correctly that he had been informed of the terms of the treaty ahead of the Austrian President Wilhelm Miklas. [119]

This courtesy did not help Schmidt's relations with the Habsburg. Otto neither accepted nor approved of the agreement and, fed no doubt with malicious rumours from Berger-Waldenegg and Starhemberg, he began his long and never-ending distrust of Guido Schmidt. For his part, Schmidt felt the pretender to the Austrian throne was unrealistic and naive. The Crown Prince's efforts to bring Schmidt round became increasingly persistent. *Otto jagt mich in den Tod* (Otto is chasing me to death) was his verdict after one of these imperial missives.[120]

The failure to square the monarchists was an inevitable consequence of Guido Schmidt's views but they were by no means incompatible with those of his boss. Schuschnigg was a monarchist; for that reason Otto was

---

1937–39 (London, 2000), p. 48

117 See GSN: Aussage Schmidt Verhör, Dec. 1945.

118 Hartlieb, *Parole*, pp. 423–424.

119 See Shepherd, *Austrian Odyssey*, p. 111.

120 GSN: Notes December 1936.

regularly kept informed, but Schuschnigg knew that the legitimist cause was on ice until a more favourable constellation in Austria's diplomatic relations could be achieved. The Habsburgs would never survive another botched restoration attempt.[121] For Schuschnigg only a favourable diplomatic environment could ensure an eventual restoration. For both men, the monarchist card was not on the immediate agenda.

The 11th July agreement was above all an attempt to win time and establish some *modus vivendi* which could give Austria the chance of survival until events strengthened the coalition against Hitler. But the Austrian Rothschilds, while undoubtedly slightly exaggerating the pernicious influence of the Treaty, were right insofar as that without some favourable developments internally and externally, "Nazi influence in Austria was bound to increase."[122]

Writing in his diary on 1st October 1937, Schuschnigg noted that the agreement had calmed the situation in Austria and that the broad masses had undoubtedly benefited from its effects (*dass der breiten Masse aller daran Interessierten dieses Abkommen zweifellos viel Gutes gebracht hat*).[123]

Schmidt would later insist that the agreement was an attempt at a diplomatic move which no responsible Austrian government could have ignored. It had the potential to win time until the western powers realised that Austria was the lynchpin of the entire European building and changed their indifference into soft support at least.

The problem with this thinking was that in 1936 there was very little sign that events would move in a positive direction for Austria. It was far more likely that circumstances would lead to negative developments, vindicating E.H. Carr's gloomy assessment of Austria's chances of survival and confirming Vansittart's belief that in supporting Austria, London was indeed backing a "losing horse."

---

121 Two attempts by Otto's father Charles to return to Hungary in the early 1920s had failed on the betrayal of his advisers and accomplices.

122 RA 57/38.

123 GSN: Notes Dec. 1936, Schuschnigg cit. Schmidt, *Aufzeichnungen*, p. 4.

CHAPTER 5

The Search for Security, 1936–1937

IF THE FIRST half of 1936 seemed in Vienna to be dominated by the Austro-German agreement, there were plenty of opportunities in the second half for Schmidt to establish his credentials elsewhere as Austria's dynamic new State Secretary for Foreign Affairs. His reputation preceded him. Before the agreement there had seemed to be absolutely no chance of reducing the tension in the country arising from disaffected Nazis. This was now no longer the case. But mending relations with Nazi Germany, as far as such a thing was possible given Berlin's ambitions, was only one of the problems on Schmidt's list of diplomatic priorities.

The Stresa Front had been formed in April 1935 when Italy, England and France, faced with growing German strength, reaffirmed the Locarno treaties of 1925 and declared their interest in Austria's independence. The Front came under much strain when Britain signed the Naval agreement with Germany in 1935 without informing Italy or France. It then collapsed with Italy's Abyssinian adventures in October of that year. This would, as Schmidt and Schuschnigg clearly saw, drive the Italians into the German camp and, once that happened, Austria would undoubtedly be the first victim of their renewed friendship. But in London Vansittart, in a typically rushed move to regain the initiative, instructed Selby to blame the collapse of the Front on Austria rather than Abyssinia. Van cynically sought to deflect any opprobrium by stressing the Austrian question. Incensed, Selby ignored the directive.[124]

---

124 SEL 6587. Van saw Austria as a useful prop for British diplomacy under pressure. This rather abusive approach would continue right up until the *Anschluss*.

The Rome Protocols, which the agreement of 11th July 1936 expressly mentioned, had been another factor in giving Austria a breather in an ever more hostile diplomatic landscape. It had been one of the foundations of Austria's Foreign Policy since Dollfuss's time. But as relations between Italy and Germany improved, its significance became less apparent. This was brought home to Schmidt and Schuschnigg when they were invited in the Autumn of 1936 to attend the funeral of the Hungarian Prime Minister, Gyula Gömbös. On 10th October, following the funeral ceremony, Schmidt made his first acquaintance with Galeazzo Ciano, the Italian Foreign Minister and son-in-law of Mussolini.

When later asked during his initial interrogations what he thought of Ciano, Schmidt was keen to play down what was an obvious antipathy, merely commenting that his relations had always been "correct" with the Italian Foreign Minister until late 1937, although Schmidt noted, *en passant*, that Ciano was "jealous [of me] because I competed with him as a youthful Foreign Minister… His appearance, his entire manner did not appeal to me (*Sein Auftreten, seine ganze Art lagen mir nicht sehr gut*)."[125]

Another possible source of antipathy was the fact that, as Schmidt recalled, Ciano always insisted that as Schmidt was "only State Secretary" and that the Austrian Chancellor remained formally Foreign Minister, meetings of Foreign Ministers should be attended by the Austrian Chancellor rather than Schmidt. Ciano himself was less polite. Recording his first impressions after the Gömbös funeral in Budapest, the Italian recalled: "Schmidt is a haggler, careerist and fop."[126]

In inverse proportion to these two men's mutual disdain, however, was Schmidt's rapport with one of the German guests at the funeral. Hermann Göring, then the Prime Minister of Prussia and shortly to be tasked by Hitler with the four-year plan aimed at bringing German rearmament to fruition was a man in many ways after Schmidt's own heart. Charming, intelligent and with an Austrian hinterland dating from his days as a child in Mauterndorf in the Lungau area of Salzburg, Göring had long interested himself in Austria's political and cultural development.[127] Göring

---

125 GSN Vienna: GS Verhör, p. 132.
126 Quoted in Gehl, *Austria, Germany*, pp. 137–138. See also *Ciano Diary*, pp. 36–47.
127 The connexion between Goring and Austria dates from his father's friend Hermann

had decided views on Austria and he had determined ambitions to become involved in foreign affairs. As the temperature between Schmidt and Ciano lowered, the chemistry between the *Reichsmarschall*, as he later became, and the Austrian State Secretary soared.

Two years later, after the German invasion of Austria, Göring made a speech in Linz in which he focussed on Austrian traits, criticising Austrian *Gemütlichkeit* and stressing that that most Viennese of vices, "Laziness (*Faulheit*) must come to an end in Austria."[128] In Guido Schmidt, he seemed to find a personality who indeed had given up these Austrian vices, if he had ever possessed them, of laziness and cosiness. Although Schmidt could be charming, no-one who worked with him would ever have accused him of being "cosy." Here therefore was an Austrian Göring felt he could work with. As the two men turned away from the larger group around them in Budapest, Schmidt deftly brought the German together with Schuschnigg. Expansively eyeing the Austrian, Göring, no doubt emboldened by his banter with the skilful Schmidt who had cleverly encouraged the German's confidence, took the Chancellor's arm and comfortably said while regarding Ciano and his entourage critically across the room: "*Herr Bundeskanzler*, neither of us needs these Italians."[129]

For Schmidt and the Austrian Chancellor, the key question to ascertain was whether the German Nazis in Berlin, having seemingly ditched their Austrian Nazi brethren under the terms of the 1936 agreement, could be persuaded to make further concessions in return for Austria moving more closely towards Berlin and away from Rome. As Schmidt would later say to Schuschnigg: "In Rome they play with fire far more than in Berlin."[130]

---

von Epenstein offering hospitality to the Göring family at the castle of Mauterndorf. After the failed Beer Hall putsch in Munich of 1923, Göring had spent his exile there. Moreover, his anti-Nazi brother Albert was living and working in Vienna as a film-maker.

128 NA Washington *Geheimakte OKW Abteilung Inland 3a50 Österreich betr. Politisches und militärisches Material über Österreich vor, während und nach dem Anschluss VII 1934–I 1939, T-77 R 798*. See also Wolfgang Rosar, *Deutsche Gemeinschaft; Seyss-Inquart und der Anschluss* (Vienna, 1971), p. 334.

129 Gehl, *Austria, Germany*, p. 137.

130 *Documents on German Foreign Policy 1938-1939*. Series D, Vol I, No 182.

For a man of Schmidt's ambition and indeed vanity, it was not difficult to be persuaded that he should travel to Berlin to take the temperature of the German "partners" in the 1936 Austro-German agreement.

The idea was initially mooted by von Papen and Glaise-Horstenau but was already implied by the protocols attached to the agreement. It did not require much effort to persuade Schuschnigg that here was an opportunity to build on the confidence engendered by the July agreement. Above all, it would be an opportunity to thrash out some of the details left unfinished in the agreement. It is evidence of the high degree of trust the Chancellor placed in Schmidt that he was able at this stage to send him to Berlin in complete confidence. Schmidt's programme, carefully worked out in advance with Papen would reconnect him with Göring and even involve a one-to-one meeting with Hitler. This last was especially important for Schuschnigg given that Hitler had drawn most of his political intelligence about Vienna from Austrian Nazis, notably, Glaise, Odilo Globocnik and Friedrich Rainer, all of whom the Führer had received for advice in the hours preceding 11th July agreement. Here therefore might be an opportunity to present a 'more balanced Austrian' viewpoint.

As Schmidt later testified, his contacts with the Nazis, especially with Göring whom he would visit two more times over the coming year were intended to reinforce the impression that he, Schmidt, would honourably defend and work for the maintenance of good relations between Austria and the German Reich. (*Aufrechterhaltung normaler and guter Beziehungen zum Deutschen Reich*). This was to be achieved without compromising Schmidt's commitment to the Austrian point of view (*ohne dabei meinen österreichischen Standpunkt aufzugeben*). These subtleties may well have been lost on Göring but it was part of Schmidt's armoury of intellectual weapons that he could listen attentively. At the meeting with Göring that November, Schmidt discussed a wide-ranging number of issues. In his note of the conversation, Schmidt recalled that Göring told the Austrian at some length that the Austrian credit market should be organised along "German lines," a move which, according to Göring, would create many more jobs in Austria. The conversation then moved onto the subject of mutual trade in military equipment. Schmidt listened carefully and then quietly questioned whether a country with the limited connexions of Austria would benefit from such a move. "Far more urgent" (and here Schmidt was moving the discussion onto territory with which he was far more familiar) was the need to help finance the development of the Austrian winter tourism industry. Even in Berlin, the interests of Vorarlberg were never far from Schmidt's mind.

This led to a most curious idea that aimed at satisfying both men's interests, namely a *Heereslieferungsgeschäft* (army supply business) which would allow Germany to support with schillings the Austrian tourist industry through sales of military equipment to Vienna. Göring insisted that this barter agreement could be implemented swiftly, even for the coming season, if Austria simply stated her wishes for military material. To this request Schmidt again played for time, not wishing to expose his limited knowledge of armament matters, by stressing that only tourism could act as a foundation for better relations between the two countries and that "without it, relations between Austria and Germany would swiftly deteriorate."[131] Schmidt realised that beneath the bonhomie of his host there were real demands on Austria aimed at increasing her dependence on Berlin at every turn.

This was equally the case when, a day later, on 19th November, the Austrian met Hitler for a brief exchange of views in the Reich Chancellery. Of this conversation, Schmidt was later after the war intensively questioned during his initial interrogation but he fielded the questions with comments on Hitler's "affectionate goodwill" towards the land of his birth. A note in the Schmidt archives, however, summarises the conversation in a more concrete way. Schmidt recalled that he had opened the discussions with Hitler by mentioning the tragedy of Dollfuss's death at the hands of Austrian Nazis, a rather indelicate matter and not, one would have thought, an obviously sycophantic way of proceeding with the Führer. There then followed a "confidential discussion" on whether the signatories of the Rome Protocols were discussing adding Czechoslovakia to their number, a clearly worrying proposition for Berlin. Schmidt could reassure the Germans that in his view even if

---

131 GSN: Note 20 Jan. 1936.

Austria and Italy were in favour, Hungary would veto such a plan. The line of questioning underlined the degree of suspicion that still seemed to exist at that time between Berlin and Rome. This would be overcome over the following months.

Schmidt was then criticised for not aligning Austria's foreign policy more closely with that of Berlin's. Schmidt's appearance a few weeks earlier at the League of Nations seemed to irk Hitler especially.[132] The German "bill" for the Agreement of July 1936 was being presented in no uncertain terms. It had also reached Berlin's ear that a few weeks earlier, at a dinner given by the Hungarian minister in Vienna, Hoffmann, Schmidt had openly vowed in the presence of German diplomats never to attend a meal where the table was bedecked with cornflowers, at that time a symbol, like white socks, of unequivocal Nazi sympathy. This point underlined the acuity of the Nazi espionage apparatus in Austria.

Even when there were no German diplomats present, there were enough Nazi sympathisers, and those in the German camp—the Polish ambassador to Vienna, Jan Gawroński, was perhaps one of the most notable—who would eagerly relate Schmidt's *piccoli difetti* to his German colleagues in Vienna.

With his subtle intelligence, Schmidt carefully evaded the more obvious traps of these encounters. Irrespective of Schmidt's personal antipathy to the Nazis, the wheels of European diplomacy continued to turn in ways that forced Austria more into the German camp and further from Rome. Schmidt's susceptibility to personal flattery gave the Germans the sensation that they were closer to him than perhaps in reality they ever were. German diplomatic reports underlined this to such an extent that Schuschnigg later briefing Selby on the visit suggested that perhaps "Schmidt had gone too far in Berlin."[133]

The 1936 agreement with Berlin was undoubtedly a massive step on the path of "reconciliation." Papen did not exaggerate when he said that "this step bore in its breast the future fate of the entire German question (*gesamten deutschen Schicksals*)."[134] In that sense Schmidt had pulled off

---

132 GSN: p. 29 *et seq.*
133 See SEL 6588: Registry of Vienna Legation telegrams with summary of contents.
134 GSN: Verhör Note 11 July 1936.

something which London would hope to achieve—and spectacularly fail—three years later. The brief "normalisation" which followed offered hope that some long-term stability might be achieved which would give Austria time for Germany to become diplomatically weakened and therefore less demanding. Yet neither Schmidt nor Schuschnigg were under any illusion that their situation could be anything other than highly fragile.

The final *communiqué* for the visit stressed Austria's interest in the preservation of a "fair and enduring peace" in Europe and acknowledged that the 11th July agreement had removed pressures on both countries. In his conversations with von Neurath, the German Foreign Minister, Schmidt went further and quoted the well-known Austrian Nazi-sympathiser and historian, Ritter von Srbik, who had written that it was not the space but the people who inhabited it who were important (*Nicht Raum sondern das Volk*).[135]

In his draft thank you letter to Göring, Schmidt referred to *Ein Volk in zwei Staaten* (One people in two states) but another hand, almost certainly judging by the style of the writing, Schuschnigg's, has crossed this out.[136] In his handwritten report on the visit to the Chancellor, Schmidt stressed that the 11th July agreement had "drawn a line under the past but that there was still some 'rubbish' *(Mist)* to be cleared." It was important that he had come as the representative of a "German state" to the capital of the "Reich." In terms of Austria's geo-political equilibrium, the visit appeared to confirm Austria's position in a new diplomatic alignment. The question was whether this attempt to reinforce Austria's independence came at an acceptable price. Certainly, Selby was not alone in accepting Schuschnigg's verdict that Schmidt might have gone too far. His French colleague Puaux shared this view.[137]

Meanwhile, the relationship between Italy and the western democracies, continued to be damaged by Italy's Abyssinian adventure and the involvement of Italian volunteers in Spain. In the spring of 1937, Schmidt accompanied Schuschnigg on a visit to Venice for a summit of the three

135 GSN: Berlin Bericht. Srbik, like many distinguished academics, moved seamlessly from *Grossdeutscher* (in the German sense) to Nazi party supporter.
136 GSN: Briefwechsel G.S. H.G..
137 See Puaux, *Mort*, p. 88.

Rome Protocols powers. That Germany was becoming closer to Italy and was therefore, as a corollary of this rapprochement, influencing more and more the direction of Italy's policy towards Austria was immediately apparent. When the Austrians arrived, they were kept waiting before meeting the Duce, while Mussolini ostentatiously visited the Nazi cruise ship *Milwaukee*, one of the KdF (*Kraft durch Freude*: "Strength through Joy") Nazi leisure organisation's excursions. The sight of the Duce silhouetted against the swastika bedecked ship in the heart of the city of the Doges was a powerful symbol for both Austrians; after all Venice had once been an Austrian possession. For others present, the action of the Italian Head of State was unequivocal. "Austria crucified on the swastika" ran the headlines of one French newspaper correspondent.[138]

The final *communiqué* revealed all too well Italy's diplomatic support for Berlin. Ciano insisted that the closing *communiqué* contain a statement that there could be no reorganisation of the Danube basin region *without* the participation of Germany. As Schmidt later recalled, nothing illustrated more vividly and comprehensively the weakening of Italy's position in Central Europe. Both Schmidt and Schuschnigg attempted to alter this formula for the final *communiqué* but in vain. Both men viewed with dismay the enthusiasm with which Mussolini and Ciano now began to push for greater isolation of Czechoslovakia, a path eagerly endorsed by Hungary's Foreign Minister, Kánya. When Schmidt protested, he was shouted down by Ciano who insisted that Prague's treaty with the Soviet Union showed that she was not interested in friendly relations with her neighbours. From this it was all too clear to see that "Germany and Italy's foreign polices were already in alignment (*zeigte sich bereits die Gleichschaltung der italienischen und deutschen Aussenpolitik*)."[139] Just in case the two Austrians had missed the message, the Italian press vociferously rammed it home, demanding that the Austrian government take more Nazis into its cabinet.

These were not the only signs of the *Gleichschaltung* of Italy's foreign policy with regard to Austria. A significant weather-vane was the Italian support for the Legitimist cause in Austria. In Venice, Mussolini made it

---

138 Ibid., pp. 88–94.
139 GSN: *Aufzeichnungen*. p. 5.

clear that whereas a year earlier he had received a high-ranking Austrian Legitimist delegation, he would not be repeating this courtesy. This *démarche* of course only vindicated Schmidt's scepticism towards the potential of the increasingly isolated monarchist cause.

Another cause of friction in Venice was Ciano's role as an intermediary between Austrian Nazis, illegal under the terms of the 1936 agreement, and the Austrian delegation. To Schmidt's immense irritation and indeed consternation, and just before the Austrian delegation was about to depart from Venice, Ciano handed over a memorandum, drawn up by the Austrian Nazi "illegals" in which they counted on the open support of Italy in achieving their aims of securing more positions in the Austrian government for Nazis. The ensuing row with Ciano cannot have improved the latter's view of the former, or vice versa. Schmidt warned Ciano that Vienna would tolerate no external interference in her internal affairs and certainly would not accept Italy as a mediator in such questions.

These exchanges marked only the beginning of the sharp deterioration in relations between Ciano and Schmidt.[140] The lack of personal sympathy between the two young strutting cockerels of European foreign policy no doubt hastened Austria's detachment from Italy's foreign policy priorities but Schmidt was surely right to note later that the whole equation of power in Europe was changing to Italy's and Austria's disadvantage. The French press lambasted the Venice summit for bringing Germany into the question of the future of the Danube basin, but Paris was in no mood for a decisive confrontation. London, meanwhile, was busy losing its interest in Central Europe now that the main bone of contention with Germany, the future of Austria had apparently been becalmed by the July agreement. With a Foreign Secretary, Anthony Eden, almost pathologically indifferent to Austria and increasingly obsessed with the Abyssinian issue, the collateral damage evident to Schmidt and Schuschnigg that

---

140 Not helped by Guido Schmidt's infant son, Nico impertinently drawing attention at a tea party to the lurid colours of Signora Ciano's nail varnish. "Why are her nails so red," the precocious five-year-old asked to the undisguised annoyance of the Italian. Information from Schmidt's grandson, Guido Schmidt, to the author, 29 March 2020.

Rome was being pushed into a stronger Germany's arms simply did not register on the Foreign Office radar until much later in the year. By then, it was far too late. Cadogan could write in his diaries over the Christmas period of 1937-1938 that it was a priority of Chamberlain's to get onto a better footing with fascist Italy but by then the damage had been done; and done irrevocably.[141] Between February and April 1938 huge efforts were made by the British Ambassador to Rome to construct the basis of an Anglo-Italian agreement but by the time it was concluded on Easter Sunday, Austria's fate had been sealed. Leo Amery visiting the Duce and Ciano on 31st March lamented—and his hosts agreed—that had the agreement been concluded six months earlier Austria could have been saved.[142]

The Venice experience revealed all too clearly that Austria was becoming increasingly isolated and had no supporters prepared to enter even the diplomatic lists to help Vienna fight its corner. It is above all in this context that Schmidt's frantic manoeuvrings with the other European powers must be seen. As 1937 progressed, it became clearer to Schmidt that Vienna's options were becoming limited in the extreme. While the British dragged their heels over the formation of some four or five power combination including Italy which could guarantee some kind of "European stabilisation," Germany grew daily more powerful.[143] Some observers, including journalists advised a stronger rapprochement between Vienna and her neighbours and the construction of a central European security system around Poland, Hungary, Czechoslovakia and Yugoslavia.[144] But this was naive. There were many circumstances militating against such a move, chief of which were the priorities of the central European states to come to an understanding

---

141 For the slowly dawning imperative for Anglo-Italian talks recognising Italy's Abyssinian claims see *Cadogan Diaries*, p.32 *et seq.*

142 See *Empire at Bay: the Leo Amery Diaries 1929–1945*, pp. 501–503.

143 Undoubtedly the idea of some form of power cooperation including the UK, Poland, Italy and Yugoslavia appealed to some British statesmen as a way of delaying "having to deal with Gemany for a few years." See *Empire at Bay*, p. 501. But the rival policy of an Anglo-German agreement eclipsed this plan within weeks of the Anglo-Italian Easter Accords being signed.

144 See for example G. E. R. Gedye, *Fallen Bastions* pp. 222 *et seq.*

with Germany which would involve sacrificing rather than guarantee-ing Austria.

The Poles were a particularly egregious protagonist in this field. The Polish Foreign Minister, Beck, visited Vienna early in 1937 with a simple message: Austria should do everything in its power to satisfy Germany and "then there would be twenty years of peace."[145] When Schmidt met Beck, a former Austrian civil servant's son, a few months later at Geneva in con-junction with a League of Nations session, Beck repeated the message. All the other neighbours of Austria held more or less similar views and they would not lift a finger to help Austria if it in any way threatened their own relationships with the Nazis. This baleful if predictable attitude infected the western powers. Holland's emissary to Vienna, Rost van Tonningen, was even more enthusiastic about the Nazis and the cause of Hitler's Germany than the Polish ambassador Gawroński.

Meanwhile, despite what he had told Hitler, Schmidt renewed attempts to mobilise some form of understanding with Prague towards the end of October. But these now foundered, not on Hungary's tra-ditional attitude towards the Czechs but on the Czech refusal to enter a closer relationship with a state which had "outlawed elections." This and the traditional Hungarian contempt for the Czechs ensured the talks never really got off the ground. It did not help that Kánya had confided in Schmidt that "of all our enemies, the Czechs are the ones everyone despises most."[146] Magyar–Czech frost would only briefly thaw after Schmidt and Schuschnigg's meeting at Berchtesgaden in February 1938 persuaded Prague that Bohemia was next on Hitler's shopping list but by then it would be too late; Hungary out of fear of Hitler would not dare enter any collective security agreement with the detested "bastard of Versailles," the doomed Czechoslovak state.

The situation in Yugoslavia was no different. The Yugoslav Foreign Minister, later Prime Minister, Stojadinović told Schmidt: "Austria's prob-lems are the internal affairs of Germany," adding unhelpfully: "Yugoslavia will never oppose the children of one people coming together."[147] The

---

145 GSN: *Aufzeichnungen*, p. 8
146 GSN: *Verhör*. Also see *Ciano* pp. 93–112
147 GSN: Archiv, Notes by G.S.

Kingdom of Yugoslavia had sheltered Austrian Nazis after they had murdered Dollfuss. German influence especially at an economic level was penetrating the country to the extent that only a British–Soviet coup in March 1941 removing the most anglophile monarch in the Balkans, Prince Paul, would arrest (and then only for a few days) Germany's domination of the country. For Yugoslavia, the Legitimist question with its implications for Croatia inevitably torpedoed any joint action with Austria or Hungary. Collective security among nations who were at loggerheads with each other over countless minority issues was simply a non-starter.

The French Foreign Minister, Delbos, visited all these countries' statesmen towards the end of 1937 and confirmed Schmidt's own view that the chances of any kind of unified response in the case of Austria was "out of the question."[148]

It was not a matter of goodwill. Both in Paris and especially in London, where the Austrian embassy was led by the charming Baron Georg Franckenstein, a former private secretary of Count Berchtold's, Austria's Foreign Minister in 1914, great sympathy was discernible for the Austrian cause, but transposing this into any form of guarantee, however soft, for Austria was an insurmountable obstacle. The fate of Czechoslovakia, a year after the *Anschluss*, was proof enough of how limited any support for Central European states would be. Schmidt was right to say that Austria simply pursued the same policy that England under Chamberlain followed, namely a policy which would avoid a conflict. In both cases it led to predictable baleful consequences. In London's case, this policy culminated in Munich. In Vienna's case it culminated in the *Anschluss*.

It is hardly surprising then that the Austrians should have grabbed at straws or even vipers to try to win time. Alone of Hitler's paladins, Hermann Göring appeared to understand and even have some sympathy for Austria. When Schmidt visited Berlin for his meetings with the German Foreign Minister von Neurath and the Führer in November 1936, he met Göring again. This meeting, like another which followed

---

148 Ibid.

it the following year, was of an official character and had Schuschnigg's unconditional approval. As Schuschnigg later recalled: "I found Göring by far the easiest to talk to in Germany."[149] Even the American diplomat, Bullitt, observed that "*Anschluss* is the final objective of Göring, but he is not in a hurry."[150]

From this first official meeting in November 1936, and with Schuschnigg's blessing, there ensued an extraordinary exchange of letters between Schmidt and Göring. In addition to the simple thank you (with no *Heil Hitler* greeting at the end), Schmidt embarked on what must be one of the most fascinating correspondences to be found anywhere in the run-up to the war. Nothing shows better his drafting skill and his undoubted ability to formulate difficult and controversial issues, in Papen's memorable phrase, "most beautifully." As the letters are unique clues to the dynamics of Austria's relations with Nazi Germany, they repay some study. In addition, they reveal much about both Schmidt and Göring's personalities and their relationship and ambitions.[151] Moreover, the originals which are in the Schmidt papers in Vienna and are here quoted from for the first time in English, with their handwritten addenda, show a warmth of sentiment which is less easily detectable among the printed extracts circulated as evidence in the Schmidt trial of 1947.[152]

---

149 GSN: Archiv, Notes by G.S.

150 Ibid.

151 GSN: Original correspondence: G.S. to Generaloberst Hermann Göring. (*General-oberst*: Colonel-General, the second highest-ranking general officer distinction in the Wehrmacht)

152 *HVPGGS*, p. 302 *et seq*.

CHAPTER 6

"Your Excellency's devoted servant!"

S chmidt's first letter runs to eight pages and was drafted with Schuschnigg's approval and the help of Theodor Hornbostel, the Political Director of the Austrian Foreign Ministry. Hornbostel, the embodiment of the sophisticated, diligent, patriotic, upright servant of the old Austrian state was arrested after the German invasion, sent to Buchenwald concentration camp and only released after much lobbying by Schmidt.

Hornbostel had begun his career in Constantinople after graduating with the highest distinction from Vienna's elite academy, the Theresianum.[153] A convinced Austrian patriot, he worked closely with Schmidt throughout the latter's tenure as State Secretary. As noted earlier, he had also helped Schmidt's drafting of many of the clauses of the 1936 agreement with Germany. It is improbable that the two men's close friendship would have weathered any hint that Schmidt was undermining the Austrian position in his correspondence with Göring. Schmidt's overture to Göring was an unambiguous but clearly officially approved attempt to open up a new line of communication going far beyond simple polite exchanges and building carefully on the concrete topics discussed during their meeting in November 1936.

---

153 The Theresianum was founded in 1746 by Maria Theresa to produce a cadre of highly educated intellectual and internationally minded, linguistically trained imperial administrators. It was abolished by the Nazis following the *Anschluss*. The boarding school was revived after the war and is now a co-educational state subsidised grammar school.

The sheer length of Schmidt's letter suggests that Göring had in some way encouraged this opening up of a novel avenue between Vienna and Berlin. It was also clearly an attempt to bypass von Papen and the "usual diplomatic channels." Schmidt referred to "taking up your offer to inform you, in a written form, of matters which cannot always be discussed in strict diplomatic paths (*auf diplomatischem Wege behandelt zu werden*)." This may have been presumptuous, but he clearly felt Göring's hint had been sincere. In any event Schmidt's presumption fell on fertile ground.

Dated 29th January 1937, more than two months after their meeting, the letter was clearly long in gestation, passing several times through Schuschnigg's hands as well as Hornbostel's. Von Papen was not even obliquely informed of the correspondence and the attempt to broaden the access to Berlin.

Schmidt's opening remarks of thanks immediately seek to establish a unique understanding between himself and his correspondent. He refers to "the atmosphere of open masculine confidence (*Atmosphäre des offenen männlichen Vertrauens*) created between us." Schmidt then moves on to find common ground with Göring in denouncing his predecessor, Berger-Waldenegg. It says a lot about Berger-Waldenegg's unpopularity in the Austrian Foreign Ministry and the general atmosphere of intrigue which prevailed there that his former Political Director, Hornbostel, not only acquiesced but collaborated in this thinly-veiled character assassination:

"Sadly I see from the dispatches of Baron Berger," Schmidt wrote, "that confused and erroneous reports about our internal affairs are reaching you... As you quite correctly pointed out with regard to Baron Berger, there are elements at work which do not approve of the July agreement (of 1936) and are determined to spread poison."[154]

Having established common ground, so to speak, Schmidt went on to counter the prevailing German misconceptions concerning Austria. It is hard not to imagine that his ear was bent in Berlin by many complaints to which he felt he should respond. He stressed that Austria was not engaged in a "persecution wave" (*Verfolgungswelle*) against the "national elements" (i.e. Nazis). This would "not be in the spirit of the amnesty

---

154 GSN: original correspondence between G.S. and Göring.

agreed in 1936." Furthermore, Vienna was "not a transit route for Soviet support for republican Spain (*Durchzugsland für sovietische Elemente auf ihrem Wege nach Spanien*)." Knowing Göring's need for detailed information, he supplied the latest statistics concerning the exact numbers of illegal Nazis arrested and incarcerated in support of his first point. In this way Schmidt hoped to strengthen Göring's hand in his "negotiations" with the other Nazis, his opponents especially in the SS, thus earning his gratitude.

With regard to Spain, he simply observed that "our world view (*Weltanschaung*) with regard to Bolshevism needs not a single word." Austria insisted on detaining anyone suspected of travelling to Spain to assist the Republican cause. Moreover, reports in German newspapers that Austria offered the cheapest ways of travelling to Spain were simply not true. It was Germany not Austria which offered the cheapest routes.

Schmidt asked for understanding with regard to his outspokenness and emphasised that it was his intention simply to present the true facts so the Colonel-General would be faithfully informed of the situation. (*Ihre Zweifel zu zerstreuen und Sie in die Lage… mit konkreten Tatsachen entgegenzutreten*).

Then with a rhetorical flourish, Schmidt addressed obliquely the issue he knew must be uppermost in Göring's mind and noted that he was offering only "an honest word, man to man, and from one German to another' (*ein offenes Wort von Mann zu Mann und von Deutschem zu Deutschem*). This of course laid the ground for Göring to believe Schmidt was supportive of an *Anschluss* between the two German states. Yet it was only an example of what the Austrians would call *Schmäh* (insincere sycophancy). Schmidt the arch *Schmähtandler* (literally: candyfloss trader) knew well how to deploy all the weapons of *schmeichelhaft* flattery and as he signed off with the *besondere Wertschätzung* (especial appreciation) for his new friend, he judged the foibles and weaknesses of his target well. Both men after all shared bourgeois tastes.

He did not have long to wait for the reply. Once again Schmidt's "beautiful" literary skills knew all too well how to prise open the Germans. On 2nd February 1937, barely forty-eight hours after Schmidt's first letter had reached Berlin, Göring sent an eleven-page response. This was encouraging, whatever the contents of the Colonel-General's reply. But as Schmidt studied the letter, he realised he had scored some positive points. Göring appreciated the clarification about Spain: "Your letter has cleared up the matter of transit to Spain… I had read in the German newspapers reports of Russian pilots being encouraged to reach Spain via Austria. As I heard no denials of this, I assumed the reports were correct. I am so happy this was an error and I will communicate that you are doing everything to prevent "red" trains going through Austria."[155]

Göring went on to thank Schmidt for the explanation of the amnesty for Nazis arrested. He clearly appreciated the statistics which Schmidt had provided, and which showed that far from "increasing persecution," the numbers of the "national opposition" in prison had fallen significantly in recent months. Even if Göring had simply dwelt only on these issues, the correspondence would no doubt have been viewed as a success but from the beginning, Schmidt had aimed to draw the German out on his views about Austria so that a meaningful and deep "conversation" could be developed. This would not only enable him to garner more useful intelligence on Berlin's thinking about Austria but also to build a relationship of trust between these two very different and yet in certain personal characteristics, especially fastidiousness of dress, also not dis-similar psychological types. Göring showed that, like Schmidt (in Ciano's assessment), he too could be a "haggler." The Austrian statistics were all very well, he insisted, but they revealed only numbers of official cases. Such information could not disclose the reality of the many coercive measures which the Austrian executive was taking against the "national opposition." Such measures included the incarceration for a week of a pregnant woman, the wife of a distinguished professor and other events which demoralised the Austrian people who struck Göring as "looking unhappy and depressed" on railway stations and other public places where he had encountered them. At the railway stations, people had only greeted him if they were sure there was no gendarme present.

Göring then went on to vent his dismay at the Austrian Chancellor, Schuschnigg, who had in the German's view, gone out of his way to banish

---

155 Ibid.

the language of reconciliation. Following the agreement of 11th July, "I spoke in my next speech" Göring wrote, "about our trust in Schuschnigg. But Schuschnigg in his very next speech, delivered the same day in Klagenfurt, referred to National Socialism as the Number one enemy (*Staatsfeind Nr. 1*)."

Such language led the German to "concerns that the fruits of 11th July are not coming." Nonetheless, Göring went out of his way to reassure Schmidt that the Austrian Nazis would fall in line with the agreement, with the possible exception of a few "hotheads (*Hitzköpfe*)." Referring to Josef Leopold, the leader of the Austrian Nazis from 1935 and a man all the Nazi leadership in Berlin found difficult to deal with, Göring continued: "I am sure Leopold and the majority of the National Socialists will support the 11th July agreement."

Göring's words illustrate, better than many contemporary documents, the problems Berlin was having with the Austrians, both within and outside the Nazi party. The fragmented landscape of political divergence in Austria gave a German political leadership already accustomed to Hitler's fragmented system considerable grounds for frustration. In theory Leopold should have been Berlin's man but as the only Austrian Nazi leader to have remained in Austria after the attempted putsch of 1934 and the murder of Dollfuss, he was imprisoned, with the result that other Austrian Nazis filled the vacuum. But these men—Globocnik, Seyss-Inquart, Reinthaller—while being Nazis, had different ideas on how best to map out Austria's future with regard to the Reich. Faced with this disarray is it any wonder that Göring seized the opportunity of having a dialogue with a clear-headed intelligent "flexible Austrian" such as Guido Schmidt?

This dialogue was all the more necessary because, as Göring summed up with realistic candour: "Unfortunately, I have to conclude that the relations between these two brother peoples are still rather far from even normal friendship. There is too much suspicion on both sides. (*Leider muss ich feststellen dass die Beziehungen dieser beiden Brüdervölker noch ziemlich weit auch nur von normalen Freundschaftlichen entfernt sind. Es herrscht noch zu viel Misstrauen beiderseits*)."

It was vital to calm down people like Leopold but how could an Austrian Nazi understand that "possession of a picture of Hitler, was enough to merit arrest by a gendarme." Göring also conceded that there were enemies of the July agreement in Germany as well as Austria. *(Ich möchte das keineswegs bestreiten)*. But the solution for banishing the "unnatural nature" of "our relations" which should "logically" be the most "intimate and close" was to remove the root cause; the different political creeds; "This unnatural state of affairs will last as long as both countries have competing ideologies." The Fatherland Front of Schuschnigg, Göring appeared to imply, simply needed to be folded into the Nazi party.

The structures, Göring continued, were the same in both countries. All the Austrians needed to do was "exchange the crusader cross (of Jerusalem, the symbol of the Fatherland Front), with the swastika." Building on this curious false premise, Göring now turned to strike a more emotional note of "in sorrow rather than anger": "I am often asked how Austria can be a German state and practice German policies and yet be so hostile to Germany." To solve this conundrum, Göring now fixed his gaze on a target he must have sensed was one Schmidt was probably less enthusiastic about defending than his chief, Schuschnigg: the Habsburgs.

The reason for these misunderstandings, as far as Göring was concerned in his letter, must lie with the former ruling dynasty: "Here the Habsburg plays a weighty role." It was Germany's right to "demand" a "clear rejection of a restoration," yet Austria tolerated the activities of monarchists even though they were opposed to Germany. The Habsburg question was not an internal Austrian question but an "integral part of German Foreign policy *(integrierender Bestandteil der deutschen Aussenpolitik)*." Germany was not working in this respect to undermine Schuschnigg. On the contrary, the German argued, "we believe we can work with confidence with your *Herr Bundeskanzler*. The ball is in your court."

Göring then revealed his own personal ambition as regards the future development of Austrian-German relations: "I should personally be delighted to play an honest role here *(aufrichtig tätig)*." Austria was in his view a "purely German state" which was "doomed" *(dessen Untergang es sein müsste)* if it continued to oppose "German politics in the long run" *(auf die Dauer eine Stellung gegen die deutschen Politik)*. The German would wish to do all in his power to bring about a clearer situation. He would personally devote his entire strength to achieve this as he knew that Schmidt and "the best *Deutschösterreicher*" would equally unite with him to work towards this end. And just in case Schmidt was under any illusions as to what that end might be, Göring concluded this remarkable letter with the sentence: "I am lucky that you found the way to develop my suggestion to have a personal and intimate exchange of views, man to man. I hope to bring the two German states together (*zwei deutschen Staaten zusammenzuführen*)."

Göring added that even though he was not sure Schmidt would agree with him, his personal sympathy for and particular appreciation of Schmidt gave him confidence to speak his mind on these issues (*mit ganz besonderer Sympathie zugetan bin*).

This exchange of letters underlines Göring's desire to play a leading role in the future development of Austro-German relations and demonstrates that Schmidt's charm and manner, which so many found offensive and ingratiating, had scored a bulls-eye with the future *Reichsmarschall*. Whatever the extent and venality of Göring's ambitions, he was clearly impressed by this young, dapper man from the mountains of Vorarlberg. Given that Schmidt had formulated his letter with the help of Hornbostel in the Foreign Ministry and had placed it in front of Schuschnigg, there can be little doubt that it represented a consensus view at the top of the Austrian government. Göring's reply offered a basis for developing another important line of communication into the German leadership and a chance to play for yet more urgently needed time. It was of course also a chance to avoid a conflict with the Reich.

It was Schmidt and Schuschnigg's intention that these "feelers" would eventually culminate in a personal meeting between Göring and the two Austrians.[156] A shooting weekend in Tyrol was thought to prove the most engaging means to lure Göring to Austria. As we have seen, when Schmidt had visited Neurath in Berlin during the late Autumn of 1936, he had also met Göring at Carinhall, following a visit to the hunting exhibition which was organised with such care by the Nazis and which attracted the interest of British statesmen, including Lord Halifax and Nevile Henderson.

---

156 See GSN: Aufzeichnungen, p.10: *Meine Beziehungen zu Göring.* (Also handwritten notes on correspondence.)

It had been during this encounter that Schmidt had been shown into a large room which Göring had explained was his "Hunting Room" (*Jagdzimmer*). Schmidt's eye had been drawn to a fine modern map of Central Europe hanging on the wall. He immediately noticed with some disquiet that the map did not show any of Austria's frontiers. Rather than draw attention to this undiplomatic omission immediately, Schmidt waited until the tour of the house was completed.

When Göring asked Schmidt whether he liked the house, Schmidt replied, "Yes very much but it is unfinished. There is something quite important missing and that is the Austrian frontier on your map." Göring was startled by this remark and immediately apologised (had he noticed?), saying that the map was not a political cartographic exercise but a simple hunting map (*Jagdkarte*). "Please accept my apologies," Schmidt's host had expansively remarked. "Do not misunderstand this: I have hunted in Rominten in East Prussia and Mauterndorf in Austria. For hunters there is only one frontier the *Reviergrenze* (game territorial limit) and no poaching!"

Schmidt pointedly replied that politics, like good hunting steward-ship, should also avoid poaching (*nie wildern*).[157]

This repartee was typical of their relationship with each other. The following autumn, when shooting at Göring's favourite lodge, Schmidt shot an old weary stag. It was named "Hermann." When Göring saw the dead animal, he exclaimed: "Look the Austrian has shot me." To which Schmidt replied with a straight face, playing on the ambivalence sophis-ticated Austrians can use with the German language: "It was not before time"" (*Es war höchster Zeit*). Göring insisted "You have done me in," to which Schmidt answered "If only!" (*Wenn nur!*) which seemed to amuse Göring no end. Schmidt obviously enjoying the repartee then said "Next time I shall bring an animal of my own, a lamb," to which Göring replied: "Good and a black sheep too, your Chancellor Schuschnigg!"[158]

---

157 GSN: Aufzeichnungen, p.11.

158 There are slight variations on this dialogue. See Guido Knopp: *Göring: Eine Karriere* (Köln, 2006) and David Irving: *Göring: a biography* (London, 2010). The version here is the one Schmidt himself referred to: Conversation with Tino Schmidt (son of G.S.) Bludenz, 28 Mar. 2019.

Given this promising personal rapport, it was perhaps doubly disappointing for Schmidt to see this relationship begin to run into the sands as 1937 developed. Yet the correspondence took on a more personal and a less political note. Schmidt became involved with Göring's brother-in-law, Friedrich Riegele, an Austrian lawyer with whom Göring had a somewhat challenging relationship. Schmidt was able to help Riegele whose businesss interests had faltered. In return Riegele introduced him to Göring's art dealer, the Salzburg-educated Kajetan Mühlmann, an art historian who has been described as the "single greatest art plunderer in history." Mühlmann would play a dubious role in Berchtesgaden the following February. On the one hand these personal connexions were useful in establishing another bond between the two correspondents. On the other it led to a dilution of the potential for progress on hard political topics.

Göring felt confident to sign this brief note off with the words: "With the German Greeting," a style, Schmidt did not feel he could reciprocate, preferring to sign off in the more formal Austrian style as "Your Excellency's devoted [servant]." Despite the seemingly politically inconsequential nature of these later exchanges, something of Schmidt's magnetism survived and Göring felt even compelled to scribble him a few lines from his yacht in August.[159]

A brief rekindling of this "special relationship" occurred after Schmidt was invited to Carinhall in early September 1937. Schmidt gushingly thanked his host for inviting him to Carinhall , "this jewel of the most exquisite artistic sensibility." (dieses Juwel des erlesensten Kunstsinnes).[160] More significantly he hinted that there had been some disagreements in their discussions. The "open talk" (a common diplomatic euphemism for frank and difficult exchanges) had "benefited both our understanding" (another diplomatic phrase suggesting divergence of views). A reference to improving imports of iron and wood into the Reich also suggested a sense that the political talks were running out of steam and that the Schuschnigg/Schmidt invitation to come shooting in Austria was in some way not acceptable to the Nazi leadership.

159 GSN: Handwritten note from Göring to G.S., 18 Aug 1937.
160 GSN: G.S. to Göring, 11 Sept. 1937.

On 11th November, Göring finally formally replied, in a twelve-page letter, to Schmidt's invitation for a few days shooting. His letter reveals better than anything else the obvious sticking points that had occurred during his meeting with Schmidt a little earlier. From the very tone of the opening paragraphs, it is clear that a new impatience has settled into the Berlin side of the Austro-German dialogue and that in the struggle between Vienna and Nazi Germany a more sinister tone was developing.

Göring opened with the polite but obviously insincere statement that "although Germany did not wish to interfere in Austria's domestic politics," there would have to be certain conditions agreed by Vienna before Göring could accept such an invitation.

This was an ominous opening. If Berlin was losing patience with Vienna and the skilful procrastination of Austrian policy administered by Schmidt and Schuschnigg, this letter of Göring's shows that his previous bonhomie was now firmly a thing of the past. His *Lieber Freund* Schmidt would understand that they were not private individuals and that "great political expectations" would follow from the appearance of Göring in Austria, especially if he met with Chancellor Schuschnigg. Therefore, it was important from the outset to outline the areas where progress and agreement could be expected.

Firstly, Göring insisted that it was high time for Austria to follow the terms of the 11th July agreement of the previous year and accept that there must be "a clearer sign of Austria's foreign policy aligning with that of Berlin's" in order to achieve the "great goals of pan-German policy" (*grossen Zielen der gesamtdeutschen Politik*). It was unthinkable that such a policy was promised in Germany while being hindered in Austria. This was a thinly veiled criticism of Schmidt, the architect of Austria's Foreign policy which under his guidance had studiously avoided both the entanglements of Spain and the abandonment of the League of Nations, despite considerable German pressure to do otherwise.

Secondly, Göring underlined the need for far greater integration than hitherto of the Austrian armed forces with those of the Reich. The Austrian army "in the sense of greater Germany, thinks in a German way," he insisted. It was time to go beyond the old slogans of "brothers in arms" and harmonise regulations and ranks of the two armies, step up the exchange of officers and unify general staff training. Germany would supply the weapons, equipment and training the Austrians needed to help facilitate this program.

Thirdly, it was necessary to strive towards a "full currency and customs union" between the two countries so that the Austrian exports of raw materials to Germany could be stepped up without the "clearing" delays which currently hindered cross-frontier trade.

Fourthly, on a political level, there remained huge obstacles to progress. This was the "most difficult" area to engage with but it was unacceptable that National Socialism should be equated (*auf die gleiche Stufe*) with Communism in Austria. It was also unacceptable that the symbols of the Reich should be banned in Austria.

"So Mr State Secretary, I am telling you the things as they really are today," he continued brusquely, changing the mood sharply from his earlier greeting of Schmidt as "Lieber Freund." It would be "in the strong interest of our Germanness" if we could orchestrate a "complete sea-change (*völliges Wandel*) in these circumstances". Göring could not "risk coming back with an empty hand." The people of Germany would say "If even Göring cannot achieve success here then who should? (*Wenn es nicht einmal Göring [schafft], wer soll es tun?*)"

Göring now played out his highest card, one which he must have known would torpedo any chance of the visit taking place. It was inconceivable, he wrote, that his visit could be kept from the knowledge of the Austrian people. He would welcome a public element which would allow the Austrians to show their enthusiasm for the concept of greater Germany. This was an impertinence to put it mildly. Göring was insisting that his visit become the focus of a huge Nazi rally, no doubt carefully orchestrated to demand *Anschluss* with Germany. This was light years away from Schmidt's idea of some discreet high-level diplomacy in the seclusion of the Tyrolean forests.

In another candid moment, Göring seemed to realise that what he was asking for was impossible. The Austrian policies had "made the relationship more difficult not less" and the problems his wishes created for Vienna was just another sign of "how impossible our relations have become." Clarity was essential and time was running out. In essence,

Göring was calling time on Schmidt's 11th July agreement and all the policies associated with it. The friendly "man to man" dialogue had become a thinly disguised ultimatum.

Obviously sensitive to the fact that his letter however acceptable to Hitler and his other paladins, would come as a sharp reality check for Schmidt, he went on to end the letter on a more conciliatory note:

> "I believe we can find a peaceful solution which respects Austria's independence if the 'national opposition' (Nazis) are allowed the same freedom of movement as that given to the monarchists."

But the threat and new bullying tone was unmistakeable:

> "You will understand that because of our friendship I do not wish a situation to arise which could have in the worst-case unthinkable consequences."

Here were the Nazi cards laid out on the baize with uncompromising clarity. Either Schmidt and Schuschnigg gave up their game of prevarication and delay or the Nazis would take "extreme measures." It was as if the original exchange had been shown to Hitler who had seen immediately that Schmidt had outwitted the future *Reichsmarschall* and had gained the time which Hitler knew was not on his side. In any event, for one reason or another, Göring had been persuaded that if he were to continue his interest in Austria he would have to move matters along from the *gemütlich* but glacial pace, Schmidt and Schuschnigg had orchestrated so carefully.

Although Göring went on to say that he was "motivated only by one thought: no escalation of the situation", this was grossly insincere, even by his standards. He was raising the stakes and at the same time pushing hard on Schmidt to fall into line. In a sentence of breath-taking arrogance and self-regard, Göring made it clear he wanted his dialogue, however one sided, to continue but that it was Schmidt's last chance:

> "I am motivated to avoid anything which damages our good personal relationship which preserves the possibility that our friendship offers you perhaps someone who can negotiate unencumbered (...*als einziger unbelastet verhandeln kann*)."

Summing up, Göring saw only three possibilities: no visit; a meeting in the remote valleys away from all cities and villages but under the conditions articulated earlier in the letter (i.e. participation of the Austrian Nazis; or a meeting with Schuschnigg on German territory near the Austrian border.

He had talked about the visit and the invitation for a long time with the Führer and while the letter he was writing was "exceptionally difficult for him," he thanked the Austrian Chancellor for the invitation. Here was the hint that Hitler had decided stop the Schmidt–Göring dalliance which he could see was going nowhere.

Schmidt's reply was to the point and to add more piquancy was sent to Göring via von Papen, a carefully calculated snub. Now that the negotiations had run into a wall, there seemed little point in keeping the line of communication secret from von Papen. No doubt Göring would forgive this deliberate indiscretion of Schmidt's.

For Schmidt, the imperative need was to salvage something of the integrity of the 11th July agreement and continue the dialogue despite the disheartening change of key. After defending the invitation and implying that his interlocutor was underestimating the importance of a meeting with the Chancellor, Schmidt went on to stress that 11th July had proved itself in many ways and that a *sovereign* Austria would always be interested in a good relationship between the two German states. This was a kick in the teeth administered with finesse to a man forever stressing the "brotherhood" and "unity" of the "entire" German concept.

Schmidt then went on to tackle the points Göring had raised. He must have known that such intellectual argument would probably fall on stony ground but the training of the Stella allowed nothing less than the full deployment of all the weapons in Schmidt's mental armoury. What followed was an intellectual tour de force.

With regard to Göring's strictures on Austria's foreign policy, Schmidt riposted that the 11th July agreement safeguarded Germany's expectations and Austria's commitments and that a sovereign Austria, the phrase is a *leitmotiv* in Schmidt's reply, would be of some use to Germany in her foreign policy aims.

Schmidt's skill was perhaps most vividly on display in his dealing with

Göring's next point, on military integration. "I suggest as a first step, a joint military exercise, to take place on the occasion of your hunting visit and in your honour. This would surely be the best way to begin closer relations between the two armies. The Chancellor would be delighted thereafter to discuss with you the ideas you mention." One cannot be sure whether Schmidt's suggestion which at first sight underlines Professor Broucek's judgment that he was "a military ignoramus,"[161] was intended from the first to be utterly unrealistic and therefore doomed to rejection. At the very least it underlines Schmidt's generally cavalier attitude towards military affairs.

With regard to trade agreements, Schmidt was on more secure and familiar ground. He promised Göring nothing less than a sketched-out plan of future Austro-German trade relations which he had already worked upon with a member of the German embassy.[162] Such an initial agreement could be signed by the Chancellor and Göring on the occasion of the visit.

With regard to Göring's political demands, Schmidt acknowledged that it was by far the most "delicate" issue. Again, he sought refuge in the agreement of 11th July 1936 which made clear in its opening clause that there was to be absolutely no interference by Germany in Austria's internal affairs. It might be better for Göring to dwell on why the "national opposition" had always made no secret of the fact that they were "unremittingly hostile towards Austria." Many problems "would have been solved long ago had this not been the case." As for Austria's attitude, the Colonel General would be directed to note that only in the recent few weeks, the Chancellor had invited Dr Seyss, a well-known Austrian Nazi-sympathiser, into the ranks of his Cabinet's advisory council (*Staatsrat*) and other Nazis had been brought into the Fatherland Front. Clearly Austria had done what she needed to achieve reconciliation, as would become abundantly clear to the German when he met with the Chancellor.

Schmidt then went on to give details of a mouth-watering program for Göring involving the "most beautiful chamois reserves of the Tyrol,"

---

161 See Broucek, *Jansa*, p. 99.
162 Presumably Keppler.

a chance to meet the appreciative Tyrolean population and a selection of breath-taking views as well as the opportunity (thrown in, one senses, at the last moment) to see a unit of Austrian mountain troops embark on one of their exercises (without their German *confrères*).

Finally, Schmidt, perhaps taking a lesson out of Göring's book, turned on the pressure on his *hochverehrter* (highly esteemed) friend by noting that a cancellation of this visit would be a personal painful disappointment for Schmidt and "difficult to explain to the world's media." But if Schmidt imagined the Nazis would be intimidated by the world's press, he was in for another disappointment. Thanks to Himmler, the Austrian Nazis had got wind of the correspondence between Schmidt and Göring, and were quick to raise the cry of treason against Göring for negotiating behind their backs. Ultimately the combined leverage of these Nazis was enough to torpedo the visit.

Whether the few days of hunting and wine would have delayed the growing menacing constellation gathering around Austria is a moot point. Göring, too, was discovering the limitations placed on his powers and his efforts to involve himself more deeply in Austrian affairs. Nonetheless, the exchange had long term consequences for Guido Schmidt which he could not have imagined in the autumn of 1937. Göring did not forget the "man to man" conversations he had had with the intelligent, ambitious and, like him, vain diplomat who nonetheless had always given him reliable information about Austria and about the fractious, uncontrollable hoodlums who made up many of the Austrian Nazi party. However frozen the negotiations between the two men now were, their friendship would persist. It is hard not to imagine an element of slight homo-eroticism in Göring's interest in Schmidt. Certainly his subsequent actions suggested a level of affectionate concern which went beyond purely diplomatic exchanges.

Meanwhile, Schmidt had not limited himself simply to this line of communication with the Third Reich. From the beginning he was quick to recognise that the western democracies would be reluctant to intervene on Austria's behalf. That did not mean he could not engage with them in the hope of winning sympathy for Austria while playing for time, during which the equation of power threatening Austria's existence could change in Vienna's favour. He briefed both the French and British ministers at length on his conversations with Göring.[163]

Schmidt would throw himself into his contacts with the western democracies with the same energy and élan that he had demonstrated in his dealings with Göring. That the results would prove so meagre was perhaps to be expected but once again the Stella Matutina training brooked no halfheartedness in the efforts to be made.

In the course of his engagements with the British Foreign Office he would learn to appreciate England and even become persuaded that British diplomacy might save Austria. In the course of this journey of discovery he would become ensnared in the greatest known security breach the British diplomatic service ever suffered in the run-up to, and indeed during the Second World War. It would prove quite a baptism of fire for this provincial "upstart," although it came closer than anything else to costing him his job.

---

163 See SEL 6588: Vienna Legation Registry of dispatches 1937. Unfortunately, this file although listed in Selby's copy of the Legation Registry in his papers did not survive the archival FO "weeding" and is not in the NA. Vansittart's papers also make reference to the Göring "conversation." See VNST II/2/26

CHAPTER 7

Diplomatic tangles: Schmidt, Vansittart and the Rome embassy valet

BEFORE ACCOMPANYING Schmidt on his tour of the capitals of the western democracies, it is perhaps worth examining his own political development at this time. Had he changed the views inherited so faithfully from the Jesuits in Feldkirch and his mentor Monsignor Seipel?

Another lecture, this time given back in his home province of Vorarlberg, offers some clues. Entitled again: *Der Mensch und der Staat*,[164] it updated his earlier thinking on the role of the state and its impact on the individual. He now attempted to respond to certain relevant issues "not just as a minister of the state" but as a "simple Austrian." "What does the state mean for people? What does it demand of us and what do we demand of it?"

As during so many periods of his career, Schmidt was at pains to emphasise his practical credentials. He was, despite his intellectual training at the hands of the Jesuits, a product of a formation which insisted that intellect without a concrete purpose was intellect wasted. Great things were expected of the Jesuits not just in terms of contemplation and prayer. Monarchs had in earlier centuries brought in the Jesuits when they had wanted to achieve what seemed impossible: to restore Catholicism in lands where heresy had taken root, to create from nothing but the soil

---

164 GSN: *Der Mensch und der Staat* (manuscript).

and barren rocks a new elite where before only an illiterate peasantry had existed. As recently as 1908 the Society had achieved precisely that in the newly annexed provinces of Bosnia-Hercegovina where they would teach Yugoslavia's greatest author, Ivo Andric, how to write.

In this context one could understand Schmidt's opening paragraph: "I come not from a world of abstract concepts but from the workshop of concrete and tangible activity." (*Ich komme nicht aus der Welt der abstrakten Begriffe sondern aus der Werkstatt konkreter sachlicher Arbeit.*)

Drawing again on a disparate range of sources, stretching from John Locke to St Paul, via Machiavelli, Hegel and Adam Smith, Schmidt demonstrated a *Weltanschauung* (world view) which underlined a liberal rather than authoritarian outlook. If Christianity was at the heart of the relationship between the Austrian state and its citizens, then the "individual rights" were the expression of a well-functioning political entity. Austria was a state which offered peace and security and improving living standards for the individual. Quoting Grillparzer's "Ode to Austria,"[165] Schmidt developed the idea that Austria was moving away from her monarchical "childhood" to a new political maturity which nonetheless retained much of the positive things of old Austria (*der Inbegriff altöster-reichischen Staatempfindens*). People who sought to disrupt this continuity were guilty—and here Schmidt was surely making a thinly veiled reference to the Nazis and the communists—of "not understanding anything at all (*krassen Unverstand*)." The state was not, as some Austrians in the 1920s had imagined—another reference to the Communists—"a cow to milk": such a state "could not endure." The socialist utopia had simply underlined the shortcomings of an impractical ideology: "Never was the state less of a republic than during the Republic," was Schmidt's verdict on the efforts of the socialists in Austria immediately following the collapse of empire. "A republic cannot be reduced to simply as much or as little its citizens derive from it." Having demolished the pretensions of the Left, Schmidt now turned his fire on the Nazis and fascists. Fascism sought to "interfere in all aspects of daily life." The "Nazis even more so." This was not the individual rights envisaged by Locke or Humboldt

---

165 Franz Grillparzer, *König Ottokars Glück und Ende* (1823), Act III.

but rather a new and dangerous form of "extreme individualism" which, unless checked, would ultimately "destroy Austria." Only the "healthy sense of the Austrian (*der gesunde Sinn des Österreichers*)" could protect the state from this danger which had already martyred one Austrian Chancellor, Engelbert Dollfuss. The *Ständestaat* (corporatist state) was a bulwark against these dangers but being based on Christian values it was, in contrast to the totalitarian systems of fascism and Nazism, capable of giving much space to the individual, allowing a "mixture of individual and universal direction." This system, much misunderstood by external observers, could be reduced to three simple words: "Freedom, Authority and People (*Freiheit, Autorität und Volk*)."

Such a system avoided the excesses of fascism and Schmidt questioned whether the individual really wanted to subsume himself in a larger entity: "Is there really," he asked, "a new generation which wants to worship the state?" Similarly, the "recurring call for a strong man and a strong state" taking on pseudo-religious forms might be a sign of the eternal desire of youth to be "excited" (*Jugend will begeistert sein*) but it could only be a means to an end, yet to be glimpsed.

The Austrian was unlikely to follow "such false paths" as he and she were possessed of their own rich heritage, little of which could bring the masses to hysteria. Rather the Austrians could follow their own path based on freedom and authority. This was not just possible but desirable and, in Schmidt's view, the "only way." The people of Vorarlberg instinctively understood this because they all had a "strong sense of freedom" (*starke Freiheitswille*) which was linked to a conviction that there "had to be a universal valid order in life *(verbindet sich mit dem Wissen dass es eine für alle geltende Ordnung geben muss)*."[166]

Schmidt went on to quote his fellow Vorarlberger politician, Otto Ender, who said "Someone has to be in charge" (*Einer muss Herr sein*). Religion had of course a role to play in this (*Das Religiöse hat hier mitzusprechen*) but Schmidt went on to distinguish between a Christian state such as Austria, and fascist Italy or Nazi Germany. "A Christian state does not mean a clerical state," he insisted, adding with a clear reference to Nazi

---

166 GSN: *Der Mensch und der Staat*, p. 27.

Germany, that a Christian state also did not mean "a political church."[167] At the core of the Christian state was a belief that "human dignity should play the leading role." The foundations of such a state were to be found in the relations of Christ towards his fellow people. In this way a "fair compromise" could be seen to be at the very heart of the idea of the Austrian state (*Kernstück unserer Staatsidee*). This "Christian foundation" was so rooted in Austrian minds and souls that it was "for most people not second nature but first"; even if, Schmidt added, "Enlightenment thought finds it difficult to accept this." Quoting the Austrian writer Hermann Bahr, who described the Austrians as *stockkatholisch* (Catholic through and through), Schmidt summed up that it was this characteristic which provided the reason why Seipel, Dollfuss and the then Chancellor Schuschnigg had acted as they did. They were all intent on building a "state which corresponds to the Austrian soul."

From the above it is clear that Schmidt had not surrendered any of his Christian convictions and was neither a fascist nor a Nazi but rather a patriotic Austrian of the same Catholic persuasion as many of his coun-trymen. Just as in the eighteenth century, Austria had developed its own interpretation of the Enlightenment which had cemented rather than challenged the ruling dynasty, so, conversely, in the 1930s, the authoritarian nature of the *Ständestaat* offered an alternative to both the blanket collective totalitarianism of Italy or Germany and the liberal traditions of the western democracies. Austria was no longer a significant power but its intellectual and spiritual legacy shone through almost every sentence of Schmidt's speech.[168] It was this Austria that Schmidt sought to defend.

The increasing pressure of Germany, expressed so vividly in Göring's correspondence, brought Schmidt quickly to the conclusion that while nothing concrete could be expected from France or England in the short term, it was essential to engage with both countries if time was to be won for a more favourable constellation of stabilising factors in Europe to

---

167 The Nazis' control of the Lutheran Church in Germany went so far as to give the Nazi party the right to appoint bishops.

168 For the way in which Austrian Freemasonry acted as a way of enveloping reform in the interests of the Habsburgs and by extension the authority of the state see Martyn Rady, *The Habsburgs* (London, 2019), Chapter 9.

emerge. Of these two western democracies, Schmidt recognised from the beginning, despite his direct experience as a young diplomat in France, that Britain was more important by far. France would, he believed, never act without British support and therefore, if Austria was to survive the hostile environment, it would be vital to establish as close a contact with the statesmen of the British Empire as was possible. A chance encounter in early 1937 on the fringes of a League of Nations meeting at Geneva brought him into direct contact with arguably the most powerful British diplomatist of his generation, Sir Robert Vansittart, the permanent Under-Secretary of the Foreign Office. Here was a man at the centre of a powerfully influential secret intelligence network which, funded by his own considerable personal financial resources, complemented and occasionally contradicted the analysis of Germany and Austria put forward by the Foreign Office and the Secret Intelligence Service.[169] Van had more than just a passing interest in Austria. While he felt support for Vienna was backing a "losing horse," he maintained an interest in developments there, not least because he knew that Austria could provide a window on developments in neighbouring Germany. This did not prevent him, as we have seen, from exploiting Austria to further his own diplomatic ends.

Vansittart had an effective informant, Group Captain M. B. Christie, a retired officer with valuable contacts in Austria. By the time Vansittart met Schmidt again in May of 1937 during the coronation celebrations in London, he already had good reasons for thinking the young Vorarlberger would be a useful contact. He had heard that Schmidt had opened a line of communication with Göring. Christie, who also knew Göring, might have told Vansittart, and it would have been confirmed by Foreign Office sources in Berlin and Vienna that Schmidt had met with Hitler and was *persona grata* in Berlin.

At that time the rearmament of Britain was just beginning and the key question for Vansittart was whether the German air force had reached "parity" with the Royal Air Force. Van had asked Hitler this question directly, following his attendance at the 1936 Olympic Games. Much

---

169 SIS Austria and Germany assessment in VNST II/2/26. (As with several other of Van's documents, his access to SIS assessments was critical to evaluating the reliability of his own sources of information.)

to Hitler's chagrin, the British diplomat, who spoke fluent German, had asked in a slightly Austrian inflected accent. Hitler had bluffed and said the *Luftwaffe* had just reached parity with the RAF. For some months afterwards it became the priority for Vansittart's intelligence service to find out whether this was really true. When Schmidt was asked for his view, he said that in his opinion, following talks with Göring and others in Berlin, he was under the impression that parity was just a bluff. Van sat up.

Schmidt was not a "Graf Bobby" figure such as he had encountered in his student days in Vienna before 1914 but a surprisingly dynamic Austrian with a very clear grasp of realities.[170] But there was more to come. Schmidt had already met Ciano a few weeks earlier. During the talks in Venice, he had picked up with his sensitive intuition a feeling that Ciano was showing off to him about "British intentions." It was as if the Italian knew exactly how London would react to any issue in central Europe. The rivalry between the two young foreign ministers was palpable and the antipathy which followed would easily have led Ciano to brag about his knowledge.

On one occasion he boasted to Schmidt that he knew everything the British Embassy in Rome thought "before they even thought it."[171] This was a clear admission that the Italians had a mole inside the Drummond embassy or had broken all the British cyphers.[172] Schmidt needed no encouragement to impart this "gem" to Van. He clearly intended to garnish his credibility with Vansittart by conveying to him an important nugget of high-grade intelligence. He did not know whether Van knew of the leak or not, but his timing was impeccable. A few weeks earlier, the ambassador's wife's tiara had disappeared out of one of Sir Eric Drummond's boxes and the subsequent lackadaisical internal embassy enquiry had thrown up the "possibility" that confidential documents also kept in the box might have been stolen.

---

170 "Graf Bobby": fictitious Austrian aristocrat of foppish but impeccable manners and limited intelligence, immortalised in several anthologies of Viennese humour in the 1920s and later much popularised in the film *The Adventures of Count Bobby* in 1961 (dir. Géza von Cziffra).

171 See GSN: *Meine Verantwortung*, p. 132.

172 Sir Eric Drummond, later Lord Perth.

Van, according to his friend and collaborator Ian Colvin, was sufficiently concerned by this tip-off from Schmidt to order immediately a
further full-blown inquiry by the head of the Secret Service, Admiral
Hugh Sinclair.[173] This enquiry, so typical of a civil service or government
internal investigation designed not to "frighten the horses" or attribute
blame which could damage promising careers, focussed ponderously on
a likely suspect in the form of a venerable locally employed chancery
servant, Signor Secundo Constantini.[174]

Constantini had worked in the British embassy in Rome since
1914. This long period of "loyal" service had ironic consequences.
Notwithstanding his being the chief suspect in a case of espionage which
has rightly been called "the most serious known breach of British security in the run-up to the Second World War"[175], Constantini and his wife
were invited to London in May 1937 for the coronation of King George
VI. His "incontestable damage" according to the internal investigation
to vital UK interests did not prevent the Foreign Office (and therefore
ultimately the British tax-payer) from funding this visit.

Constantini, "an inside agent unable to resist temptation," had
"abstracted documents and cyphers, photographed them and following
their copying, returned the documents." He had also made duplicated
keys to all the embassy safes and passed these to the relevant Italian
authorities. The SIS report[176] speculated that this had been going on
since the mid-1920s but the embassy reaction to the report was to dismiss
its conclusions with what has been rightly called "incredible carelessness,
tinged with a sublime confidence in British methods." Irrespective of
when they had begun, there is no doubt that the leakages continued right

---

173 See Colvin, *Vansittart*, pp. 56–58.
174 I am indebted to Professor David Dilks for pointing me in the direction of his work
  on this subject, notably: "Flashes of Intelligence" in *The Missing Dimension*, ed. D.
  Dilks and C. M. Andrew (London, 1984) and his masterly study "Appeasement and
  Intelligence," in *Retreat from Power: Studies in British Foreign Policy of the twentieth century*, volume 1: 1906–1939, ed. D. Dilks (London, 1981). For Constantini's possible
  role as a "double agent" see Owen Chadwick's *Britain and the Vatican during the Second
  World War* (Cambridge, 1986), p. 298.
175 Dilks, "Appeasement and Intelligence," p. 150 *et seq.*
176 Y775/775/650 FO 350/2

up until 1940 when on the declaration of war, the embassy was closed.

There has been a recent trend among some well-known journalists to discount the value of intelligence in geo-politics.[177] "Intelligence gathering is inherently wasteful," they cry, but lest anyone should imagine Signor Constantini's efforts were nugatory, we should consider the strong links between Foreign Policy and intelligence in this particular case. Schmidt would not have taken the risk of imparting such an important piece of information if he did not consider the leaks from the British embassy in Rome to be affecting the way Mussolini and Ciano conducted their policies towards Austria.

The recent evidence from Italian sources confirms beyond doubt that in this case, it is no exaggeration to say that Mussolini's entire Foreign Policy was based on the fruits of Constantini's efforts. A few examples will suffice to convince the most sceptically minded cynic of the value of this intelligence:

1. In 1935, as the Abyssinian crisis developed, a large part of the British Home Fleet was moved to Gibraltar in an attempt to intimidate Italy. Mussolini was presented with copies of signals from the Admiralty to the fleet indicating that supplies of ammunition were pitifully low and that other technical difficulties would impede any "demonstration." His marginalia, much in the style of Kaiser Wilhelm, indicated his contempt for British attempts to bully him and his determination not to be intimidated.

2. In 1936, Anthony Eden circulated to the key European embassies including Rome a highly confidential report entitled "The German Danger," indicating that it was "vital to complete rearmament" and that therefore some kind of "holding deal" with Hitler was necessary. Eden urged "the utmost secrecy" Mussolini showed the document to the German Foreign Minister, von Neurath, who eagerly showed it to Hitler, not least to "disprove Ribbentrop's illusions." Ciano used it to great effect during a conversation with Hitler to demonstrate that London would never come to a lasting

---

177 For a current example see Max Hastings, *The Secret War: Spies, Codes and Guerrillas, 1939–1945* (London, 2016).

accommodation with Germany or Italy and that "Germany should be under no illusions."[178] Attached to the report was a dispatch from Sir Eric Phipps, the British ambassador in Berlin, branding Hitler and his paladins as a gang of "dangerous adventurers." This made a profound impression on Hitler who commented that the British empire had also been founded by "dangerous adventurers." A few days after this meeting, Mussolini and Hitler declared the Axis.[179]

3. In early 1937, two dispatches from the British minister in Belgrade, Ronald Campbell, quoting first, the Yugoslav Prime Minister, Stojadinović, relating a conversation with Ciano warning that all Foreign Office documents of any relevance were with the Italian ambassador in London Dino Grandi "within hours," and then second, Prince Paul, the Regent of Yugoslavia, stating that his agreement with Italy, just about to be concluded was "meaningless." This indiscretion so infuriated Mussolini that he eagerly torpedoed the "gentleman's agreement" he signed with Belgrade on 25th March 1937, one of whose clauses respected the independence of Albania. Italy occupied Albania at Easter eighteen months later and eventually agreed with Hitler on a plan to partition Yugoslavia.[180]

4. In mid-May 1939 Chamberlain issued a confidential report to Henderson in Berlin underlining London's determination to stand by Poland militarily and not just act as a non-participating guarantor of Polish independence. A copy of this was sent by Mussolini to Hitler with the result that a week later the Pact of Steel between Italy and Germany was proclaimed on 22nd May in Berlin.

5. In July 1939, following a visit to Rome, the King of Greece arrived in London where he was exceptionally scathing in his personal evaluation of Mussolini's personality. These comments rankled so

---

178 Dilks, "Appeasement and Intelligence," p. 150.

179 Professor Dilks leaves open the possibility that this document was leaked from a source, possibly Russian, in London to the Italians. See Dilks, "Appeasement and Intelligence," p. 150 *et seq.*

180 Campbell to Eden 10.iii. 1937. R 1687/224/92/ FO 371/21198.

much that it was a contributing factor to Mussolini's intemperate and ill-starred invasion of Greece a few months later.[181]

Three of these examples occurred before the *Anschluss* but it was doubtless of interest to Schmidt that the report of Sir John Maffrey of the Colonial Office advising that there was simply no "British interest" affected by the Abyssinian crisis landed in the last week of February 1936 on the eve of a critical sanctions debate in the League of Nations a few weeks later. To underline how toothless British threats were, Mussolini took the opportunity of publishing this document in its entirety in the *Giornale d'Italia*. Schmidt quickly realised that these leaks fuelled Mussolini's resentment of the British and their condemnation, undermining the attempts to repair fences between London and Rome that alone might ensure that Mussolini would not be driven increasingly into Hitler's arms. It would be several vital months before the British could put Abyssinia behind them and try to move to an understanding with fascist Italy.

Until Schmidt's "indiscretion" the Foreign Office enquiry had been lacklustre. The wheels of the official investigation into the British embassy leak had ground on ponderously. "I do not believe in such a thing as an expert on security measures," the investigating officer unpromisingly began his report noting that there was an increase in danger especially during the "dead" periods between 1 p.m. and 5 p.m. and 8.15 a.m. and 10.15 a.m. when the chancery was usually unmanned (!). The investigating officer also noted that the "Italian policeman at the gate should be regarded as a menace rather than a safeguard."[182]

It was a matter of concern that the Head of Chancery, Mr Noble, had left explicit instructions for the windows of his office to be closed and locked and yet they were habitually found to be open. Although the safe combinations were considered fool proof, it emerged that a recently departed First Secretary had left a note of the combination on a piece of

---

181 A fine irony this given that the debacle which awaited Italian troops forced the Germans to delay Barbarossa by a crucial six weeks thus affording the Red Army the unquestionable advantages of "General Winter" in their campaign against the *Wehrmacht*.

182 *DBFP* 2nd series, vol. XV, p. 648.

paper at the top of a pile of documents in an unlocked diplomatic box. It was equally to be regretted that the press office was "rather inclined to retain for longish periods" confidential papers. But it was the accessibility of the ambassador's quarters to "native servants" which was the principal concern together with an awareness that internal telephone communications were easily compromised by certain "brand new instruments" placed on desks.

When Vansittart read this report at the beginning of March 1937, he minuted that it was "essential" that the four "native chancery servants" be "removed at once." Following Schmidt's disclosure he redoubled his efforts to clear up the Rome chancery with a full blown investigation by the chief of the Secret Intelligence Service but what followed is a textbook example of how the bureaucracy of a great office of state, albeit in an undoubtedly declining imperial system, can neutralise instruction from the highest authority.

After various "consultations," the new Permanent Under-Secretary Alexander Cadogan advised caution. (Vansittart had been moved to the "new" position of Chief Diplomatic Adviser at the end of 1937 following protest at his high-handedness from Chamberlain and others.) And caution quickly became inertia. No doubt the protestations of the Rome embassy to the Quirinal were partly to blame. Cadogan's private secretary, Clifford Norton, had observed earlier, it was just "a scare about Rome." "As regards our missions abroad, we believe our cyphers are safe." In a wonderful piece of oblique jargon designed to see off all interference, Norton continued: "We should resist attempts to simplify and weaken the system." After all, "all reasonable precautions are taken." Moreover, Norton concluded, "all the evidence points to our telegrams in cypher to Rome being 'safe'. I do not think the Italians can read our cyphers" and that should be "an end of the matter." After all Ciano's perceptive comments might simply be intelligent guesswork.[183] Thus was arguably the most influential breach of security and Guido Schmidt's most significant contribution to the British Foreign Office quietly put to bed until rumours from other European diplomats reopened the case in the

---

183 Minute C. J. Norton 16 March 1937, DBFP 3rd series Volume V p 648.

immediate aftermath of the war. By then, the authorities felt they could no longer proceed against Signor Constantini because he was "no longer an enemy national."[184]

Schmidt, even with his experience of an equally byzantine bureaucracy in Vienna, could be forgiven for thinking that the efficiency of the Foreign Office would quickly identify and even eliminate the leak, towards which he had so generously alerted Vansittart. Certainly, Schmidt's acuity in these matters compares most favourably with that of the British in whom he confided so freely. He would soon experience at first hand the brutal realisation that far from acting on his tip, the leaks were not only continuing but were about to become highly dangerous to the progress of his own career.

On 27th September 1937, he dined with Vansittart in Geneva, on the occasion of another League of Nations meeting. This time, it seems that the conversation became quite animated with regard to the personalities of Mussolini and Ciano. Perhaps Schmidt found the superb French wines Van served after a trying day loosened his tongue. In any event he felt sufficiently expansive to dwell on certain traits of the Italian statesmen. The dinner did not have an "official" character and Lady Vansittart was present. Perhaps Vansittart had told Schmidt that following the Austrian's tip-off the enquiry had been sanctioned and concluded successfully. This would certainly have buoyed Schmidt to imagine he had helped the great office of state of a great empire which Van represented. In any event, as the conversation turned towards the rather strained relations between England and Italy, Schmidt was rather indiscreet in his descriptions of the Duce and his son-in-law. Vansittart carefully made a transcript which he then sent on to Anthony Eden, no doubt thinking the Austrian's comments would amuse the Foreign Secretary.

Unfortunately, within a week, a copy of this report, courtesy of Signor Constantini, translated rather badly landed on Ciano's desk causing a

---

184 Chadwick speculates that Constantini also worked for the Germans and the Vatican; see *Britain and the Vatican*, p. 298. But regrettably the reason Constantini was allowed to remain in his post was entirely the result of Treasury bean-counting which prevented "native" servants in the Chancery being replaced with more expensive expatriate staff. (Dilks to author, 5 Aug. 2020.)

veritable diplomatic storm.[185] Mussolini sent a personal envoy, Salata, to the Austrian Chancellor with an unequivocal demand for Schmidt's head. As Schuschnigg recalled: "I told him that the Italian version must be based upon a mistake or an outright falsification since nobody, except Lady Vansittart had been a witness to the conversation."[186]

However, these remarks were considered so injurious that neither Mussolini nor Ciano felt they could just let the matter drop. A week later Salata returned with a copy of the letter from Vansittart to Eden. This was, Salata insisted, irrefutable proof that the Italian government was correctly informed about the incident. Schuschnigg kept his nerve: "I informed the ambassador that it must be a misunderstanding." Still the Italians refused to forgive or forget. The following week, no less a figure than Filippo Anfuso, one of Mussolini and Ciano's most trusted ambassadors arrived in Vienna to issue a formal complaint. Anfuso was closely involved in the intelligence operation which had so brilliantly penetrated the British at virtually every level of their diplomatic communications and while he was careful not to reveal his source, supplying as a distracting "red herring" a reference to a "high ranking member of the British Foreign Secretary's immediate entourage," it is clear that the document came from the same treasure trove as so many of the others, the Rome embassy, with whom Eden had felt compelled to share the joke.

Anfuso insisted that "there could not be the remotest doubt about the authenticity of the Italian information." At the very least Dr Schmidt should "be employed—if at all—in some other capacity than that of State Secretary for Foreign Affairs." Nothing demonstrated more vividly the bond between the two Stella alumni than this extraordinary performance of support for Schmidt by his chief in the face of overwhelming pressure from the one country Vienna traditionally counted upon to support its

---

185 This most elusive of documents would seem to refer to the memo penned by Van to Eden which is FO 371/21114 6256/109/3, but appears harmless enough. The passage which would have perhaps caused the Duce offence as the colloquialism may not have been familiar to the Italians and may have gathered intensity in translation was Schmidt's apparent reference to the Duce "kicking against the pricks." See 109/3, page 288. However, it cannot be excluded that the troublesome document also was "weeded" to spare Foreign Office and in particular Van's blushes.

186 See Schuschnigg, *Austrian Requiem* (London, 1947), pp.111–113.

independence. The Chancellor and his State Secretary weathered the storm and Schuschnigg displayed an impressive coolness under fire: "I replied that I could not doubt for one moment the accuracy of my own information in spite of the photostatic copy before me and that I believed firmly that the whole incident must have its roots in a linguistic misunderstanding on the part of Lord Vansittart." Schuschnigg must have known from Schmidt that the English diplomat was fluent in German and that Schmidt was fluent in English and that therefore any room for linguistic misunderstanding was decidedly limited. Nevertheless, Schuschnigg (and no doubt Schmidt who, despite the Italian insistence not to inform him must certainly have been consulted), probably knew that it was unlikely that Van's fluency in German would be known to Rome. No Italian diplomat interacting with Vansittart would ever have had the remotest reason to attempt to hold a conversation with him in German.[187]

The "lost in translation" ruse worked and as Schuschnigg later reported: "A few weeks later I met Count Ciano in Budapest on the occasion of the Rome protocols annual meeting. During this conference I brought up the incident of the secret report once more. Ciano admitted at once that the possibility could not be denied that Lord Vansittart had misunderstood Dr Schmidt's remarks."[188]

In any event the Italians pleaded the need to safeguard "their source in London" as a reason for not dwelling on the affair, another plausible but deceitful evasion. This, the last meeting of the signatories of the Rome Protocols before the German invasion of Austria was no doubt concerned with the escalating crisis which would wipe Austria from the map of Europe within a couple of months and place any Italian reservations about Schmidt into an altogether more complex if irrelevant context.

---

187 Significantly, Selby after the war in a letter to *The Times* accused Van of misrepresenting Schmidt's views in this dispatch. See *The Times*, 26 Aug. 1947.

188 See Schuschnigg, *Austrian Requiem*, and Max Löwenthal, *Doppeladler und Hakenkreuz: Erlebnisse eines österreichischen Diplomaten* (Innsbruck, 1985) for the Austrian perspective on this incident.

CHAPTER 8

The run-up to Berchtesgaden

AS WELL AS defending Schmidt, Schuschnigg appears to have been at pains to protect Vansittart whose reputation came under sustained attack after the war.[189] In his memoirs, the Austrian Chancellor went out of his way to praise the diplomat as a "true and understanding friend" of Austria to be remembered with gratitude. No doubt the importance of British goodwill was uppermost in the Austrian Chancellor's mind but the Austrian was also aware how during the critical days of February 1938, Van had pushed more than anyone the idea of a referendum which Schuschnigg so fatefully pursued.

In May 1937, the coronation of George VI gave Schmidt, accompanied by Hornbostel, the chance to immerse himself briefly in London society. As well as meetings with Vansittart, he also spoke at length with Anthony Eden who recalled the conversation in a memorandum which suggests that the Foreign Secretary's interest in Austria remained slender.

In an attempt to enlist the Foreign Secretary's support for Austria, Schmidt had repeated his tactic with Göring of trying to invite the English statesman to Austria for a few days of recreation, an opportunity for informal discussions between Eden and Schuschnigg. But just as his invitation to Göring had fallen on stony ground, so too did his overture to Eden.[190]

Schmidt had suggested, naturally enough, that Eden might like to attend—unofficially of course—the Salzburg Festival for a few days.

---

189 Especially from Selby who did not allow the outbreak of peace to persuade him to bury the hatchet. See Chapter 16.
190 Eden memorandum: FO 371/21120, 11 May 1937.

Eden's presence in Salzburg in the summer of 1937 would have been a tremendous boost to Austrian morale even if there had been no "conversations." "Salzburg," Schmidt insisted, speaking absolutely truthfully of the city in the 1930s, "is the home of Anglo-Austrian cultural relations."[191]

But Schmidt had not reckoned with Eden's Olympian disdain, not untypical of his class, for high culture. Austria, a small country, was for Eden always a huge nuisance.[192] As Selby observed: "Eden always carefully avoided Vienna."[193] Eden, observed that "Salzburg would be rather difficult to fit in." He would wish to "switch off" from all political and diplomatic engagements and reserve the month of August for "purely recreational purposes." The condescension and crassness of Eden's reply still leaps off the page nearly a century later. If London wished to send a message of dazzling clarity to Vienna that it would never lift a finger for Austria then Eden's memorandum must be reckoned to be a masterpiece of candour. It even went on to suggest that Schmidt had proposed that London could best serve Austria's interests by making "no direct allusion to Austria" but rather "by showing a general interest in Central European Affairs." As this contradicts Schmidt's invitation to Salzburg, one is left to wonder whether Eden was not putting into Schmidt's mouth his own views which certainly chimed with "not referring to Austria specifically by name."[194] Just in case Schmidt might have thought Eden's distance from Austria as somehow untypical, a speech by the former Minister of War, Duff Cooper, around the same time, noted that "England would not establish a large army for eventual deployment on the continent." Unsurprisingly, this caused consternation in the Austrian press.[195] Unabashed, Schmidt continued to try to enlist what friends he could, ably assisted by his minister in London, George Franckenstein.

---

191 For an example of the powerful attraction Salzburg and especially the Café Bazar exerted in those days on young Oxford undergraduates, see Osbert Lancaster, *With an Eye to the Future* (London, 1967), pp. 98–99.

192 Otto von Habsburg would later describe him as the "greatest enemy of an independent Austria." See interview with Otto von Habsburg: *Otto von Habsburg in Gespräch* ORF Radio Oe 1, 12 August 1997.

193 SEL 6587 "Eden always carefully avoided Vienna…"

194 Eden memorandum FO 371/21120.

195 See *Neue Freie Presse*, 26 May 1937.

The relationship between these two men was not easy, not least because Franckenstein always imagined Schmidt could have done more to enlist British support, a view convincingly contradicted by the above exchange with Eden and Duff Cooper's speech quoted in the previous paragraph. After his visit to London, Schmidt felt there was little he could expect in terms of tangible support from London until the European situation had changed. Key to that was the need for London and Rome to mend fences over Abyssinia. Schmidt supported this proposition with everyone of influence he met in London. Encouraged by Vansittart, he continued to hope that some form of "soft" guarantee by the Western powers might emerge over the coming months. In the end the short-lived Easter Accords between Rome and London which might have provided a basis for such a guarantee came just a few weeks too late.[196]

Given this backdrop it is hardly surprising that Schmidt's contacts with Vansittart were intensified. For Schmidt Van was a key partner not only on the diplomatic stage but also in the important area of Anglo-Austrian finance. On 15th September, following the dinner between the two men and Hornbostel, Van used his contacts with the Bank of England to follow up on a request by Schmidt that the Austrian loan of 1930 which had saved Otto Ender's government be renegotiated. The 7% coupon if appropriate then had, in the slightly improved economic situation of 1937, seemed to the Austrians rather punitive. A note attached by the relevant Treasury official to Van's memo notes that "on general grounds we could show a desire to assist Austria in her difficulties." There was widespread support in the City which was "fully in sympathy" for Austria although the private bondholders might well prove "a little sticky."[197] The influence of the House of Rothschild would certainly help.

Schmidt's hopes and actions took place against a backdrop of increasing domestic tensions as 1937 drew to a close. The illegal Austrian Nazi party had become more and more dependent on the personalities of the Nazi leadership in Berlin (thanks partly to the improved communications

---

196 Leo Amery discussed this with Ciano and Mussolini six weeks after the Anschluss. All three men agreed that had the agreement been signed six months earlier Austria could have been saved. See *Empire at Bay*, p. 501.

197 FO 371/21114 File 6256/109/3.

with the Reich arising from the 1936 agreement). As a result, the Austrian Nazis presented a splintered front which reflected the fragmentation the party displayed in Germany. Josef Leopold, hitherto the only Austrian Nazi leader received personally by Hitler, found his position challenged by others during his time in prison. The more extreme views of the other Nazis, especially the Carinthians such as Odilo Globocnik, persuaded Schuschnigg in February 1937 to hold a meeting with Leopold but this brought no compromises or progress. Another meeting with a leading Austrian Nazi, the lawyer, Friedrich Reinthaller, also brought no result. Reinthaller was prepared to find a means of restoring legality to the Austria Nazis in the context of some "National Action" but his demands went too far for either Schuschnigg or Schmidt.[198] At the other end of the spectrum from Reinthaller's and indeed Göring's attempts to bring Austria closer to the German Reich economically, stood the Austrian SS, directly answerable to Himmler whose priority was to ensure that by the time Austria fell into German hands, a powerful Austrian SS structure would have been established, ready to take charge of the country at the word of his command. Unlike the Austrian SA, which theoretically owed its allegiance to Leopold, the Austrian SS was ultimately largely indifferent to the Austrian Nazi hierarchy.

Faced with such a disparate and unpromising cast it is perhaps unsurprising that Schuschnigg turned to an Austrian Nazi sympathiser of a Catholic inclination, Arthur Seyss-Inquart. Seyss was a lawyer, from an aspirant middle-class background with Bohemian roots. It was tempting to imagine that a practising Catholic such as Seyss would be immune to the wilder pagan elements of the National Socialist *Neuheidentum*. Ultimately, however, this would prove a costly error of judgement: Seyss attended early morning mass on 11th March 1938, but this did not give him pause for thought before he delivered Berlin's ultimatum to Schuschnigg a few hours later.[199]

In the summer of 1937 Seyss-Inquart still seemed a man Schuschnigg and Schmidt could work with. He was admitted to the *Staatsrat* (Council of State Cabinet). Schuschnigg hoped Seyss would handle the tricky Nazi

198 See Schmidl, *März 1938*, p. 22 *et seq.*
199 See Chapter 12.

press and also the ever more fractious and fragmented Austrian Nazi leadership. Together with Guido Zernatto, a Carinthian poet who was now the General Secretary of the Fatherland Front, Seyss was to "deal" with the Austrian Nazis' internal demands while Schmidt continued to face the growing German pressure to "unify" Austrian Foreign Policy with that of the Reich.

By the end of the year 1937, it became increasingly clear to Schuschnigg that the time he hoped to win by appointing Seyss to the Council of State a few months earlier was running out. Lord Halifax's visit to Berlin and Berchtesgaden in November 1937, in theory unofficial and in connexion with a hunting exhibition, did not openly touch on the Austrian question. Although Halifax was only Lord Privy Seal, the future arrangements in Central Europe were superficially discussed.[200] For Stefan Zweig, privy to sources of reliable information concerning Anglo-Austrian relations, there was little doubt that the Halifax visit was giving Hitler the green light to move more aggressively against Austria. The "holding deal" with Hitler, of which Eden had spoken "with the utmost secrecy," and which was linked to British rearmament was becoming daily more expensive but it would be the Austrians who would pay the price.[201]

Meanwhile, Schuschnigg gave an interview to the *Daily Telegraph* in which he openly stated that National Socialism was "irreconcilable" with Austrian politics. This was typically honest but unhelpful. For many of the Austrian Nazis, this interview was taken as an irrefutable proof that the 11th July agreement of 1936 had been broken. Leopold ordered those Austrian Nazis loyal to him to organise a shadow government in Linz ready to take power if Schuschnigg failed to appoint at least two Nazi ministers and then organise new elections. The SA with its own secret networks in the Austrian police and armed forces would support this move.

On the 25th January, the Vienna *Gauleiter*, (a Nazi title then devoid of any validity or meaning outside the party), Dr Leopold Tavs, published an interview given some months earlier to a Prague newspaper which claimed that the Nazi party operated in Austria in an almost quasi-official way

---

200 See Lois Schwoerer, "Lord Halifax's visit to Germany," *The Historian*, vol. 32, No. 3 (May 1970).

201 See Eden VNST Van II 2/13.

from the Vienna Teinfaltstrasse, close to the Burgtheater, where it had an illegal cell. This may not have been planned as a provocation, but the interview had immediate results. Twenty-four hours later, the Teinfaltstrasse was raided and during the search the police stumbled upon Leopold's plans for action. The detailed description of what obviously amounted to some kind of putsch took everyone including von Papen and Schmidt by surprise. Far from winning time to develop some kind of compromise acceptable to Schuschnigg and the Nazis, Nazi policy appeared to be accelerating the process of another violent attempt at an Austrian Nazi takeover. Particularly disturbing were documents which revealed intimate links between the Austrian Nazis and German railway and other officials, and their plans to increase Nazi propaganda in Austria. Details of the ill-named "Planetta" Munich Student club, commemorating the murderer of Chancellor Dollfuss, also augured badly for future relations between Vienna and the Reich. Seyss's presence in the Council of Ministers was clearly incapable of controlling the Austrian Nazis and contributing to the strategy to win time. A far more radical approach would be needed.

A meeting between the two chancellors, Schuschnigg and Hitler, had long been mooted by von Papen. Contrary to the accusations levelled at the time, and after the war, that such a meeting was Schmidt's idea, the evidence of all the available documentation, including the Schmidt archive, points conclusively to the fact that the meeting was neither an initiative of Schmidt's nor the result of his lobbying Schuschnigg. Neither man was under any illusion concerning the likely outcome of the meeting. Yet in the desperate effort to "win time" until the Anglo-Italian rapprochement could lead to a stabilisation in European diplomacy, no avenue could be left unexplored.

Any visit to Hitler was certainly going to be easier if the ground was well prepared. Von Papen was sympathetic, and Guido Schmidt had worked well with him in the past. Schuschnigg trusted Schmidt to ensure there would be no unpleasant surprises by working on a joint programme of discussion points which could be agreed well in advance of any meeting. But here the whimsical nature of a totalitarian regime showed its unpredictability when, without warning, Papen was informed on the 4th February that he was being recalled.

The fallout from the Blomberg-Fritsch crisis in Germany which Hitler exploited to tighten his grip on the military and force out two generals (Werner von Blomberg and Werner von Fritsch) did not only involve the German military.[202] On a diplomatic plane, the old school diplomat von Neurath was replaced by the arriviste and committed Nazi "von" Ribbentrop, then ambassador in London. A number of other diplomatic and military appointments followed strengthening the grip of the Nazi party on both institutions. At this turbulent time, it suited von Papen to accelerate planning for a summit between Schuschnigg and Hitler so that the impression that he was being ignominiously sacked could be forestalled. Whether the results of the summit could have been in any way different had the meeting been more carefully prepared remains a moot point. Von Papen's recall was only one of a number of dissonant factors which, almost by pre-ordained authority, dominated the internal and external political situation as 1938 unfolded.

By the beginning of 1938, tensions were also rising in the western democracies. In London the news of Van's promotion to the position of Chief Diplomatic Adviser was formally announced. Schmidt reacted as if one of the most vital props of his policy had been destroyed. Beaming, Papen greeted him with the news: *Ein Begräbnis erster Klasse!* ("A First-Class Funeral!"). No doubt Schmidt did not show by the slightest change of expression what he was really thinking—the experienced diplomat shows no surprise—but given the depth of the bond between Van and Schmidt, the loss of this direct line to the head of the Foreign Office was disquieting.[203]

Ironically, it came hard on the heels of Van's antagonist, the pro-Austrian Selby being "kicked upstairs" to the embassy at Lisbon. Just before he was dug out himself, Van had finally managed to remove Selby from his position of studied insubordination in Vienna. His first attempt in 1935, when he had persuaded Anthony Eden to offer Selby a straightforward

---

202 The Blomberg–Fritsch crisis involved the removal by dubious methods of the two generals, who were considered politically unreliable by Hitler. The affair was at the time wrongly interpreted by many to herald an increase in opposition to Hitler from within the ranks of the *Wehrmacht*.

203 Mentioned *en passant* in Palairet's correspondence to Van, VNST II 2/16.

exchange with Palairet, had failed thanks to Selby's court connexions. By the summer of 1937, Selby's resistance had wavered and the offer of promotion had proved impossible to resist not least because his advice from Vienna had been so studiously ignored. Not once had Van passed onto the cabinet Selby's recommendations that "Austria should be at the forefront of our negotiations with Germany."[204] Palairet, from Van's, if not Austria's point of view, would prove far more compliant. Both Schmidt and Schuschnigg appeared at the Westbahnhof in silk hat and tails to see off Selby. Schmidt gave the departing envoy a set of three exquisite Augarten porcelain horses to "complete your collection." No doubt the gift was heartfelt because Selby had done more than any other Englishman to support Austria through the First Republic's most challenging years.[205]

In a fascinating letter from the British minister, Palairet, to "his old friend" Van, dated 11th January 1938, Palairet observed that Schmidt had asked him no less than four times over two days what the "promotion" of Van meant and "was greatly relieved" when Palairet explained that Van's influence in the Foreign Office had substantially "increased" with the promotion.[206] New to events in Vienna, Palairet misled London, but this comment of his illustrates that he was also no less capable of misinforming his Austrian hosts. It should have been obvious even to Palairet that the appointment was a polite way of neutralising Vansittart's influence in the great office of state he had controlled for so many years.[207] Nonetheless, as he wrote: "I said the exact reverse… that it meant an increase not a decrease of your influence." This was an unhelpful misrepresentation which would encourage both Schmidt and Schuschnigg to overestimate Van's influence in the critical days ahead.

---

204 SEL 6587 Selby had according to this correspondence with Arthur Murray benefited from intervention at the highest levels of the court and much advice from Willie Tyrell, a formidable Foreign Office diplomat and ambassador to Paris, and Lord Perth who had helped him draft the first reply to Eden's letter 'offering him Stockholm'.

205 GSN: Copy of letter to Selby 3 Oct. 1937 (original in SEL 6588).

206 Schmidt's sensitivity to the appointment of Van suggests that Van through his intelligence network may well have had another direct line to Schmidt or Schuschnigg which has gone unrecorded.

207 Palairet to Vansittart 11 Jan, 1938 in VNST II 2/16.

Schmidt wrestled with the implications of Van's new appointment—he had after all entrusted highly sensitive information to Van a few months earlier and had suffered through his indiscretion in the Eden memorandum. At a more practical level, both men had worked well together to secure some relief from Austria's creditors in the City of London.

Vansittart's successor as permanent Under-Secretary was Sir Alexander Cadogan, a less colourful figure who cared very little for Austria (perhaps as the result of his posting there in 1914) and who adopted an altogether more conventional and arguably more conscientious approach to his duties. Van would still be able to influence Austrian affairs but in London his voice had become less powerful.

That Austria's fate was still taking up much space in Van's mind is shown by a secret memo dated November 1937 noting that the "Austrian desire for *Anschluss* was only too natural." "Shut off from the realities of the German Nazi regime, the Austrian people only saw a grandiose resurrection of the Reich whilst they themselves scraped along as a small detached unit of *Deutschtum* under a system many of them believe to be a dictatorship more oppressive than Hitler's."[208] This memo indicates that Van, despite his rather reckless encouragement of Schmidt, had evolved his position from backing "a losing horse" in Austria to realising it was probably not even going to be allowed to race.

Like Van, Palairet was not a varsity man and some mischievous gossips thought he had only passed into the Foreign Office because he had two cousins who were top county cricketers and the cricket loving examiners had confused him with one of them. He had converted to Catholicism after the First World War in no less a church than Notre Dame de Paris and was considered upright, sound but not very bright and utterly lacking in imagination.[209] These were not qualities to help him understand the tortured meanderings of Austrian foreign policy under Guido Schmidt. His telegrams would prove to be a textbook of how even the most

---

208 VNST II 2/13 Most Secret: *Memorandum on internal situation Germany*, November 1937.

209 A useful quality in a bureaucrat, albeit unhelpful in an ambassador. I am grateful to John Jolliffe for this appreciation of his late uncle's career. Conversation with the author, 60 St James's Street, Nov. 2019.

experienced and well-meaning diplomat, when new to his post, needs a few months of calm before penning a dispatch if he is not to make an utter fool of himself.

Such a helpful "breather" was denied to Palairet. Because of their remoteness from the reality of the situation, his reports from Vienna must be some of the most embarrassing analyses ever penned by a British diplomat *en poste* during a major European crisis.[210] They had no effect on British policy as the British system, then still well-oiled and experienced at dealing and minimising the influence of any "duds" carried on regardless. Palairet was asking reasonable questions concerning the loyalty of Schmidt and they would appear to be questions which resonated in London.

Undoubtedly the decision to remove Selby was unhelpful for Schmidt who at the ultimate crisis point of his career and country was forced to interact with an ill-informed and increasingly hostile envoy. The imminent crisis was undoubtedly expected by elements within the Foreign Office, even though most were almost certainly hoping for a "peaceful" absorption of Austria by Germany over the coming months. In any event the Austrophile, excellently connected and perceptive Selby was replaced by one of the "least sharp knives" in the Foreign Office drawer.

The changes in personnel appeared to reflect more important imminent and unsettling moves in the Foreign Office. Within a few weeks, Eden, finally finding his relationship with Chamberlain fractured beyond repair, would resign to be replaced by Halifax, a statesman possibly only marginally less indifferent to Austrian hopes of independence. This change would cause consternation in Europe. Ciano and Mussolini felt it would be the prelude to Eden becoming Prime Minister in "two months and all of us being in uniform in four."[211] At all levels of British policy-making it implied again a far less "pro-Austrian" approach as the crisis gathered momentum.[212]

---

210 See below Chapter 10.

211 *Ciano's Diary*, p. 60 *et seq.*

212 This view is also strongly implied in *Diplomatic Twilight, 1930–1940* (London, 1953), Selby's memoirs, but was given added credence by a review in *Economist* which noted "Selby was promoted out of Vienna to be got out of the way." See *Economist*, 20 June

The situation in French diplomatic circles was no more promising. France was beginning to undergo one of its frequent political crises leading to a change of government which would see the removal of the energetic Léon Blum twice as the Austrian crisis unfurled, thus ensuring that there was absolutely no chance of Austrian affairs rising near the top of any French political agenda. In any event, as Schmidt had recognised already, there was no possibility of French intervention without British support. His meetings with Eden strongly implied that such support was unlikely until a new diplomatic constellation had emerged.

The French ambassador in Vienna, Gabriel Puaux, was more staunchly pro-Austrian than the new British envoy and recognised the necessity for French interests of maintaining a sovereign and independent Austria, yet his dispatches evinced no commensurate commitment from the Quai d'Orsay. Moreover, the realisation that he was increasingly ignored in his own capital made him over sensitive to Schmidt's "realism." In August 1937, attending the manoeuvres of the Austrian army in front of the Italian, Hungarian and German military attachés, Puaux had remarked provocatively to Schmidt that his foreign policy was creating "a new triple Alliance in Europe." Schmidt had answered sharply that there was absolutely no question of Austria building any blocks, rather it was the French with their alliances and ententes who preferred such moves. Puaux's disdain for Schmidt appears to have grown into something approaching hatred from that moment.[213]

A few months earlier, at the beginning of May 1937, a dispatch by the Austrian military *attaché* in Paris, Colonel Jahn, had reported that French policy with regard to Austria was "completely dependent on London" and would be unlikely to engage in any robust steps to promote a new "Danube policy." Paris urged Schmidt to draw nearer to Prague and detach Austria from the German–Italian sphere but, apart from "moral support" and "sympathy," France appeared increasingly detached.[214] The

1953.

213 Puaux, *Mort*, p. 93

214 Quoted by Erika Weinzierl in "Die französisch-österreichischen Beziehungen Jänner–März 1938 nach den Berichten der Österreichischen Botschaft in Paris" in Kreissler, *Fünfzig Jahre danach*, p. 29 *et seq.*

only constructive note had been tentatively struck by the French military *attaché*, Colonel Salland in March 1936 when he had suggested to the Austrian Chief of the General Staff, General Jansa, that France might be interested in selling arms to Austria and that this could be followed by the establishment of a French military mission in Austria. This suggestion along with another proposing joint regular staff contacts between Paris and Vienna was quickly ruled out of court as a potential "infringement of Austrian neutrality." [215]

At the 1938 New Year Reception for the diplomatic corps at the Elysée, the secretary of the French Foreign Minister, Alexis Leger (the poet Saint-John Perse), noted to the Austrian ambassador that he admired the extraordinary skill in which the "nuance-rich" Austrian policy of Schuschnigg's continued to preserve Austria on "a tightrope." Leger stressed, however, that it was vital to win time for British and American rearmament. More pithily, an article a few days later in the *Figaro* pointedly referred to Austria as one of Germany's priorities for 1938. [216]

A few weeks earlier, the French Foreign Minister Yvon Delbos had been briefed in person on conversations between Göring and Halifax in which the German had spoken quite openly about Berlin's plans for incorporating Austria into the Reich. Shortly afterwards, Delbos preached conciliation and compromise when he embarked on a tour of eastern European capitals. The Chautemps government practised its efforts to win time through a policy of "understanding" towards Germany. Although this coincided with Schmidt's policy, it provided Schmidt with all too little evidence of any French solidarity in the event of matters coming to a head in the new year.

Whatever the limitations on the diplomatic front there were two groupings in Austria which could have offered some support for Schuschnigg ahead of any meeting with the Führer. At first glance, both groups would appear to have been at unreconcilable ends of the Austrian political spectrum: one was the monarchist Legitimist movement for which Schuschnigg had much personal sympathy. The other

---

215 See Jedlicka, "'Die Aussenpolitik der Ersten Republik'" in *Vom Justizpalast zum Hel-denplatz* (Vienna, 1975).
216 See *Le Figaro*, 22 January 1938.

was the socialist working class who had so far not been entirely seduced by the Nazi propaganda, unlike so many of their better off comrades of the lower middle classes. As many historians attribute Austria's failure to 'withstand' the *Anschluss* as directly attributable to her internal political divisions, it is worth exploring the plausibility of these two groups offering any meaningful alternatives to the policies pursued by Schmidt and Schuschnigg in the weeks immediately preceding the Berchtesgaden meeting.

The groups had more in common than is generally supposed. Both groups, unlike the fractured Nazi party leadership in Austria, could command without credible rivals the loyalty of nearly all their followers. Otto von Habsburg, the pretender to the Austrian throne, and the trade unionist leaders could certainly mobilise their "people." Indeed the two groups even offered to cooperate with Schuschnigg (and each other) ahead of the *Anschluss* and their failure to contribute to the events which followed can be regarded as a lost opportunity but it was also the result of nearly two decades of internal rupture culminating in the "civil war" of 1934. This had shaken the foundations of the state and the efforts of Schuschnigg to build some kind of Austrian consensus within the model of the corporatist state.

Schmidt in any event would have been convinced that these were not players critical to the process. Undoubtedly, Schmidt believed that only he could square the circle of Vienna's relations with Berlin thanks to his contacts with the Nazis around Göring's brother-in-law, Franz Hueber, and the art dealer Kajetan Mühlmann. Even before Schmidt had entered the Austrian government in 1936, he and Schuschnigg had cooperated closely on sensitive issues to do with the Nazis.[217] After Glaise was brought into the government, Schmidt could demonstrate the superiority of his own Nazi contacts. In the process he had worked hard (and successfully) to neutralise Horstenau's influence, something the soldier bitterly resented. For Glaise, Schmidt resembled "a Balkan diplomat" in his mannerisms and behaviour.[218] More than anyone else in

217 See next chapter.
218 See Paul Broucek (ed.), *Ein General in Zwielicht: die Erinnerungen Edmund von Glais-es-Horstenau* (Vienna, 1984), pp. 152–153 *et seq.*

the Schuschnigg government, Schmidt was *ein schlechter Kamerad* (a bad comrade). The State Secretary had completely marginalised the general's influence in Schuschnigg's government. Such a stance did not augur well for building bridges with the representatives of the proletariat or indeed the monarchists.

His youth and intellectual arrogance made him impatient with other actors in the drama and his influence on Schuschnigg meant that an almost total opacity descended on Austrian decision-making as the crisis of 1938 approached. It was as much this lack of transparency as internal divisions which ultimately frustrated the efforts of monarchists and socialists to play any meaningful role in the February and March days which spelt the end of Austria.

CHAPTER 9

Princes and Marxists

COULD A DEAL between Schuschnigg and the Marxists of Vienna have staved off the inevitable? Had Otto von Habsburg returned to Vienna to replace Schuschnigg, might the country and especially the army have rallied around him to resist more forcefully the German aggression?

The pretender to the Austrian throne, Otto von Habsburg, was no stranger to Nazism. The eldest son of the last Emperor of Austria, Charles, who had died in exile in Madeira in 1922, he had studied in Berlin at the time of Hitler's rise to power. Adolf Hitler had been educated in Habsburg Austria, had gone to school with Ludwig Wittgenstein, and had cut his political teeth on the anti-semitism and German nationalism of Karl Lueger's Vienna. He was keen to meet the pretender to the Austrian throne and extended several invitations, but the Archduke always refused. When asked why many years later, Otto replied: "I had read *Mein Kampf*, one of the more onerous duties I discharged on behalf of Austria. Despite the tiring length and boring prose, it was absolutely clear to me that whoever believed in what was in this book could never be a friend of Austria."[219]

At the time, he was even more blunt, saying, "I absolutely reject Nazism for Austria… this un- Austrian movement promises everything for everybody but really intends the most ruthless subjugation of the Austrian people. The people of Austria will never tolerate that our beautiful

---

219 Interview with Otto v. Habsburg, October 21 1983, Lower Austria.

Fatherland will become an exploited colony and that the Austrian should be a man of the second category..."[220]

By the time the Austrian crisis began absorbing the energies of Europe's diplomats, Chancellor Schuschnigg had gone a long way towards preparing the ground for an eventual restoration of the Habsburg monarchy once political and diplomatic conditions were favourable. He had been a loyal Imperial and Royal officer during the closing stages of the First World War and had remained faithful to the oath he had sworn to the Habsburgs. In 1935, he had repealed many elements of the so-called Habsburg confiscation laws which had expropriated all Habsburg property in Austria and prevented members of the family who did not renounce their claims from visiting Austria.

Moreover, although Otto von Habsburg, as the heir to the throne who had never renounced his title, was still not allowed to enter Austria, he was kept in touch with all relevant political developments by Schuschnigg. In the early days of March as the crisis developed, Otto would have an aircraft on permanent standby at Steenokkerzeel in Belgium to fly him to Austria if Schuschnigg permitted.

But Schuschnigg, like Schmidt, was under no illusions that any attempt at a restoration of the monarchy at that time would spell the "ruin" of Austria.[221] However much Schuschnigg sympathised with the Legitimist cause in Austria, he had come to see the dangers inherent in inviting the Archduke to return to take up the reins of his inheritance. Schmidt had shown time and again how the Balkan states would never show solidarity with Vienna while the restoration issue remained live. His correspondence with Göring had confirmed, if confirmation were needed, that Otto's return to Austria would be the *casus foederis* for a full-scale German invasion. As the winter of 1937 progressed, even Prague, which had spoken so warmly about Austria, according to Delbos, made it abundantly clear that this warmth did not extend to the young Archduke. Otto was only in his mid-twenties and was a rather more impetuous young man than

---

220 John Gunther, *Inside Europe* (New York, 1936) p. 321.

221 Schuschnigg's actual word to Joseph Roth, 2 March, Vienna: quoted in Christopher Brennan, "Deux semaines avant le fin d'Autriche', *Europe: revue littéraire mensuelle*, Nos.1087–1088 (Paris, 2019). See below.

the measured and mature elder statesman of the European Parliament he became famous for in the 1980s. His father had been dead for more than ten years and his mother Zita, a strong personality, had brought the eldest of her eight children to accept unquestioningly the responsibilities of his birthright. Surrounded by loyal courtiers and supporters, Otto existed in a bubble which reinforced the feelings that he was not just a Crown Prince in waiting but already an emperor for whom the eighteen-year-old republic of Austria was just some unfortunate ephemeral blip in the century-old history of Habsburg rule. He was openly impatient for the "Republican experiment" to end and to return to the city of his birth.

As the faithful servant of the Emperor, Schuschnigg knew that there could be no experimenting with the monarchy. Either Otto returned to a safe, stabilised, loyal Austria or he remained for life as a pretender in Stennockerzeel. To place him on the throne only to find that he was hurled from it once again either by some violent German *Anschluss* or the disaffection of his people would have been to ruin the dynasty for centuries. Not even the Habsburgs could survive two depositions in so short a space of time. That at least was the view of Schuschnigg's biographer R. K. Sheridan writing during the war.[222] What was Schmidt's role if any in all this? The *alter ego* of the Austrian Chancellor was inevitably consulted over the Legitimist question and how such a restoration would "play" in the European capitals. If the reaction towards Schmidt of such monarchists as his predecessor at the Foreign Ministry, Berger-Waldenegg, was anything to go by, Schmidt counselled the utmost caution. Schmidt was painfully aware that, with the exception of Mussolini's earlier receptivity to Legitimist delegations, the idea of a Habsburg restoration was regarded with undiluted hostility among Austria's neighbours, and with considerable scepticism in Paris and London. The fact that Schuschnigg moved in the space of three years between 1935 and 1938 from enthusiastic support to extreme caution can be attributed to his growing awareness, certainly mostly through Schmidt, of the unhelpful international climate. It did not help that from the beginning Schmidt, who had been too young to serve in the First World War as a *k.(u.)k.* officer, was intuitively sceptical of the dynasty's relevance to the modern world.

---

222 R. K. Sheridan, *Kurt von Schuschnigg* (London, 1942).

Recently published confidential documents from the Habsburg family archives reveal just how far Schuschnigg travelled, under Schmidt's "guidance" in terms of his own disposition towards a future restoration of the dynasty.[223] On 7th January 1935, while Schmidt was still working in the office of President Miklas, the two men journeyed alone to Switzerland where, in a remote Benedictine monastery at Einsiedeln, barely fifty miles from the Austrian frontier, they met with Archduke Otto and his life-long private secretary, Count Heinrich Degenfeld. Degenfeld's record of the conversation is an astonishing document which shows all too poignantly how close Schuschnigg was to organising a full-blown restoration, less than six months after becoming Chancellor in July 1934.

The paper entitled "Preparations for the Restoration" is a verbatim account of the conversations the two Austrians had with the Crown Prince. In it the Austrian Chancellor commits to bringing about a full restoration of the dynasty by the end of the year 1935 "even if it leads to a serious European conflagration." German objections to such a move would "be resisted by force." To compare this unreserved enthusiasm on the part of Schuschnigg with his later correspondence with the Crown Prince is instructive. When in the early days of March 1938, Otto's brilliant but alcoholic private secretary, the writer Joseph Roth, arrived in Vienna with a personal message of support from Otto, Schuschnigg made no bones about rejecting the Archduke's offer. "A restoration would be the hundred per cent ruin of Austria," he told Roth.[224]

Those who accused Schmidt of having "undue influence" over Schuschnigg tend to think of the Austrian Chancellor in terms of "introspection and weakness."[225] Schuschnigg's personality was undoubtedly very different from that of his predecessor, the "miniature Metternich" Engelbert Dollfuss who was something of a showman and undoubtedly possessed substantially more charisma. But the idea that Schuschnigg

223 See Habsburg Family archives: Degenfeld Verbatim Memorandum *Vorbereitung der Restauration*: 7 January 1935 Einsiedeln (Switzerland) meeting EZH Otto von Habsburg with Kurt Schuschnigg and Guido Schmidt.

224 Brennan, "Deux semaines."

225 See Otto von Habsburg's verdict quoted *in extenso* in Gordon Brook Shepherd, *Uncrowned Emperor* (London, 2003).

was a mere cypher does not stand up to close analysis. He prized duty, honour, friendship and his faith above all other considerations but he was clearly in command of his own opinions. That he was open to Schmidt's reservations about a restoration would seem to be proven. Legitimists were undoubtedly right to suspect Schmidt of having acted as a brake on their aspirations. His egotism, background and intelligence made him unlikely material to be a fawning courtier and he must have regarded the archaic, unreconstructed atmosphere around the Archduke's "court" with considerable antagonism. He had neither the patience nor the temperament to play the obsequious lackey. Moreover, Schmidt was the senior official running the office of the real Austrian head of state, President Miklas, a position which he would no doubt have imagined afforded him a little more respect than that which the courtiers around Otto would have accorded the young man who, in their view, was just a "kleiner Beamter" (junior official) of an illegitimate entity.

Schmidt's scepticism towards the Habsburg monarchy would have been reinforced by his experiences once he took over the Foreign Affairs portfolio as State Secretary. That he voiced his concerns to his chief is undoubtedly the case and that he shared with him his reservations about a restoration vigorously is equally incontestable. Schmidt's personal "universal foreign policy" which was characterised cynically by the Polish Ambassador Gawroński as "peace to all nations, neighbours and people of good will," was incompatible with a restoration. This reality gradually assumed a larger part in the Chancellor's thinking than it did before Schmidt was appointed State Secretary for Foreign Affairs. [226]

Compare Schuschnigg's almost reckless statement in 1935 that he would engineer a restoration "irrespective of a European conflagration" with his language a few years later in a letter to the Crown Prince dated 2nd March 1938. While still addressing Otto as "Your Majesty" Schuschnigg strikes a very different note: "The fundamental principle which serves as the pillar of Austrian ideology is: Service for Peace." [227] This is the language of Schmidt and his "universal foreign policy." If proof were needed of the young State Secretary's influence over the Chancellor

226 Gawroński, *Moja Misja*, pp. 32–39.
227 Quoted in Sheridan op. cit. p. 241.

during the course of 1935-1938, than Schuschnigg's attitude towards the restoration question furnishes an accurate barometer. Schuschnigg reached this view with the help of his trusted advisor but it would be an exaggeration to imagine it was simply foisted on him by Schmidt. The "mind-meld" between the two men at this stage was such that there was not a sliver of space to be found between them on key issues of policy, even if as we have seen Selby had reported in 1937 that Schuschnigg had felt his State Secretary had "gone too far" in Berlin.[228]

Schuschnigg's apparent *volte-face* gave Schmidt's critics on the Legitimist side plenty of ammunition to fire at him, not only in the run-up to the Second World War but afterwards. Schuschnigg and Schmidt's distance from the monarchist cause also seems to have infected some non-Austrian players, notably among some of the diplomats *en poste* in Vienna during the crisis, including Palairet and his number two, Mack.[229] Both British diplomats appear to have absorbed the distrust and negativity the monarchists felt towards Schmidt. Brook-Shepherd, the *Haus, Hof und Staat* historian of the Habsburgs in the British language would, as late as 2003, write that Schmidt was the most "dubious of Schuschnigg's counsellors" while not providing a shred of evidence to support this accusation.[230]

If Schmidt influenced Schuschnigg over the Legitimist cause, did he play a similar role in dampening potential feelers put out by the Socialists towards Schuschnigg in the run-up to the crisis of 1938?

It did not help that Schuschnigg and Schmidt were remote from the interests of the working class whose anxieties were not an area where Schmidt's intellect and contacts or indeed upbringing offered any insights. His links to the other part of the political spectrum always appeared to him to be more relevant.

The problem both Schmidt and Schuschnigg had with the Socialists was simple: the Social Democrats had for years been even more vociferous than the Nazis in calling for *Anschluss* with Germany. For them

---

228 SEL 6587–6589.
229 Henry Mack, then *chargé*, later Head of the Political Mission as part of the office of the British High Commissioner to Austria during Schmidt's trial.
230 Brooke Shepherd, *Uncrowned Emperor.*

uniting with Germany was not so much the fulfilment of an ancient racial dream but the beginning of a new proletarian Europe. Otto Bauer, the leading Socialist dogmatist of his time, had been forced into exile after the 1934 crisis but, before then, he had striven to organise Austria's incorporation into the Weimar Republic of Germany. His slogan was "Unite now with the Red workers of Germany: Union with Germany is union with Socialism." Despite the rise of Hitler, the Socialists had remained for several years the *Anschluss* party par excellence.

By 1938, this enthusiasm for *Anschluss* with an avowedly Nazi Germany had of course waned but the question was whether enough of Marxist solidarity really existed to help Austria resist Nazi Germany. Could the leaders of the trade unions and the working classes really forget the trials of the "Civil War," of 1934, the execution of their leaders like Koloman Wallisch? It was unlikely—eighty years later the subject still divides opinion in Austria—and for both Schmidt and Schuschnigg it seemed as if the "Red Peril," if no longer *aktuell*, was nonetheless unlikely to support the *Ständestaat* in which workers had no privileges or rights. It did not help that Schmidt was perceived in socialist circles to be hostile and deceitful in matters concerning their movement.

In 1936, two influential members of the British Labour party, Messrs Ammon and Silverman, both members of the British parliament[231] arrived in Vienna to ask for an extension of the amnesty Schuschnigg had offered the Nazis to include Socialists. To the MPs' chagrin, the Chancellor refused to see them ("even though he was negotiating with the Nazis," they recalled) and they had to make do with Schmidt who assured them that the Chancellor was about to abolish the system of multiple sentences for one offence under which the Socialists had suffered so severely. But after the two parliamentarians had departed, the system remained unchanged. For G.E.R. Gedye, the correspondent of the *Daily Telegraph* this amounted to early evidence of Schmidt's deviousness and venality.[232]

---

231 Charles (later Lord) Ammon and Sydney Silverman.

232 See G. E. R. Gedye, *Fallen Bastions* (London, 1939), p. 201. For Gedye, Schmidt was the "poor little man" who imagined thanks to his "overweening conceit" that he was going to "outwit both Hitler and Schuschnigg and become the ruler of a Nazified

Worse was to follow for those in England who followed Austrian affairs from the perspective of the Left. For Gedye, Schmidt was only a "thinly disguised Nazi," part of the "Nazi Trojan Horse" which was plotting Austria's destruction.²³³ Given that Gedye enjoyed impeccable contacts with the Socialist leadership in Vienna and was writing in 1939, barely a few months after the German absorption of Austria, we can safely assume that his words represented the views of the leadership of the Austrian workers. If they shared Gedye's view that Schmidt was merely "Hitler's willing tool," it is hardly surprising that their reservations about coming to any kind of cooperation with Schuschnigg were so powerful. Schmidt was not especially hostile to the working class, but he had no time for the Marxist element. It is significant that when, five minutes before midnight, Schuschnigg finally met in the first week of March with the Socialist leadership in Vienna, Schmidt was absent. As far as they were concerned, he was "Hitler's principal agent."

Although the criticism that Schmidt influenced Schuschnigg in his dealings with this important group is exaggerated (Schuschnigg needed no-one to reinforce his own distrust of the Marxists), it contains a small kernel of truth. When Schuschnigg came to power, many of the Socialists argued that, like his predecessors Fey and Dollfuss, the new Chancellor did not have a "clean bill of health." He had been directly responsible at the Justice ministry for the execution of several socialists involved in the 1934 uprising. He was an *Arbeitermörder* for most of the workers. Initially, however, Schuschnigg was inclined to "reward" them for not having supported the Nazis in their putsch against Dollfuss but within a few months (and once again following Schmidt's appointment as State Secretary for Foreign Affairs), the line against the Socialists became harsher and less conciliatory. Undoubtedly pressure from Italy and Germany played a role. Schmidt tried to replace or at least supplement unreliable Italy as the guarantor of Austria with the western democracies, but these proved elusive. The guarantee which would alone have saved Austria proved impossible to extract in time from Paris, Rome and London. Meanwhile Italy demanded that none of Dollfuss's work against the "Red Antichrist"

Austria," p. 207.
233 See Gedye, *Fallen Bastions*, pp. 206–208.

be undone. The corporatist state with its strong clerical ethos was not an easy bedfellow of conventional Marxism and a distrust of the masses was something Schmidt and Schuschnigg shared. As scholars of the Jesuits, they well understood the primacy of elites. The "love affair" between the Society of Jesus and the dispossessed had begun already in the 16th century and indeed had led to their suppression in 1773, but in the world inhabited by Schuschnigg and Schmidt, these ideas did not apply to Austro-Marxism. Those who imagine that Schmidt acted as a brake on Schuschnigg's desires to embrace the proletariat are surely far from the mark. Schuschnigg did not need Schmidt to develop his own instinctive aversion to the "dictatorship of the proletariat," his experience as an officer on the Isonzo front during the First World War when communist subversion had contributed earlier to the disaffection of several regiments remained a vivid memory.[234] Even so, Schuschnigg would leave no stone unturned to save Austria including—though rather late in the day and partly under British pressure—consulting the Socialists.

Schuschnigg was keenly aware that Austria's image abroad was partly influenced by his attitude towards the "Left." When the attempts to motivate the western democracies into a more robust policy towards Austria began in earnest in the Autumn of 1936, Schuschnigg rejected the *Heimwehr* and sacked its crypto-fascist leader, Prince Starhemberg. As the crisis approached, Starhemberg had his last encounter with Schuschnigg and offered the support of his "troops" to deal with the Nazis on the streets of Vienna, Schuschnigg insisted that he would prefer other methods which would not affect the public opinion of the democratic countries, "in particular Great Britain."[235]

Perceptions are real and there can be no doubt that the accusation on the "Left" that Schmidt, as a businessman, was somehow viscerally hostile to the working class would play strongly into the hands of his critics after the war. The entire fabric of the Corporatist State by suppressing workers in 1934 deserved, in this interpretation, to be found guilty for all the misery which followed. This was a view which would be forcefully articulated during Schmidt's trial and certainly persists in Austria even

234 See Bassett, *For God and Kaiser,* Part 3.
235 See Starhemberg, *Between Hitler and Mussolini.*

Guido Schmidt as a pupil of the Stella Matutina College in Feldkirch. His Jesuit tutors found him "diligent, hardworking and *highly ambitious*."

Maria Chiari. Born in Trieste, highly intelligent and devoted wife who had grown up in the *beau-monde* of the old Habsburg empire.

Love at first sight. Maria Chiari's confidence on the ski-slopes of St Anton had seduced Guido Schmidt into taking lessons with the great Austrian slalom skier, Rudi Matt.

The perfect bureaucrat. With President Wilhelm Miklas. Schmidt's elevation to President Miklas's *chef du cabinet* brought him into contact with all the foreign missions in Vienna.

The two "up and coming men" of European diplomacy. Guido Schmidt as State Secretary for Foreign Affairs with the Italian Foreign Minister Galeazzo Ciano in 1936.

Above: Schmidt, the Austrian Chancellor Kurt Schuschnigg and Mussolini in Venice. The Duce snubbed the Austrians by keeping them waiting while he boarded a Nazi cruise ship.

Below: Schmidt and his German counterpart von Neurath at the time of the signing of the Austro-German agreement, the highpoint of Schmidt's diplomatic career and a brief respite for Austria from German pressure.

Schmidt with Adolf Hitler following the successful conclusion of the Austro-German agreement. Schuschnigg later told the British ambassador Selby he felt "Schmidt had gone too far in Berlin."

Monsignor Ignaz Seipel.
Austrian Prime Minister
and the shrewdest cleric in
central Europe. Impressed by
Schmidt he not only helped
his rise through the Austrian
bureaucracy but also performed
Schmidt's marriage ceremony in
1931.

Generaloberst Hermann Göring, the
"least uncouth" of Hitler's paladins.
So impressed was he by Schmidt
that he sent a plane to Vienna
to rescue the Austrian from the
clutches of the local Nazis after the
Anschluss.

Right: Franz von Papen: *Ein Herr* in Schmidt's view: the charming servant of Hitler's designs on Austria. As Hitler's envoy to Vienna he worked closely with Schmidt on the Austro-German agreement and was the catalyst for the ill-fated visit by the Austrian Chancellor and Schmidt to Berchtesgaden in February 1938.

Below: Honouring Austria's war dead; Schmidt never joined the Nazi party and never, as a point of honour even after the *Anschluss*, ever gave the Hitler salute.

"Van" : Robert Vansittart, the Permanent Under Secretary of the Foreign Office, who ran his own personal intelligence service funded from family funds and which made use of Schmidt as a valuable source of information on the "most serious" security breach at the British embassy in Rome.

W.H.M.Selby, the British Minister in Vienna; a staunch admirer and defender of Guido Schmidt, he resisted Vansittart's attempts to make Austria the scapegoat for the failure of the Stresa front.

Above: Schmidt with Neville Chamberlain (leaning over to engage a German princess) and assorted aristocrats at a reception given at the Austrian embassy in London in 1937.

Below: On trial for high treason in Vienna. Schmidt conducted his own defence with the help of the Viennese partly Jewish lawyer Rudolf Skrein who had endured house arrest during most of the war.

Theodor von Hornbostel, the epitome of the incorruptible patriotic Austrian civil servant. After spending much of the war in Dachau his testimony in favour of Schmidt proved critical in the trial of his former chief.

Guido Schmidt in happier days in his beloved Vorarlberg. His sparkling sense of
humour and musical talents (on horn and organ) captivated friends and strangers alike.

The family man: Guido Schmidt with his son Nico, later the Chairman of Austria's most influential bank before 1998, the CreditAnstalt.

up to the present day.[236] But however brilliant Schmidt's gifts for making enemies, it would surely be a mistake to overestimate his talents and imagine one man alone could simultaneously have frustrated two such disparate and influential groups as the Legitimists and the Marxists in their attempts to rescue Austria's *Bundesstaat*.

236 See Conclusion.

CHAPTER 10

The Summons to the Eagle's Nest

BERCHTESGADEN IS STILL a place which evinces mixed feelings among Austrians. The small Bavarian village which became the country retreat of Adolf Hitler, thanks to that most enigmatic of Hitler's paladins, Martin Bormann, appears harmless enough at first glance. It seems spotlessly arranged like a picture book. Berchtesgaden remains the tourist destination *par excellence* for those on the journey of the "Third Reich theme park." After the war, families with property on the Austrian side of the Untersberg, the "house" mountain of Salzburg, were advised not to cross the German frontier even though this "green border" was neither controlled nor guarded.[237] Such reserve was based on an almost collective aversion to the place which had meted out such widely publicised humiliation to the Austrian Chancellor Kurt Schuschnigg in February 1938. The place and date were inextricably linked in the post-war patriotic Austrian psyche with the destruction of their independence and sovereignty. If "Munich" was a word synonymous with shameful appeasement for a particular generation of Englishmen, so, too, was "Berchtesgaden" equated with humiliation for a generation of patriotic Austrians.

On the 11th February 1938 at 11 p.m. the express from Vienna's Westbahnhof pulled out with an additional sleeping carriage. In it were the Chancellor and his *intimus*, Guido Schmidt. Upon arrival in Salzburg

---

237 This was particularly the case for several families in Grödig (despite the construction after the *Anschluss* of a still extant "Neue Heimat Strasse"). Conversation Dr Raimund Kerbl, 22 June 2018.

some five hours later, the sleeping car was detached from the main train and shunted into a siding close to the Salzach river. None of the local authorities had been informed that on board were the Chancellor, his military adjutant, his private secretary, and his state secretary for foreign affairs.[238] After a hearty breakfast at the Hotel Bristol with the *Landeshauptmann* of Salzburg, Franz Rehrl and the District Head of Security, *Oberst* Bechinie-Lazan[239] to discuss measures if the Austrians did not return, a car would pick the two men up and drive them over the nearby frontier to the Ober Salzburg and a summit with the German Führer. As Schuschnigg later recalled: "A few plain clothes men were on duty... At about 9:30 am our car came. We had been told that Hitler could not receive us before 11 a.m."

What had happened in Austria to produce the circumstances for such a meeting? Once again Schmidt was to be seen as the source of this ill-omened engagement but, as always, the causal chain of events was much more complex. It was also rapid and multi-faceted. We have seen that by the end of 1937, it was increasingly obvious to Vienna that the diplomatic situation with regard to Austria was deteriorating sharply. Lord Halifax's visit to Germany in November 1937 had lasted only five days but he was shortly to replace Eden as Foreign Secretary. Rightly or wrongly he was seen as bearing "gifts" to Hitler in terms of British concessions, not only on colonies but also on Austria.

The reports which reached Schmidt's desk at the Austrian Foreign Ministry from his envoys throughout Europe were disquieting. There was above all a sinister consistency about them:[240] "our reports concerning the visit of Lord Halifax to Hitler all stated that the Austrian question stood high on the discussion agenda. Negotiating with Hitler over Austria could not mean anything good and in reality this was absolutely the case.

---

238 There is a surprising lack of consistency in the historiography concerning who accompanied the Chancellor (see below, note 271).

239 Colonel Bechinie-Lazan, scion of a family which had offered Austria military service for generations was later murdered in Sonnenstein extermination camp in 1941. Rehrl was later arrested in 1944 in connexion with the July plot.

240 For Halifax's visit see L. Schwoerer, "Lord Halifax's visit to Germany November 1937" in *The Historian* (May 1970, Vol 32, number 3). For Schmidt's diplomatic information re the Halifax visit see GSN: *Aufzeichnungen*, p. 9.

It would be later reported that the Italian ambassador in London had given a British newspaper in confidence" (courtesy yet again of Secundo Constantini in the British embassy in Rome), "even before Halifax's departure, full details of the discussion agenda. Italy had the gravest concerns that London and Berlin would agree behind their backs."

The extent to which Halifax conceded Austria to Hitler can be gauged by the British press coverage ahead of his visit. To the dismay of the Austrian minister in London, Baron Franckenstein, it appeared to express the briefings of the principal Foreign Office press officer, Rex Leeper, faithfully. As we have already seen in connexion with the infamous E.H. Carr memorandum, extolling Austria as an inevitable part of Germany, Leeper could be relied upon to relay a British propagandist view which not only emphasised Britain's lack of interest in Austria but also reflected "his master's voice." As an Australian he had inclined, perhaps unsurprisingly, towards a pro-Russian, pan-Slav view with regard to Central Europe. This invested him with an indifference towards Austrian issues in general and Vienna's struggles with her larger neighbours in particular.[241]

An "op-ed" in the *Observer* published as Halifax visited Hitler in Berchtesgaden showed clearly how successful Leeper had "done his work." The article noted that "in no circumstances" would Britain "resort to arms to preserve Austrian independence." On the same page, the influential editor of the paper, James Garvin, argued forcefully that the key to "world peace" was an "understanding" between Britain and Germany. In this context he noted that the "process of German unification" had not yet been "completed." The "incorporation of Austria" into some system which involved closer unity with other Germans was "unavoidable." It was "as natural as the unification of Germany achieved by Bismarck" (!). Moreover, Garvin continued, "without such a unification, the Austrians would have "no secure or significant future." This question, however, was something the "Germans themselves" must sort out. "England had nothing to do with it." It would be "the height of insanity" to interfere with this. The Dominions would never agree to London resorting to arms to support Austria. For good measure and having articulated so

---

241 *No Kangaroos in Austria*, privately printed paper on Austro-Australian relations by Reinhold Gayer (Salzburg, 2015).

perfectly British appeasement policy towards the key to Central Europe, Garvin went on to describe Czechoslovakia as "an unnatural and ahistorical state." The *Observer* at that time was one of the most influential newspapers in the country. Owned by Viscount Astor, it had impeccable links with the key controlling elements of the British establishment. Its views reflected a British consensus at the highest echelon of policy making. The same family owned *The Times*, another shameless supporter of appeasement.

This baleful theme was taken up by the *Evening Standard* and the *Manchester Guardian*. The former speculated that Germany had demanded a plebiscite in Austria to "create clarity" while the latter dwelt on the inescapable fact that Austria would soon be "peacefully abandoned" by Britain and France. According to its correspondent in Berlin, "the European situation could not be better for a solution to the Austrian problem to be found which does not put at risk the cause of European peace."[242] These reports created consternation in the Austrian mission in London and Franckenstein moved swiftly to counteract the gathering view that the preservation of Austria was no longer a *sine qua non* of European peace. But when the hapless Franckenstein attempted to meet with Mr Leeper, this (relatively junior) official claimed that he could not meet with the minister for several days as he was "rather busy." Well might Schmidt recall that while London was served brilliantly by Franckenstein and Vienna benefitted from having "one of her best, able and committed" of her envoys in London, Franckenstein was, for all the success he achieved in arousing sympathy for Austria, completely "unable to alter the fundamental line of British policy towards Austria."[243] As Schmidt later insisted: "I am totally convinced that no other Austrian either in Vienna or in London could have acheived any more." In this, he was almost certainly correct.

The British press reports which had such a depressing effect on the Austrian *emigré* community in London, including Stefan Zweig, were a straw in the wind. A few weeks before Halifax's visit to Germany, Schmidt

242 See *Manchester Guardian*, 21 Nov. 1937, and *Observer*, 30 Nov. 1937. Also Franckenstein to Schmidt in *HVPGGS*, pp. 535–536.

243 See GSN: *Aufzeichnungen*, p. 9.

had again initiated talks between Prague and Vienna to explore whether the "two threatened" central European states might undertake a closer cooperation together with Hungary. The cooperation envisaged by Schmidt was first and foremost to be developed along commercial and trading lines but with a view to a future political alignment which would enable all three countries to stand together against external threats. The talks with Prague were burdened by the issues of the Legitimist claims, the different political systems, and the fact that the Czech province of Moravia was still viewed by many Austrians, including the Chancellor, Schuschnigg, as "Vienna's strongest hinterland," and its people as "part of the Viennese population."[244]

These talks however soon ran into the sands on a different issue, one that did not involve Austria directly, namely border adjustments between Slovakia and Hungary. Well might Schmidt observe "the seriousness of our situation might have given the Hungarians and the Czechoslovaks pause for thought and to renounce their claims against each other, but it was not to be."[245] The old Hungarian disdain for the arriviste Czechs stymied any progress. Budapest had in any event cut a deal with Berlin and under the influence of Rome had become a passive member of the emerging *Gleichschaltung* with regard to Austria. A similar development appeared to be in motion in Yugoslavia which was becoming more and more dominated by German strategic considerations with regard to the future of southeastern Europe. Its Regent, Prince Paul, was an anglophile—he was married to the Duchess of Kent's sister—but he well understood that Germany had to be lived with and that London could not offer much tangible support in the event of any conflict with Berlin.

Unable to count on either France or England or indeed Austria's closest neighbours, Schmidt turned to Poland but here the mood was unmistakeably pro-German. The Polish Foreign Minister, Beck, had, as we have seen, urged Schmidt to surrender to the "German Moloch" and thus "guarantee the peace of Europe for at least twenty years."[246] Beck's man in Vienna, Gawroński, was "ardently pro-German." Even the League

244 See Schuschnigg, *Austrian Requiem*, p. 144.
245 GSN: *Aufzeichnungen*, p. 10.
246 GSN: Verhör, p. 7.

of Nations representative in Vienna until 1936, the Dutch diplomat Rost van Tonningen, was a Dutch National Socialist completely sympathetic to the Nazis.[247]

A week after Halifax's visit to Hitler, the French Foreign Minister, Yvon Delbos, came to central Europe on a tour of the relevant capitals to discuss the Austrian question amongst other issues. His briefings left Schmidt in no doubt that Vienna could count on absolutely no support from Prague and that French efforts to garner any help had failed totally.[248]

There remained Italy but, as we have seen, the mood music was uncertain there. In the absence of any concrete steps by London (as opposed to "wishful thinking" in Cadogan's phrase) to entice Mussolini back from his embrace with Berlin, the reaction of Italy towards any German encroachment on Austria was bound to be very different from that which had accompanied the failed Nazi putsch of 1934.[249] Vansittart and other British figures may have hinted that there would be an energetic attempt to prise Italy back from Germany's orbit but the talks between Perth and Ciano and Mussolini in Rome were only just starting.

Faced with this hapless, and indeed hopeless diplomatic situation it is hardly surprising that Schmidt, along with Schuschnigg, began to look carefully at the need to step up the dialogue with the unfriendly giant neighbour to the north west.

Other factors also played a role. The interview published on 22nd January in a Prague journal with Leopold Tavs, the so-called *Gauleiter* of Vienna, which provoked the Vienna police to conduct a search of the Nazi headquarters in the Teinfaltstrasse, appeared to give the Austrians legitimate grounds for imagining they had somehow the "moral high ground" in a negotiation with Germany.

The Blomberg–Fritsch affair strengthening the Nazi party's control over the army appeared at first to herald the beginning of a new crisis which again, incorrectly, was perceived in Vienna as if it might make Hitler

---

247 Rost van Tonningen (1894–1945) later appointed "liquidation commissar" in Nazi-occupied Holland.

248 Delbos briefing to Schmidt's diplomatic representative in Prague quoted in *GSN Aufzeichnungen*, p. 8.

249 See *Cadogan Diaries*, entries Dec. 1937.

more open to concessions. Rumours of a coup against Hitler by the military high command and other non-party elements were rife. Meanwhile, Papen's recall served as a catalyst for speeding up thoughts of a summit. Although clearly a man of venal ambition and a convinced supporter of Hitler, Papen was nonetheless perceived by Schuschnigg and Schmidt to be much more amenable than his possible successors: Josef Bürckel, the anti-semitic Bavarian *Gauleiter* of the Saar or Hermann Kriebel, another Bavarian, a former Consul-General in Shanghai who was a personal crony of Hitler's. Compared to these mediocrities, Papen was indeed *Ein Herr*.

Papen's recall focussed minds. Although von Papen had made many suggestions for a summit between the two Chancellors, there had so far been no official invitation, partly because Schmidt had insisted that there could be no meeting between the Austrian and German Chancellors unless certain pre-conditions were accepted by the German side well in advance of the meeting. Schmidt's terms, agreed in advance with Schuschnigg, were inflexible. There could be no alteration of the 11th July 1936 agreement, whose foundation was a commitment from Berlin to respect Austria's sovereignty. This commitment and the equally important concession by the Nazis not to interfere in Austria's internal affairs were immoveable points which were "the basis of our relations."[250] For Schmidt any remaining points of contention were to disappear (*aus der Welt geschafft werden*). The illegal Nazi party in Austria was to be disbanded *etc. etc.*

However, the rapport between Schmidt and Papen if it were to deliver practical results was now time-limited. Papen, after he had received his *unverzüglich* (instant) dismissal at the hands of a junior official in the German Foreign Ministry in Berlin on 4th February 1938, had immediately rung Schmidt. The following morning he appeared in Schmidt's office "a completely broken man (*völlig gebrochen*)" but still capable of venting his spleen against the decision and, above all, the manner in which it had been carried out (*gab seiner Verärgerung insbesondere über die Art der Behandlung ungehemmt Ausdruck*).

The following day, Papen saw Schmidt again. This time he brought

---

250 GSN: Verhör, pp. 15–16.

the news that von Neurath had been replaced as Foreign Minister with Joachim von Ribbentrop, then Hitler's ambassador in London. Ribbentrop had been lampooned in the press as "Herr von Brickendrop" after he had committed the ultimate breach of etiquette at the court of St James by greeting the King with a *Heil Hitler* salute.[251]

It is a sign of Schmidt's genius for facing the most sticky situation undeterred that he, rather than Papen, saw immediately the potential in the fluidity of the new arrangements. He had never got on well with Neurath and the inexperience of Ribbentrop might deliver some advantages in the difficult days ahead. Above all, as he said to von Papen: "the changes in the Reich confront us with a completely new situation." For Schmidt this was always a challenge to be embraced. Papen seems to have been obsessed still with the mode of his sacking and when the two men parted on the 5th, the German had decided to go immediately to see Hitler to protest at the manner of his dismissal and seek clarification on the grounds for the decision. As Schmidt later recalled, "I did not expect to see Papen in Vienna ever again."[252] (*Ich war der Meinung, dass Papen überhaupt nicht mehr nach Wien zurückkehren werde*).

Yet two days later, on the 7th, who should appear in the chancellery but Papen. This time he did not bother to see Schmidt but went straight to the Chancellor Schuschnigg. In his briefcase was a formal invitation from Hitler for the Austrian to visit him in Berchtesgaden. Schuschnigg accepted immediately (without consulting Schmidt) but the Chancellor also mentioned the conditions he had agreed much earlier with Schmidt concerning the agenda of any meeting.

It is not beyond speculation, especially as Schmidt was accused at the time and ever afterwards of "laying a trap for his chief," that the idea of accelerating the invitation as a means of helping Papen salvage something of what looked like the end of his career *and* securing the long-awaited summit on Austrian terms was a seed carefully planted by Schmidt in Papen's mind. Schmidt was certainly capable of such sophisticated

---

251 This faux pas which filled those who witnessed it with that sense of mild injury courtiers so convincingly convey, soon became a byword for poor German manners, crass behaviour *etc. etc.*

252 GSN: Verhör, p. 16.

thinking. Von Papen was to all intents and purposes unemployed. Why shouldn't he (unwittingly or consciously) work for Schmidt? Both men would benefit in their careers from having organised the summit which might just finally solve the Austrian problem peacefully, or at least delay the evil day of annexation. Moreover, such a move could be a significant milestone in the development of the Anglo-German friendship which the English media had been crying out for a few weeks earlier. Given that events turned out rather differently than planned, it would be equally plausible for both Schmidt and Papen to wish to play down their roles in the ill-starred meeting during their subsequent trials at Vienna and Nuremberg respectively. But we are in the realms of speculation here.

Schmidt himself always vehemently denied that the visit to Berchtesgaden was his idea. He had not been present at the first meeting between Papen and Schuschnigg and therefore could not have influenced the Chancellor's decision to accept the invitation in any way. That supposition was, in his words, "an historical lie (*eine historische Lüge*)." Schuschnigg saw the visit as having a purely unofficial character and had initially wished to travel alone to Berchtesgaden. Only when von Papen indicated that Ribbentrop would be present, did Schuschnigg ask Schmidt to join him. The decision to go to Berchtesgaden was the Chancellor's "own affair" (*eigene Angelegenheit des Kanzlers*).[253] He feared that not accepting the invitation might give Hitler grounds to provoke some act of force against Austria. As Schmidt commented: "We all knew the language of Hitler and could imagine his saying that he had offered a chance to regulate Austro-German affairs, but the Austrian leadership had rejected it *etc. ...*"[254]

In any event, there are none of Schmidt's fingerprints on Schuschnigg's acceptance of the sudden invitation from Hitler. In the absence of any evidence to the contrary, it is hard not to accept Schmidt's assertion that "I was practically incapable of influencing the Chancellor's decision (*ich konnte praktisch gar keinen Einfluss auf die Entscheidung des Kanzlers ausüben*)." Moreover, his chief exonerated him later. Referring to the Berchtesgaden debacle in his memoirs published shortly after the war,

253 GSN: Verhör, p. 17.
254 GSN: Verhör, p. 17.

Schuschnigg later wrote: "I cannot remain silent when silence could be interpreted as an attempt to shirk the responsibility which I have to bear myself. The discussions with Hitler were completely in line with my publicly announced policy and I have to bear the exclusive responsibility for them."[255]

Schmidt shared the view that a failure to accept Hitler's invitation would have been "risky (*absolut riskant*)." This view was powerfully supported by Mussolini who also advised that it was essential for Schuschnigg to accept the invitation. Both the French and British envoys were also consulted and, according to Schmidt, "Even if I cannot remember their words exactly, I believe I can assert (*behaupten*) that neither of them suggested we should not go."[256] (It would of course have gone well beyond both envoys' instructions to have intimated such a course of action.) Both envoys could do little more than simply "wait and see." Any reservations expressed by the diplomats of the western democracies have gone unrecorded.

On the other hand, Papen, once engaged on the project and convinced of its beneficial effect on his remaining career prospects, threw himself into the task with great vigour. If Schuschnigg had had any lingering doubts about the visit, they may well have been dispelled by dangerous and ultimately inexcusable advice from von Papen. He was convinced that the moment to negotiate with Hitler was especially favourable The crisis in the German army following on the heels of the Blomberg–Fritsch affair had provoked enormous excitement in the world's media and Hitler was keen to calm the situation with a personal foreign policy success. Schuschnigg would perhaps be able to exploit this and win important concessions for Austria and finally "stabilise" the relations with Germany. For Schuschnigg the thought of winning a breathing space also played a role. Above all, he was playing for time, as he and Schmidt had done in 1936. But the circumstances in 1936 were different and any idea that

---

255 Schuschnigg, *Austrian Requiem*, p. 166

256 GSN: Verhör, p. 17. According to Cadogan's diary, he was largely uninformed about the Berchtesgaden visit until it had taken place. See *Cadogan Diaries*, p. 48: 17 Feb. "Only news we have is from Franckenstein." Once again Palairet appears to have been "out of touch."

this new encounter might simply "fine tune" the 1936 agreement was a dangerous illusion.

To be fair, neither he nor Schuschnigg imagined for a moment that they would meet Hitler on terms approaching any kind of equality.[257] Both men hoped that Papen, despite his demotion, might act as a "friendly" observer and would be better disposed towards Schuschnigg than any successor. After the war, Schuschnigg may have exaggerated his surprise at the asymmetry in the equation of power during his meeting. But, as his letter informing the Austrian President of his decision to accept the invitation reveals, he was under no illusions as to the difficulty of the encounter and the likelihood of tangible success: "I rather feel," he wrote to the President on the afternoon before his evening departure for Salzburg on 11th February, "that this visit is unlikely to produce any positive results."[258] To Schmidt, a note confirmed this lack of optimism: "I am reminded of Bismarck's phrase that the Bavarian is the half-way station between humanity and an Austrian."[259] These were old jokes but they betrayed almost a Viennese frivolity with regard to the men they would now be facing in Berchtesgaden. To that end, Papen had done his work well, albeit unwittingly. Like von Papen, the Austrians had little idea as to the harshness of what awaited them in reality. They joked that it would have been better to send the Nobel prize-winning physician Wagner-Jauregg in their place. He, after all, was "the expert on dementia paralytica" and could therefore have a more useful conversation with Hitler than either Schuschnigg or Schmidt.[260]

Although the visit was organised in a great hurry—barely three days elapsed between the formal invitation and the visit—it was far from being a "blind date." A detailed programme had been quickly worked out in advance by Schmidt. The points of these *Punktationen* had been left to negotiations between the Austrian Nazi Arthur Seyss-Inquart (since the previous summer a member of the State Council) and Guido Zernatto, a state secretary who was also the general secretary of the Fatherland Front.

---

257 GSN: Schuschnigg to Schmidt internal correspondence, 11 Feb. 1938.
258 GSN: Copy Letter H.B.K. (Herr Bundeskanzler) to President Miklas, 11 Feb. 1938.
259 GSN: Note H.B.K. to G.S., 10 Feb. 1938.
260 Ibid.

Schuschnigg and Schmidt judged Seyss to be a "good Nazi," an Austrian patriot and a staunch Catholic, an intellectual and a man of sensibility. A friend of the art historian and carefully camouflaged senior SS officer Kajetan Mühlmann, shortly to become Göring's art dealer, he had also, like Schmidt, befriended Göring's brother-in-law, Franz Hueber. Compared to the brutish Leopold, now utterly discredited following the Teinfaltstrasse raids, Seyss appeared to be the voice of reason. Although Schmidt was at pains later to deny the degree of his familiarity with Seyss, he had worked with Seyss on the so-called cultural "sub-committee," as Glaise-Horstenau's diaries reveal. This group had met in Berlin in the Autumn of 1936 to discuss cultural and press relations following the Austro-German agreement.[261]

It certainly suited Schmidt and Schuschnigg to be in touch with this more moderate, more cerebral Nazi grouping with its close links to Göring. Already in March 1937, Schuschnigg, following a brief encounter in February, had had a two-hour meeting with Seyss-Inquart. Glaise-Horstenau noted in his diaries that the two men had spent three quarters of the time discussing Beethoven and one quarter of the time issues of high politics. Guido Zernatto, the poet-politician who had set up the meeting and was present when it took place in Schuschnigg's apartment recalled: "After an extensive and stimulating discussion over music and the symphonies of Anton Bruckner, the conversation turned to questions of *Weltanschauung* and politics... he (Seyss) had carefully prepared his views. The formulations he employed suggested his ideas were not spontaneous thoughts but well thought out ideas... he was from beginning to end seized by one idea, that of uniting all Germans in a *Volksreich*. It was far too early to determine the form of this entity, but it was clear to Seyss that Austria would be called upon to play an extraordinary role in this new arrangement. From his description he appeared to favour a federal structure with a monarchical apex. He rejected any form of political *Gleichschaltung* (forced standardisation) for Austria, and an independent Austria was taken for granted. Rejecting any form of illegal activity or subterfuge he favoured cooperation,

---

261 See Broucek, *Glaise*, vol. 3.

joint responsibility and joint programmes (*Mitarbeit, Mitgestaltung, Mitverantwortung*).[262]

It was perhaps a sign of the limitations of his upbringing—Seyss was educated at a simple Gymnasium in Moravia—that this self-professed Catholic could find elements of Nazi ideology compatible with his faith. It remains a mystery to this day how the future *Reichkommissar* of Holland, responsible for the murder of the Catholic saint of Jewish birth, Edith Stein (Sister Teresa Benedicta), among tens of thousands of others, reconciled his faith with his political beliefs.[263]

The impact of Seyss's call for positive engagement and cooperation was undeniably favourable and from that moment, Schuschnigg encouraged Schmidt to keep in close contact with Seyss. Schmidt's mother-in-law warned him not to trust him but it was logical that, even before Hitler's formal invitation to Berchtesgaden was received, the programme agenda for the discussions should be worked out in advance in coordination with Seyss. It helped both Schuschnigg and Schmidt that Seyss was a man of legal training and therefore able to keep up with Schmidt's rigorous thinking. No doubt Schmidt and Schuschnigg hoped that by drawing Seyss into the equation more fully, the rowdier and more extreme elements of the Austrian Nazis could be marginalised. They did not realise that as far as the Nazi Germans were concerned, Seyss, of whom Hitler had barely heard of before Berchtesgaden, was at best a useful "softie" and at worst a useless nonentity. Within weeks of Berchtesgaden, Seyss would enjoy the dubious distinction of fulfilling both these roles simultaneously for Berlin with perfect aplomb.

While they thrashed out the details, Schmidt and Schuschnigg deployed all means at their disposal to maintain the secrecy of the meeting, aware of the risks that were being taken. If Schmidt had tipped the western democratic envoys off—they received copies of the formal invitation—he had laid a blanket of secrecy across the whole of the Ballhausplatz. With his usual distance from the military, Schmidt had

262 Guido Zernatto, *Die Wahrheit über Österreich* (New York, 1938), pp. 178 ff. Also see Rosar, *Deutsche Gemeinschaft*, p. 99 *et seq.*
263 See Broucek, *Glaise.* Also see Rosar, *Deutsche Gemeinschaft: Seyss-Inquart und der Anschluss,* Vienna 1971.

not bothered to inform either Glaise-Horstenau, the "crypto-Nazi" (and a man the Nazi Seyss regarded as a lightweight) in the Schuschnigg cabinet nor, perhaps more importantly, General Jansa, the chief of the Austrian general staff.

Jansa would be informed in the most Viennese of ways, by chance that evening when he attended an aristocratic ball in the Hotel Imperial with his daughters, one of whom, after dancing with an inquisitive diplomat, rushed up to her father and asked, "Is it true that the Chancellor has gone to Berchtesgaden for a meeting with Adolf Hitler? I told my dance partner that I should ask my father as he was the senior officer in Austria and would of course know."[264] The flabbergasted Jansa left the party immediately and eventually found Hornbostel in the Foreign Ministry who confirmed what his daughter had told him in the "Imperial." Of the key personalities of the Austrian administration only the mayor of Vienna, Richard Schmitz was informed so that he might be ready to take over the reins of government if the two men failed to return, a possibility which was more credible than is generally supposed.

By the afternoon of 11th February, the points to be discussed, the so-called *Punktationen* had been agreed and Seyss had forwarded them to Berlin. He already had authority from Schuschnigg to make whatever contacts with officials of the Reich he thought fit.[265] Moreover, Schuschnigg had seen them and expressed his satisfaction with the points. The Chancellor failed to realise that Seyss would be entirely on the "other side" if it came to any disagreement or debate over ambivalent formulations. During the early evening of the 11th Seyss had discussed the programme with the Chancellor in detail and given no indication of how in reality they might be received by Hitler. By the time Seyss had met with other Nazis in his own office and gathered more information about what the Führer was expecting (notably certain further demands which had been indicated concerning government posts far and beyond what had been discussed between Zernatto and Seyss) it was too late to inform Schuschnigg. As Seyss testified at Nuremberg later, "In the meantime,

---

264 See Broucek, *Jansa*, p. 668.
265 A point slightly reluctantly conceded by Schuschnigg at Guido Schmidt's trial. See *HVPGGS*, p. 444 *et seq.*

the Chancellor had travelled to the railway station and I had absolutely no possibility of informing him about this."[266] As Professor Schmidl has pointed out, one of the paradoxes of the February and March 1938 crisis was that while the Austrian Nazis were often harnessing the latest technology, flying between Vienna and Berlin, the Austrian statesmen always preferred the night train's wagon-lits.[267]

The *Punktationen* was a document of a dozen points, several of which contained elaborate subheadings. In essence, they attempted to reaffirm the foundations of the Austro-German agreement of 1936 while conceding several tactical points to Berlin. The ambivalence which had served the Austrians so well was apparent in much of the language, formulated with characteristic vagueness in many areas. For example, it was agreed that the Austrian government's press office would engage a "personality" to deal with questions arising from the "so-called national" press and the German media. Yet who this "personality" might be was left in doubt deliberately.

While these details were being worked out with Schuschnigg's approval, Schmidt and von Papen devoted their energies to the drafting of a joint press *communiqué* and—as the tradition of Austro-German treaties seemed to demand—a secret codicil.

The press release, also agreed by Schuschnigg, offers us the best guide to what Schmidt and his chief were aiming to achieve in the ill-starred summit at Berchtesgaden. It is therefore worth quoting in some detail:

> "The Austrian and German Chancellors met on 12 February in a sincere and confident discussion with regard to the changing relations between the two German states and agreed upon the following points:

> 1) The agreement 11 July 1936 will be reinforced in all its substance and any activity harmful to its foundations will be condemned.

> 2) Convinced that these conditions will allow the Austrian Chancellor to restore (through the attached measures, see Appendix B) Austria's already improving internal harmony, the German Chancellor commits to take steps which not only preserve the precise contents of the 1936

---

266 IMT Volume 16 pp.188 *et seq.*
267 See Schmidl, *März 1938*, p. 93 *et seq.*

agreement but also exclude any interference on the part of *Reichsdeutsche* party officials in Austrian affairs. This in particular applies to any direct or indirect moral or material support for any individuals and groups in Austria dedicated to undermining the Austrian Chancellor's peace-rein-forcing policies. Furthermore, the German press and other media should be influenced so as to not undermine but support morally, the peace-re-inforcing policies in Austria.

3) Both chancellors, in the expectation of long-term friendly relations between the two German states created by these terms have focussed on developing relations in key areas:

(A) Foreign Affairs

(B) The Military sphere

(c) Commercial sphere[268]

With regard to (A) both states committed to a regular diplomatic ex-change of information on issues of mutual concern. Where requested Austria would "extend its moral, diplomatic and press support for the wishes and actions of the German Reich insofar as these concern peace-ful acts with regard to joint German importance or the revision of the unjust clauses of the dictated peace."

With regard to (B) experts from both sides would meet within a month to draw up an appropriate agenda which would include military intelligence sharing, an officer exchange programme, procurement con-vergence of equipment, weapons and ammunition, the regular encour-agement of joint veteran activity, and General Staff talks.

The commercial clauses were more sensitive as they touched again on a common currency and a customs union between Austria and the Reich but even they were framed in ambiguous language and it can be seen quite clearly from this draft press release that Schmidt had done his work well. He had placed the 11th July agreement at the heart of the talks, and he was pressuring Berlin to accede to Austrian demands for a public renunciation of all illegal Nazi activity. In return Seyss, a devout Catholic

268 See Rosar, *Deutsche Gemeinschaft*, pp. 204–205 for full text in German.

and therefore in Schmidt and Schuschnigg's eyes, a man of moderation within the Nazi camp, would be elevated to full cabinet rank. The Nazis were pushing for the Interior and Security portfolio, including the police for Seyss, but there is ample evidence to suggest Schuschnigg thought at this stage he could get away with eventually simply offering Seyss the Ministry of Justice.[269] It is certainly significant that in neither the *Punktationen* or the draft press *communiqué* worked on by Schmidt and Papen is there any reference to a particular post for Seyss.

Far from being a completely spontaneous and ill-planned expedition, Schuschnigg's visit to Berchtesgaden had as much planning as the circumstances permitted and, even if the Chief of the General Staff was not informed, the Salzburg garrison regiment was put on high alert. It should not be forgotten that in the prevailing atmosphere of those days, the fear of Nazi informers and spies was everywhere. To regard Schuschnigg and Schmidt as behaving recklessly in going to Berchtesgaden is to underestimate the preparatory work Schmidt had done ahead of the summit.

For him, as for his boss, it was seen largely as a way of using the 1936 agreement and its published German declaration of respecting Austria's sovereignty as a means of gaining more time for the long-awaited British-Italian rapprochement to yield fruit and usher in a new diplomatic alignment which could offer a soft guarantee of Austria's independence.

Even if Schuschnigg realised that the "other side" now knew exactly what cards were in the Austrians' hands, neither he nor Schmidt were to know that the Germans had no intention of negotiating or making any concessions. Neither Austrian knew that Hitler's patience was running out and that his hatred of Austrian methods was rising. Hitler, the Austrian who had been at school with Wittgenstein, knew all the byzantine ways in which old official Austria had waged policies of delay and opacity. He was determined to bring an end to obfuscation and ambivalence.[270]

---

269 Ibid., p. 207.

270 The question arises to what extent Hitler was encouraged to step up the pressure through being informed of the British diplomatic move in Rome to secure some form of agreement pledging support for the status quo in Europe. Ever wary of Italy's reaction to the issue of Austrian absorption, Hitler sent three weeks later the high-ranking SS officer Prince Philipp of Hessen to sound the Duce out and assure the Italian that their border would remain on the Brenner. The Führer's unbounded

For Schmidt the 1936 agreement was the outer bastion which safe-guarded Austria from direct German interference and preserved Austria's internal equilibrium. For Hitler it was the bulwark on which attempts at "persuasion" and Nazi subversion had been wrecked. Schmidt and Schuschnigg thought the agreement could be preserved and even rein-forced. Hitler knew it had to be destroyed. To this end he summoned generals, booted and spurred to give the impression that he merely had to nod for a full-scale German invasion of Austria to take place. It was a bluff that carried more than a hint of menace.

As if to underline the sheer inevitability of Austria's imminent humil-iation and destruction, a senior SS officer travelled from Vienna in the same train as Schuschnigg and Schmidt, although unlike them he would be going straight on to Berchtesgaden and the comfortable rooms of the Hotel Post. It was Kajetan Mühlmann, Schmidt's contact man with the Austrian Nazis and the man who perhaps more than anyone else had been responsible, as Göring's favourite art dealer, for bringing Schmidt onto the most important stage of the Third Reich. After breakfast with Papen, Mühlmann would meet Ribbentrop who would arrange the meeting with Hitler that day so as to keep Hitler fully informed about Austrian "conditions." The haphazard nature of this meeting suggests a certain improvisation, although at least one author has implied that Mühlman's access to Hitler was only possible on account of his high rank in the SS.[271]

Schuschnigg's arrival with Schmidt on German territory, however, was not haphazard. At the German frontier post, a few miles out of Salzburg, von Papen waited for the Austrian party to arrive. The German, Schuschnigg later recalled, was "in the very best of humour." As the car began to climb the road to the mountain beyond, the *Hausberg* of Salzburg, the Untersberg, the familiar profile of the Austrian mountain began to recede and the more jagged outline of the Kehlstein swung

---

relief (and pledge of eternal gratitude) at Mussolini's agreement suggests that he indeed was less than completely confident that Rome would not react negatively to his *coup de main*. He appears to have been rather more confident of London's unhes-itating compliance. See below p.128, *Ciano's diaries*, p. 69. For the Berlin–London–Rome diplomatic triangle leading to the Anglo-Italian "Easter accords" see Richard Lamb, *Mussolini and the British* (London, 1997), pp. 208–218.

271 See Rosar, *Deutsche Gemeinschaft*, p. 209.

into view. Shortly after passing through the village of Berchtesgaden, the party transferred to a tracked vehicle for the final ascent up the mountain road, built in record time in 1937 under Martin Bormann's supervision, with the help of forced labour, twelve of whom died in the construction. The first jarring note was struck by Papen who asked the Austrians if they would mind if "some German generals" who were "by chance" visiting the Führer that particular day were also present in the Kehlsteinhaus. Schuschnigg exchanged glances with Schmidt but neither man offered any objection.

After all, as Schuschnigg later recalled, "I had no choice in the matter."[272]

---

272 Kurt von Schuschnigg, *Austrian Requiem* (London, 1947), p. 19.

CHAPTER 11

A "Unilateral Conversation"

B Y THE TIME the Austrian party[273] had reached the Berghof, several picturesque villages had been passed occupied mostly by faithful SA men, many of whom were Austrian Legion Nazis who had fled the Republic after the failed putsch of 1934. Like figures from a Breughel painting, they stared and grimaced as the architects of their exile swept past them.

Upon arrival, Hitler, flanked by General Keitel, the newly appointed head of the *Wehrmacht* High Command (OKW), General Sperrle, a *Luftwaffe* commander and General von Reichenau, a motorised unit commander from Dresden, greeted the Austrians with formal heel clicking and salutes. After introducing each other's staff, in Schuschnigg's case, Schmidt and Colonel Bartl, his personal adjutant, Hitler led the Austrian Chancellor into a rather ponderously furnished study on the second floor of the house.[274]

---

273 It is surprisingly difficult to pin down who precisely apart from Schmidt and Schuschnigg were in the Austrian party. Broucek notes that the two men were accompanied to Salzburg by the Chancellor's private secretary Baron Viktor Eugene Fröhlichstal and his personal adjutant Colonel Georg Bartl. But Fröhlichstal remained in Salzburg in case of difficulties (see below). See Broucek *General in Zwielicht*, p. 186 *et seq.* Apart from Schmidt's private secretary Otto Peter-Pirkham, a Nazi sympathiser, there was an unnamed police official. See Reinhard Spitzy *How we squandered the Reich* p.175.

274 Schuschnigg's private secretary Baron Fröhlichstal had stayed behind in Salzburg to coordinate the response should the Austrians fail to return. See Broucek: *Glaise* op cit p. 188

Historians are generally agreed that Schuschnigg was "browbeaten" by Hitler and that a humiliating day was now spent by the Austrian being insulted, bullied and threatened by Hitler. No doubt it suited both Schuschnigg and Schmidt to emphasise the asymmetry of the meeting and to play up the hectoring and "rude" tone of their host.[275] Berchtesgaden gave the game away and from that moment Austria was doomed. But the reality was rather more complex. While Schuschnigg was placed under a great deal of psychological pressure and subjected to all the weapons of "impression management" and, above all, prevented from smoking in Hitler's study, he was not quite the weak, broken figure to which the historiography usually alludes.

The Austrian opened the conversation complimenting his host on the view but Hitler coldly noted that they were not here to "discuss the weather." Schuschnigg began on what he believed was the secure untouchable ground of the 1936 treaty but this only provoked his host even more. Thus began a conversation which Schuschnigg would later recall as being rather "unilateral." When Schuschnigg indicated that Austria only wished to continue "the friendly policy" towards Germany, Hitler exploded that "Herr Schuschnigg," as he impolitely called his guest, had done "everything possible to avoid a friendly policy towards Germany." First proof of this was the complacent Austrian decision to remain a member of the League of Nations after Germany had decided to leave. "No-one asked us to leave," Schuschnigg responded, but Hitler only shouted, "It was self-evident that you had to leave the League!" So far the temperature of the meeting had been chilly but both men had kept their nerve. Hitler now raised the stakes by launching a long list of Austria's sins with regard to Germany down the centuries. It was as if all his neuroses concerning the land of his birth needed finally to be aired to the Austrian Chancellor.

Although Schuschnigg would later avoid ordering the Austrian army to resist the German invasion by stating he never wished there to be a repeat of the German *Brüderkrieg* as German nationalists called the Austro-Prussian war of 1866, he was nothing if not an Austrian patriot

---

275 See, for example, Richard Evans, Max Hastings, David Faber, Tim Bouverie, Norman Stone, Richard Overy *etc.*

when it came to dealing verbally with Germany. Hitler began to rant that "Austria has never done anything that would ever be of any help to Germany. The whole history of Austria," he insisted, "was just one act of uninterrupted high treason." Austria's treason towards Germany had scarred her past and disfigured her present but, Hitler insisted, "This historical paradox must now reach its long overdue conclusion and I am determined to make an end of all this."

Schuschnigg simply parried the thrusts and noted calmly that he was fully aware of the *Reichkanzler's* views on Austrian history but "you will understand that my opinion in these questions differs basically from yours. Austria's entire history is inseparable from that of Germany and the Austrian contribution is far from negligible." This assertion caused Hitler to lose his self-control: "Zero, absolutely zero: that is Austria's contribution to Germany. Every national idea has been only sabotaged throughout history by Austria. The Habsburgs, the Catholic Church, they both engaged upon this sabotage unremittingly."[276]

There then followed a heated discussion which showed all the ambivalence of an Austrian's attitudes towards Germany. When Schuschnigg suggested Beethoven was an Austrian, Hitler insisted he came from the lower Rhineland. Schuschnigg retorted that Austria and Vienna was the land of Beethoven's choice, implying that had Beethoven remained in Bonn no-one ever would have heard of him. Developing this theme, Schuschnigg rather provocatively added that "nobody would, for instance, refer to Metternich as a German from the Rhineland."[277] These were intellectual points, but Schuschnigg's host could take losing the odd argument on semantics. His "mission" was altogether of a more serious kind: "I have an historic mission and this mission I will fulfil because Providence has destined me to do so. I thoroughly believe in this mission: it is my life."

Schuschnigg had long ago learnt from the Jesuits that *mit einem ruhigen Gesicht beherrscht man die Welt* (a calm face conquers the world) and no doubt his expression was inscrutable.[278] Hitler attempted to pene-

---

276 The text from Schuschnigg, *Austrian Requiem*, pp. 20–30.

277 Ibid., p. 21.

278 Blanka von Korwin to author, Trieste, 6 June 1979.

trate this with an attempt at drawing the Austrian's sympathy by referring to his own religious feelings: "And I believe in God! I am a religious man although not in any denominational sense of the word."

No doubt Schuschnigg would have realised he should simply sit back and humour his host by calmly listening. Hitler meandered over his successes in Germany noting that he had hoped to unite the Catholic and Protestant churches there, but the two churches had refused to cooperate. Therefore "I decided that my task would be achieved without the Churches and if necessary, notwithstanding the Churches because who is not with me will be crushed."

Just in case Schuschnigg did not understand this theological point of view, Hitler clarified his thought: "Look around you in Germany today, Herr Schuschnigg and you will find there is but one will. I was predestined to achieve this task; I have chosen the most difficult road that any German ever took; I have achieved the greatest things in the history of Germany, greater indeed than any German but not by force. I am carried along by the love of my people." The police in Germany when he appeared in public were there simply to curb the "boundless enthusiasm of the German people" not for Hitler's protection.

Schuschnigg responded with subtle and typical old Austrian insincerity and superiority: "I am quite willing to believe that, *Herr Reichskanzler.*" This was a familiar piece of condescension for Hitler and it seemed to get under his skin: "I could call myself an Austrian with far more reason than you," he snapped. This was a thinly veiled reference to the fact that Schuschnigg was born in modern Italy on Lake Garda and that his family was of Carinthian Slovene origins. In Schuschnigg, despite all his talk of Austria as the Second German state, Hitler was confronting everything he despised in the land of his birth, the multi-racial, multi-national, multi-confessional empire of the Habsburgs. Beneath his seemingly innocuous insult was the nub of the matter. Hitler believed in the racial superiority of the Germans and the national idea whereas Schuschnigg represented, indeed personified, the multinational Austrian empire he had been born into. This was the exact antithesis of everything Hitler and the Nazis stood for. Otto Habsburg had known this when he had refused to meet Hitler.

Schuschnigg now rather skilfully moved the conversation back onto the imagined safer ground of the 1936 agreement. If there were issues arising from the inevitable coexistence of the "small state along the larger one," then his host should enumerate them. The Austrian Chancellor added: "we will do everything to remove obstacles to a better understanding as far as it is possible." Austria wished nothing more than to live in peace and fulfil its "historic mission in Central Europe." Again, Schuschnigg was demonstrating his intellectual superiority in the hope that this could provide some semblance of equality in the "unilateral" discussion, even though he realised that the equation of power between the two men left little scope for a satisfactory outcome. Hitler realised that this intellectual and theoretical fencing was unlikely to progress matters. He moved onto the attack on a more menacing note: the vulnerability of the Austrian frontier with Germany: "You have made ridiculous efforts to mine the bridges leading to the Reich... do you think you can move a pebble in Austria without my hearing about it the very next day?... I have only to give an order and in one single night all your ridiculous defences will be blown to pieces."

Here was an escalation and the threatening tone continued: "Perhaps you will wake up in Vienna to find us there—just like a spring thunderstorm—and then you will experience something Herr Schuschnigg. I should like to spare Austria such a fate because such action will mean blood. After the army, my SA and the Austrian Legion will move in and nobody will be able to stop their just revenge—not even I. Do you want to make Austria another Spain?"

These were sobering words but Schuschnigg insisted that a German invasion would not only mean bloodshed but would also provoke outside intervention: "We are not alone in this world and such a step would probably mean war." Here were words perhaps inspired by Schmidt's dialogue with Vansittart, but his host was better informed. If the Austrian hoped that this reference to some unspecified help might inhibit Hitler, he was mistaken. Hitler knew, as Schmidt did, from Halifax's visit that there could be no help from London and that without London's support Paris would not intervene. He was less sure about Italy but if he could move before London cemented a new agreement with Rome any hopes Schuschnigg might have of Italian support would also be rendered nugatory.

Hitler moved swiftly to let his guest know these realities with a thinly-veiled reference to Halifax's visit in November. "I see eye to eye with Mussolini; the closest ties of friendship bind me to Italy. And England? England believe me Herr Schuschnigg will not move one finger for Austria. Not long ago, an English diplomat sat in the very chair you are now sitting in. And outside this window hundreds and hundreds of Austrian men and women, desperate, starving in rags with misery written across their faces passed by. All of them had come here to see me, to implore me as their saviour to put an end to their misery. I showed these people to the Englishman and he grew very silent and no longer contradicted me. You cannot expect any help from England."

The Englishman in this case was Nevile Henderson, the British ambassador to Berlin and a staunch critic of Schuschnigg and Guido Schmidt.[279] No doubt Hitler was exaggerating because, for all his faults, Henderson could usually be relied upon to defend the official British position staunchly. But the British official position implicitly was encouraging German policies with regard to Austria as long as violence was avoided. Henderson had already made this clear when he had said to the Austrian minister in Berlin, Tauschitz, a few months earlier: "You Austrians are Germans: why make all this fuss? You are just as German as Germany"[280] There is some dispute over the exact wording of Henderson's *gaffe*. He later defended himself vigorously by saying he had only said that should the Austrian people one day want an *Anschluss*, there could be no moral argument against them implementing their wishes, a hypocritical formulation vividly illustrative of the *déformation professionelle* of diplomacy.

Hitler continued: "The world must know that it is unbearable for a great power like Germany to have every little state on her borders believing that it can provoke her... the persecution of National Socialists in Austria must have an end or else I shall put an end to it."

And so the "discussions" continued with Hitler threatening action and Schuschnigg attempting to hold the line of the 1936 agreement whereby the Reich recognised that there could be no Nazi party in Austria. Hitler's

---

279 See N. Henderson, *Failure of a Mission* (London, 1940), p. 119 *et seq.*
280 See GSN: Verhör, p. 56. Also see Eden's gentle admonishment of Henderson: 22/6/37 FO 800/268 and Peter Neville, *Appeasing Hitler*, pp. 28–31.

pressure increased as he gave the Austrian Chancellor less than two hours to come to terms. "I can only wait until this afternoon. Think it over carefully Herr Schuschnigg. You should take these words literally. I do not believe in bluffing."

Gradually the Nazi leader was wearing his guest down but after two hours he had not extracted any meaningful concessions from the Austrian. Nevertheless, the fact that Hitler had not alluded to either the *Punktationen* or the draft press release or indeed showed any interest in discussing either of these two documents was ominous. As the two men walked to the dining room where they were served by "exceptionally tall and remarkably handsome" SS stewards in white tunics, this "impression management" designed to intimidate and emphasise the discipline and greatness of Germany was not lost on Schuschnigg.

Conversation over lunch was largely inconsequential. The generals but not Schuschnigg's staff joined them. The Austrian noticed a particularly fine Madonna by Albrecht Dürer on one of the walls. When he complimented its piety (and by implication its Christian resonance), Hitler defensively responded to the Austrian: "My favourite picture; because it is so thoroughly German."

After lunch Hitler did not appear and as the Austrian waited, he debriefed Schmidt on the discussions. For the first time, the Austrian Chancellor was allowed to smoke. As a chain-smoker, the two hours with Hitler and the one hour at lunch had been rather difficult for him. While the two Austrians talked, watched by the German press chief Herr Dietrich, a young man in a black SS uniform appeared, the son of a famous surgeon from Vienna. This was more impression management, designed to give the guests a sense that Austria's natural inclination was towards *Anschluss*. Most Viennese surgeons were of Jewish origin but this young man, it was explained, had opted for "the future" rather than "the past." Although both Schuschnigg and Schmidt were aware that discussions had not been very encouraging so far, both men were convinced that more concrete issues arising from the 1936 agreement would be ventilated that afternoon. Nevertheless, it was clear that any thought of the Austrians perhaps having the upper hand or moral high ground in these discussions was illusory.

While the two men preserved their calm and discussed superficialities, Hitler was preparing to meet Göring's art dealer and agent, Kajetan Mühlmann. Before that encounter Hitler quickly agreed with Ribbentrop the points of the German draft document which would be presented as a *fait accompli* to the Austrians, who would be told to sign before being allowed to leave the Berghof. This document was not based on the *Punktationen* and the very modest programme Schmidt had outlined and agreed with von Papen. Rather, its scope and tone were far more intrusive and dictatorial than anything either Schmidt or Schuschnigg, or indeed von Papen had imagined. According to Papen, both he and Schmidt were shocked at the tone of the Note which was nothing less than an ultimatum.[281] Schmidt's face, according to Papen, when he saw this document was one of the greatest "astonishment." As he digested the contents of what was an unwarrantable and wholly unacceptable interference in Austrian sovereignty, Schmidt grew more and more angry, speaking sharply to von Papen at this breach of trust. The exchange was overheard by Nazi officials in the room who were taken aback at Schmidt's vehemence.[282]

The *grosses Forderungsprogramm* (great demands programme) showed that the "new" German diplomacy had evolved significantly since 1936 and had little time for the Austrian nuance or ambivalence which had served Schmidt so well during the drafting of that agreement.

The document began with a demand that the Austrian Chancellor implement *within a week* all the following measures:

1) The Austrian government commits that Austrian Foreign Policy will be coordinated with the Reich with regard to all issues of mutual interest.

2) The Austrian government recognises that National Socialism is not incompatible with the realities of Austria and that with regard to the Austrian constitution, no measures will be carried out which prohibit National Socialist activity. The Austrian Chancellor will declare in public his understanding for an acceleration of the integration process bringing

---

281 It is hard to believe Papen, given that his assistant at the embassy in Vienna, Keppler, had together with Mühlmann worked on these points, with Papen's approval. See Papen, *Memoirs*, p. 414.

282 GSN: *Aufzeichnungen: Grosse Forderungsprogramm.*

Nazis into the Fatherland Front (*Volkspolitische Referate*).

3) The appointment of state councillor Seyss-Inquart as Minister of the Interior with responsibility for security to be subordinated directly to Berlin with the understanding that he will introduce measures which support the activities of the National Socialist movement in Austria.

4) A complete amnesty for all Nazis. The decision on whether any of the released figures are allowed to remain in Austria to be decided in agreement with both governments on a case by case basis.

5) Compensation for any loss of income, pensions *etc.* arising in the past as a consequence of National Socialist activity in Austria. The abolition of all measures introduced to financially punish party members.

6) All commercial discrimination towards members of the Nazi party to be ended.

7) The newly agreed cooperative press relations between the two countries will be reinforced by the removal of minister Ludwig and commissioner Adam.[283]

8) Military relations between the two countries will be secured by the following measures:
   a) The appointment of Glaise-Horstenau as minister for the army.
   b) Regular officer exchange programme involving at least 100 officers.
   c) Regular staff talks.
   d) Regular veteran reunions.

9) All discrimination in the armed forces against Nazis to cease and where possible be reversed.[284]

10) The assimilation of the Austrian economy into that of the Reich to be effected by the appointment of Dr Fischböck as Finance Minister.

Any issues of contention concerning security will be discussed exclusively with Seyss-Inquart.

While this Carthaginian programme was presented to a shocked Schuschnigg and Schmidt, the latter again addressed Papen in angry tones, loudly and brusquely berating the German for breaching the understanding that the programme agreed in Vienna would be the exclusive

---

283 Eduard Ludwig: Head of the Government Press Service; and Walter Adam Homeland Commissioner.

284 A reference to the reinstatement of Nazis dismissed from the Austrian armed forces.

basis for the talks. As there are several witnesses to Schmidt "having a go at von Papen" and everyone who came across Schmidt remembers he had a violent temper, there can be little doubt that the State Secretary was surprised by the "new programme."[285]

Meanwhile, Hitler had his meeting with Mühlmann. As the two men met alone and no other record exists of this conversation other than Mühlmann's testimony under oath at Guido Schmidt's trial, we must accept, albeit critically at least, the basic outline of the account. He described the encounter in the following terms:

> "Around quarter to six in the evening I was telephoned by Ribbentrop who said I would be collected in ten minutes and presented to the Führer… I found Hitler in an extraordinarily excited state. He was very pale, looked dreadful and made an appalling impression."[286]

This was hardly the description of someone who had his teeth well into the Austrian Chancellor's soul. Rather it shows that Schuschnigg had demonstrated some resilience towards Hitler and that his calm and dignified manner had even unsettled his interlocutor.

Mühlmann continued:

> "Hitler said that he had invited me to see him to know whether the agreement which Schuschnigg had proposed [sic!] was acceptable to the Austrian Nazis. 'I am determined to solve the Austrian question today even if it means spilling blood'."

The next question the Führer posed to the art dealer revealed vividly that contrary to popular legend, Schuschnigg had stood his ground and had even frustrated the Nazi leader: "Would Schuschnigg," Hitler asked, "even respect a treaty?."

To this strange insecure probing, Mühlmann replied: "I do not know him personally, but I do know Seyss-Inquart's view of him and he believes that Schuschnigg would respect his commitments. I am therefore convinced that this would be the case, although of course under the condition that Austria's independence was respected."

Hitler said nothing to this, and the silence was broken again by the

---

285 *"Er ist wirklich vehement an die Menschen losgegangen"*: author's conversation with Tino Schmidt-Chiari, 29 March 2019, Bludenz.
286 *HVPGGS*, p. 244.

Austrian art dealer: "However one condition will be the recalling of Leopold." Hitler regarded his guest from head to toe and asked "Why?" Mühlmann explained but Hitler only looked at him again from head to toe, not wishing to be drawn on the subject.[287] Hitler now asked his guest about Seyss. Did he have enough support in the Nazi camp to implement a policy of reconciliation? Was he not after all a Catholic?"

If Mühlmann's testimony is even only partly correct it seems to imply that Hitler's mind was still plagued by doubts about who would be the best candidate to lead the absorption of Austria into the Reich.

Meanwhile Ribbentrop and Schmidt together with Schuschnigg were fighting over the ultimatum. It was largely thanks to Schmidt's mental agility and grasp of drafting that the document Ribbentrop presented to them could be revised in favour of the Austrians. Nothing demonstrated more vividly Schmidt's intellectual superiority over Ribbentrop than this rearguard action to water down German demands.

The first point Schmidt attacked was the time-limit. The German document suggested 18th February (a week hence) as the deadline for all the German demands to be met. This was impracticable and Schmidt limited it to the appointment of Seyss, the changes to the government Press service, and the amnesty and a few financial points.[288]

With regard to foreign policy (point 2), Schmidt struck out the phrase "coordination with the Reich" and replaced it with the far more innocuous "diplomatic exchange of thoughts (*Gedankenaustausch*)." He added the sentence that "moral, diplomatic and press support" for the Reich would be offered after "evaluation of the possibilities (*Massgabe der Möglichkeit*)."

On the question of integrating Nazis into the Fatherland Front (point 2), Schmidt came up with a characteristically ambivalent formulation whereby such steps could only be taken for "certain individuals" rather than the blanket all-embracing process stipulated in the German

---

287 In fact, within days of this meeting Leopold was recalled to Germany. See Rosar, *Deutsche Gemeinschaft*, p. 212.

288 See GSN: Schmidt amendments: *Definitive Fassung des Protokolls von Berchtesgaden v.12.II.1938* (Gegenüberbestellung/Entwurf Protokoll). Also Rosar, *Deutsche Gemeinschaft*, pp. 210–212.

document. Moreover, such "entry" would be "only possible under certain conditions (*unter bestimmten Vorraussetzungen*)." This was a major block to German demands. Schmidt chiselled away even at the use of the term National Socialist movement (*Bewegung*) preferring the altogether more restrictive "National Socialists."

On the issue of the amnesty for National Socialists (point 4) Schmidt struck out the catch-all phrase, inserting instead the much narrower definition of "Nazis convicted in Austria." With regard to the replacement of Ludwig and Adam in the governmental press service, again Schmidt removed this clause, replacing it with a less radical phrase promising the involvement of Dr Wolff[289] in the press office but not mentioning either Ludwig or Adam.

It was perhaps the military demands of the Germans which Schmidt neutralised most effectively. Instead of accepting the appointment of Glaise as Minister for the Army, Schmidt simply scratched that clause out replacing it with a harmless reference to an unspecified "change in the chief of the general staff." Here Schmidt knew what he was doing. FML Jansa had been in the sights of the Nazis for a long time but hitherto Schuschnigg had resisted all pressure to remove him. Jansa, however, as Schmidt well knew, was overdue for retirement and therefore could be, if necessary, relatively uncontroversially dropped during the following weeks. Moreover, Schmidt struck out the clause stipulating a minimum of 100 officers for the exchange programme, replacing it with a "maximum of 100 officers." (Not bad redrafting for a "military ignoramus" under intense pressure of time and the threat of imminent violence.)

On the economic conditions, (point 7) Schmidt revisited the text even more radically, replacing the "assimilation" of Austrian commercial activity into the Reich with the more neutral "intensifying of commercial ties" between the two countries. The demand for Dr Fischböck to be appointed Finance Minister is met with a clause noting that he should be given a responsible but again unspecified position.[290] Although subse-

---

289 Wilhelm Wolf, a Nazi who would succeed Schmidt for two and a half days as Austrian Foreign Minister following the Anschluss. His Catholicism disarmed his critics initially. Family connexions with Schmidt also played a role in his appointment.
290 GSN: *Definitive Fassung*.

quent events rendered all these points meaningless and therefore more or less forgotten, there can be no doubt that Schmidt's performance as a negotiator working under unparalleled pressure was little short of magnificent.

These were ultimately all small victories but even Schmidt's sternest critic, the British minister in Vienna Michael Palairet, would later report to London that given the circumstances, it was remarkable the Austrians "did not have to concede more." For once Palairet was right. Schmidt had excelled himself in a near hopeless situation, no doubt motivated by the sense that he should try to save what could be saved.

That he was able to modify at all the German document is astounding given that just as he was working on the points with Ribbentrop, anxious not to mark the beginning of his new role as Foreign Minister by being complicit in a diplomatic failure, Schuschnigg was again summoned to see Hitler. By now Hitler had finished his meeting with Mühlmann and was pacing up and down in his study in a state of high excitement. During the meeting he had been twice interrupted by Ribbentrop to be told that Schuschnigg (or rather Schmidt) was resisting key parts of the document including the appointment of Seyss-Inquart.

When Schuschnigg re-joined him, Hitler pushed the original German draft towards the Austrian Chancellor and simply said, indifferent to Schmidt's revisions: "Herr Schuschnigg I am making one last effort. Here is the document. There is nothing to be discussed about it. I will not change one single iota and you will either sign it as it stands or else our meeting has been useless and I shall decide tonight what the next steps will be." Again, far from simply giving in to Hitler, Schuschnigg prevaricated saying that the appointment of ministers and the introduction of amnesties for prisoners were the responsibility of the Austrian President, Miklas. Therefore, there was no question of offering any guarantee to his host that the document would be acceptable. "You have to guarantee that," Hitler insisted. "I could not possibly *Herr Reichskanzler*," Schuschnigg coolly replied.

Hitler paused on hearing Schuschnigg's reply and was silent for a few seconds as if pondering his next move. He then exploded in rage, appearing to lose his self-control. He ran to the doors, opened them, and shouted "General Keitel! Where is Keitel?." Turning back to Schuschnigg he simply said: "I shall have you called later."

As it happened, just at that moment, Keitel was enjoying a polite if insincere conversation of superficialities with Guido Schmidt who had briefly broken off from his discussions with Ribbentrop. As soon as he heard Hitler's voice calling him, Keitel who had been perfectly friendly if somewhat stiff towards Schmidt, changed his manner immediately and became almost actively hostile towards the Austrian. Marching off to find Hitler, he neither heel-clicked nor saluted but strode off self-importantly giving an impression of "outspoken enmity."[291]

Schmidt felt a "decisive moment" had been reached and when Schuschnigg re-joined him, he told him that he would not be surprised if they were both arrested within the next five minutes. In fact, Hitler had simply wanted to indulge in some more impression management. When Keitel arrived to find him grinning and not needing the soldier's presence, the slow-witted general at first could not understand. Gradually it dawned on him that he was just a *Statist* on the stage of a drama which did not directly concern him.

The impression management had its effect: a subdued Schmidt and von Papen were now called into Hitler's study to be told again of his historic mission to solve the Austrian question once and for all. Then Schuschnigg was called in to be told that the points following Schmidt's revisions were "now agreed" and that three days would be granted to implement them. "I have decided to change my mind—for the first time in my life," Hitler said, adding "But this is your last chance."

According to Mühlmann, it was neither Schmidt nor Schuschnigg who "won" this three-day extension but the art dealer who persuaded Hitler to give the Austrian Chancellor a little more time. According to Mühlmann, Hitler had simply said "Alright. I should have preferred to march in but I shall give him a last chance."[292]

Towards evening, the document with all of Schmidt's revisions was brought in, signed by Hitler and Ribbentrop on behalf of the Reich and Schuschnigg and Schmidt on behalf of Austria. Given that Schmidt was

291 G.S. *Aufzeichnungen*
292 Rosar p.213

seen to be *grossdeutsch gesinnt* by the Germans, Schuschnigg felt it useful to give Schmidt the title of Foreign Minister, a bauble which in practice meant nothing to either man but might give the Germans the sense that the Austrians would be more cooperative. The promotion would give Schmidt more authority in his dealings with Ribbentrop with whom he had established a rapport (and over whom he had total intellectual dominance). As the Austrian party, accompanied by Papen, left the Berghof and returned to Salzburg there was a sense of relief but both Schuschnigg and Schmidt were silent. After five minutes, Papen tried to lighten the mood with the remark "Now you know what the Führer can be like at times. Next time it will be entirely different... he can be so charming."

Schmidt might have been tempted to repeat his offer of the previous week to Papen that perhaps he would like to go to Berlin to be Austrian ambassador (if he found the Führer so charming), but if the thought crossed his mind, he did not speak. Perhaps his German escort, led by the Austrian SS officer, Reinhard Spitzy, gave him grounds for caution. It would later emerge that had Schmidt and the Chancellor refused to sign the document, Spitzy's men were under orders to stop the car in a copse at the edge of a ravine, stand the Chancellor, Schmidt and their ADC against a tree and shoot them dead before placing the bodies in the car and crashing it over the precipice.[293]

---

293 See Sheridan *Kurt von Schuschnigg: A Tribute* 228-229. Spitzy always denied this and indeed was happy to engage in a post-war correspondence with Schuschnigg. His commitment to the Nazi ideology followed him to the grave. Charlotte Szapary to the author 8.8.2005

CHAPTER 12

The Four Week Respite

A FTER A BRIEF few hours in Salzburg, where a suite at the Oesterreichischer Hof [294] was put at Schuschnigg's disposal, the Austrians re-joined their train and returned to Vienna. Reports that the Austrian Chancellor holed up in the *kaisergelb* hotel along the Salzach are wide of the mark, although at least one source recalled hearing the Chancellor screaming at the ever attentive Room Service to leave him in peace.[295]

The violence of Hitler's language had shocked both Austrians. Schuschnigg realised time had run out and Schmidt who adopted a more positive gloss on the talks could not persuade his boss that there was still something to be saved. Schuschnigg saw starkly the ruin of his policies and everything he had striven for personally. The Germans would increase the pressure relentlessly now. Indeed, barely had the two Austrians been back in Vienna then the German *Abwehr* under Admiral Canaris began to initiate a skilful series of military activities designed to give the impression of an imminent invasion of Austria.[296]

For Schuschnigg and Schmidt the challenge was almost the opposite: to give an impression that there was simply no crisis and that despite

---

294 Today, following its acquisition by the Gürtler group from the Segur Cabanac family the Hotel Sacher.

295 E. W. to author Salzburg 26.6.1986

296 For the *Abwehr* dimension of "Operation Otto" see Bassett *Hitler's Spy Chief* p.147

the intimidation visited upon them in Berchtesgaden and the growing military menace, neither they nor their government should be in the least bit anxious. Retaining an appearance of confident optimism especially with regard to the foreign diplomats was the key. As Schuschnigg later recalled: "any panic, any excitement might provide the spark which would start the conflagration."[297] This approach did not preclude the briefing in some detail by Schmidt of the relevant foreign envoys.

As it happened, two days after Berchtesgaden, on the evening of February 14th, there was the annual state reception for the diplomatic corps. The French Minister Puaux insisted this event had been organised to celebrate Schmidt's elevation to the position of Foreign Minister, but this was an obvious *canard* as even in Vienna a ball at the Hofburg could not be organised at two days' notice.[298]

That same day, the prisoners' amnesty was announced by President Miklas. Any diplomat with good contacts in the city was sure to see that Austria's relations with Germany were about to change. Despite or perhaps because of his pro-German sympathies, one of the best informed diplomats was the Polish Ambassador, Gawroński. He was a personal friend of Starhemberg's and a supporter of the Prince's form of "Austro-fascism." He had always been rather sceptical of Schmidt, dubbing him "naive and hopelessly unrealistic" in his policy aspirations. Ahead of the annual reception he asked for a detailed briefing which Schmidt proceeded to give saying that the discussions had been "amicable" and that much progress had been made in setting Austro-German relations on a stable course. As the Pole later recalled: "This meeting lasted the best part of three quarters of an hour. Schmidt said that Austria could be very happy with the agreement and went on to praise himself and the Chancellor for their sterling efforts. It was entirely the result of such efforts that they had managed to emerge from the talks with the small concessions that they had won. I have rarely in my entire career as a diplomat had to listen to such an avalanche of falsehoods in so short a time, so flowingly uttered from such a high ranking official, as I had to that afternoon from the mouth of Dr Guido Schmidt."[299]

297 G.S. *Aufzeichnungen*
298 Puaux p.106-108
299 See Gawroński, *Moja Misja*, p. 511. See also 469–474. It should be borne in mind that

Unfortunately, this distrust among the diplomats did not just extend to pro-German ministers, the representatives of the western democracies were equally concerned. Puaux made no secret of his views of Schmidt's "treachery."

The British minister, Palairet, was more calibrated, preferring to dwell on the fact that the German manoeuvres taking place on Bavarian territory with a clear intention of threatening the Schuschnigg government were seen correctly as a bluff by Schmidt.[300] Schmidt had conceded to the British envoy that the talks had been a challenge. Palairet reported that the Berchtesgaden meeting had been "extremely difficult."[301] But the two men still clearly did not enjoy any rapport. When the Englishman asked Schmidt if the appointment of Seyss was simply "the first step towards Austria's Nazification," Schmidt immediately countered by saying that this was unlikely, as Seyss was a "practising Catholic." The British envoy was far less cynical than his Polish colleague and clearly took Schmidt's briefing at face value concluding: "it is astonishing Dr Schuschnigg was able to give away as little as he did when one considers the circumstances of the meeting."[302]

Schmidt had clearly decided to be more open with the British envoy and he confided that he had received "a very favourable impression of Ribbentrop." Papen had been "helpful" but as Palairet admitted in a rare note of realism, all in all Schmidt's "optimism was decidedly shattered" by the meeting. When, rather unhelpfully, Palairet "took him to task" for his earlier "misplaced optimism," for minimising the dangers of the meeting when he had announced the imminent Berchtesgaden summit, Schmidt replied with annoying but typically skilful insouciance that "he had seen no object in telling me then how pessimistic he really felt."[303] This riposte no doubt ruffled Palairet's feathers even more. The exchange was another example of how Schmidt's playful and sophisticated Austrian

---

Gawroński here was writing in hindsight when it was all too easy to ignore Schmidt's efforts at Berchtesgaden.

300 FO 371/22312 213 *et seq.* R1826.
301 *DBFP* 2 5162/XIX, p. 895.
302 Ibid., 569.
303 FO 371/22312 214.

sensibility played poorly with the Englishman's more straightforward mindset, although it underlined Schmidt's conviction that he had to give London a relatively unvarnished version of the Berchtesgaden meeting.

Nevertheless, Schmidt had maintained a convincingly reassuring countenance when dealing with the Englishman and Palairet could report on 19th February, a few days later, that he fully expected "a few months calm."[304] This message was eagerly greeted in London where Eden minuted on Palairet's dispatch: "I do not think we need expect any dramatic development in the immediate future." These embarrassingly unrealistic observations speak volumes about London's lack of grip on Austrian events and lack of insight into European developments.

Palairet made two other equally inaccurate observations the following day in another dispatch to Eden which revealed he was still finding it difficult to obtain reliable information in Vienna. First, he reported that "as it was, no programme was drawn up" ahead of the Berchtesgaden meeting. This was demonstrably false, as we have seen, but it was his second observation which emphasised his remoteness from the realities in central Europe. In an extraordinarily irrelevant speculation he attributed Hitler's tough attitude at Berchtesgaden partly to a desire to "balance" the "blow to prestige" which "the fall of the Goga government" in Bucharest had inflicted. This strange excursion back into the political arcana of his earlier posting reveals perhaps more than anything else, Palairet's desperation to sound authoritative and be on top of a rapidly evolving situation which was clearly racing away from him.[305] It was all happening far too fast: he had neither had the time to develop his own contacts at a senior level or to form a mature judgement on events. This disadvantage was to have grave consequences for Austria and ultimately the peace of Europe in the days ahead.

At this stage, by the middle of February, Palairet's scepticism towards Schmidt was about to harden into something far more critical, thanks mostly to his close friendship with his French colleague, Gabriel Puaux.[306] Both envoys had served together in an earlier posting in Bucharest so

304 *DBFP* 2/XIX 530.
305 FO 371/22312 213
306 See Puaux, *Mort* for the French diplomat's highly selective account of the crisis.

it was hardly surprising that the Englishman sought the advice of his French friend. New to a complex and fast-moving situation, Palairet came to rely more and more on Puaux's views or, more accurately perhaps, his prejudices. Puaux found Schmidt overbearing, young and far too pro-German. For his part Schmidt found Puaux slightly pompous, self-important and viscerally hostile to anything German but above all completely ineffective. Whatever words of support for the government in Austria he uttered, Puaux could not deliver any tangible support from Paris. Puaux had met the French premier Leon Blum and had told him buoyantly "Austria lives" to which Blum had grimly replied "(only) by a miracle."[307]

Schmidt's character failings did not endear him to many others of the diplomatic community. His colleague Martin Fuchs, the press *attaché* in the Austrian embassy in Paris would later recall: "this companiable man... who would languidly flick the ash of his cigarette into a nearby pot-plant and who affected a look of boredom at most briefings was truly loathed."[308]

The chemistry between Puaux and Schmidt became increasingly negative. Schmidt often kept Puaux waiting and went almost out of his way to demonstrate that he did not take him as seriously as he took von Papen.[309] Madame Puaux eagerly joined in her husband's critical views with regard to Schmidt, not hesitating to share her hostility with Palairet. Thus Schmidt's elevation from State Secretary to the title of Foreign Minister was seen by Madame Puaux as something he had boasted about to her already before the Berchtesgaden summit when he had said something "very agreeable was going to happen to him."[310] For Palairet, Schmidt's elevation to Foreign Minister post Berchtesgaden was "a very black mark" against him.

Identifying more and more with the French point of view, Palairet

---

307 Puaux, *Mort*, pp. 90–93.

308 See Martin Fuchs, *Showdown in Vienna* (New York, 1939).

309 For Schmidt's poor time-keeping with Puaux see Karl Karwinsky in *IMT interrogation supplement A* (Washington, 1947), 3855, p. 589.

310 FO 371/22312 220. Palairet again preferring to dwell on the optics rather than the fundamentals of the situation.

failed to realise that Schmidt had been appointed in the first place to manage Germany and that his "promotion" had to be seen in terms of minor concessions and token optics to prevent Berlin demanding more substantial concessions. Schmidt's reference to something very agreeable being about to happen to him could easily have been a typically Austrian verbal provocation or indeed referred to some event of rather less importance.[311]

When with thinly veiled sarcasm, Palairet congratulated Schmidt on his promotion, Schmidt "made light of it" and answered with unambiguous candour that it "made no difference and that he would continue to work under the Chancellor's instructions."[312] Palairet remained unconvinced, and it is hard not to accept that his reservations about Schmidt were also shared by those to whom he was reporting in London who may well have encouraged them.

As the news of Berchtesgaden reached London, Eden faced questions in the House of Commons on 16th February. The Labour MP Bellenger asked "whether in view of the fact that the integrity and independence of Austria are declared objectives of Britain's Foreign Policy," Eden might care to comment on the Berchtesgaden discussions.[313] Eden knew what was coming next and as the files of the Foreign Office show, there had been a flurry of effort during the previous week to find every relevant statement the UK had made over the previous three years concerning Austrian independence.[314] Bellenger continued and asked the inevitable question: "Would the Foreign Secretary give an assurance that the policy of His Majesty's Government in relation to the integrity and independence of Austria remains the same as stated by him on a previous occasion in this house?" Eden based his reply on what his staff had dug out and no doubt his own convictions. In four days' time he would resign, ostensibly over appeasement of Italy with regard to Abyssinia. Faced now with the dilemma of Austria he preferred to continue the weak tropes of appeasement. "My recollection," he replied, "is that what I said then was that His

---

311 The *agréable* event might well have been to do with his family rather than politics.
312 FO 371/22312 222.
313 See *Hansard* House of Commons, 16 February 1938
314 See FO 371/22312 210–224

Majesty's Government desired in central Europe, as elsewhere, peace and good understanding. That is certainly our policy."

Asked by Arthur Henderson whether His Majesty's Government would "stand by the joint declaration by three governments [i.e. Stresa] of February 1934 to the effect that they reaffirmed the interest of this country in the integrity and independence of Austria," Eden gave a most unhelpful reply: "That was a declaration by three governments: Britain, France and Italy. Italy has not yet consulted His Majesty's Government." There had in fact been a separate declaration with regard to Austria in 1934 but Eden happily acquiesced in the question's intellectual laziness by implying, in a highly misleading fashion, that Austria's independence was primarily a concern of Italy. The diplomats of Germany and Italy in London took Eden's statement for what it was, namely a strong disavowal of any British interest in the independence of Austria. The Italian ambassador Count Grandi reported to Ciano on 18th February: "I would not wish to leave Your Excellency the impression that Chamberlain has in mind any plans for resisting Germany over the Austrian question. Austria is not the battleground between Chamberlain and Eden; only Italy is."[315]

Eden was only articulating what his government's policy had been with regard to Austria for the last few months. Already on 2nd December 1937, Eden had told Ribbentrop in London, "Austria is of much greater interest to Italy than England. Furthermore people in England recognised that a closer connexion between Germany and Austria would have to come about sometime."[316] Eden's indifference to Austria was once again on parade in the most vivid of ways.

"A closer connexion between Austria and Germany"? Had this not been the policy of Guido Schmidt? Yet Schmidt was determined that such a "connexion" would not come at the price of Austria's sovereignty and this made him not entirely candid with London which did not share these scruples. It would have been so much more helpful for Eden if the Austrians simply had rolled over and accepted Hitler's demands. As this was something Schmidt would never contemplate, he felt more and more constrained in some of his dealings with the western democracies.

315 Colvin, *Vansittart*, p. 188.
316 Ibid.

Gradually in February he came to realise that the long promised diplomatic realignment which could lead to a soft guarantee of Austria's
independence was a mirage. Even if the British and Italians could put
Abyssinia behind them, the ensuing accord would not arrive in time for
Austria. This "failure" to submit Austria entirely to London's policies was
at the root of the distrust towards him felt by the British and French ministers in Vienna. As the first weeks of 1938 progressed, this distrust built
up into a crescendo of hostility towards Schmidt on the part of Palairet. It
is easy to see in the British diplomat's vilification of Schmidt an attempt to
shift blame for the hapless shortcomings of British foreign policy. While
Germany was growing stronger, Britain sought to play for time to boost
her own rearmament but her priority increasingly was above all to achieve
an understanding with Germany. Austria was in this context but a useful
"chip" to be surrendered on the board at the appropriate moment. Such a
surrender would require eventually a convenient scapegoat for the vacil-
lations of British policy. Yet Palairet's aversion was largely personal. As the
weeks went by, it became, even to the surprise of some of his colleagues
(but clearly not all of them) in London, almost pathological.

Palairet's suspicions had been building up for some time. It is hard
not to think that this line of argument found favour in the Foreign Office
and offered one strand of reporting for which the Legation could offer
something of substance. So much of Palairet's correspondence was so
wildly out of touch with events, it was almost inevitable he would become
obsessed with the easy to grasp theme of Schmidt's untrustworthiness.[317]
Already on 30th December, a secret report from the Legation had
focussed on rumours of Schmidt's disloyalty.[318] By 3rd February Palairet
was writing to Ingram at the Foreign Office almost gleefully that Schmidt

---

317 Palairet may well have been encouraged not just by Puaux but also his *chargé* Mack
and even Vansittart. But on this the documents are silent. Van may easily have shared
the conviction that Schmidt was too "pro-German" (or rather too pro-Austrian) and
therefore, like Selby, unable to "fit in" to Van's long term but unrealistic and disin-
genuous programme for Austria to enjoy eventually some soft form of guarantee
from Italy, France and London. The later Palairet correspondence on Schmidt's reaction to Van's promotion suggests a direct line of communication existed between
Schmidt and Van. See below note 332 on p. 116 and p. 79.

318 FO 371/22320/1047/191/3 Palairet to Ingram.

was likely to be replaced by Ludwig, the former head of the Federal Press Service who, although being "very unpopular with British and American correspondents," was also "not much liked by the Germans."[319]

This was a rumour remote from any reality but a week later, Palairet was confidently predicting Schmidt's imminent dismissal: "the information is once more that the Chancellor will shortly dismiss Guido Schmidt." Palairet points out (rather to his disappointment, one suspects) that "no concrete instance of disloyalty to the Chancellor or anything of that kind is mentioned," but he continues: "Schmidt's over-weening ambition has led him to try to show himself as being more responsible for Austrian foreign policy than he actually is." Given that the preparations for the Berchtesgaden summit were in full swing when Palairet was composing this, it would be hard to find a more egregious instance of an envoy being more out of touch at a critical time with the reality of the decision-making process of the government to which he was accredited.

By 20th February, in the aftermath of Berchtesgaden, Palairet felt sufficiently confident of his prejudices and suspicions concerning Schmidt to report them to London where the head of the Central department, Noble, annotated: Berchtesgaden had "thrown a most sinister light on the part played by Dr Schmidt who seems to have entered into an intrigue with von Papen inspired by considerations of personal advantage for both of them."[320] His colleague Nichols scrawled on the report: "the very dubious Dr Schmidt" is "very ambitious and preparing the way (with German friends) for his own advancement." Palairet followed up with an astonishing private letter of 20th February to Orme Sargent, the Assistant Under-Secretary: "Ought not Dr Schuschnigg's eyes be opened to the double dealings of his Foreign Minister? ... he could restrain his power for mischief if he clearly realised the danger." Palairet's solution to this conundrum was unprecedented and novel: "It seems to me the only person who could undertake this delicate job would be Franckenstein. His long and very successful term of office as Austrian minister in London would enable him to speak to the Chancellor with more authority than anyone I

---

319 Ibid: For Ludwig and his personal vendetta against Schmidt see GSN: Verhör and Chapter 15.
320 FO 371/22312 210.

can think of: Puaux might be able to do it but I am sure you will agree that such a warning should come from an Austrian not a foreigner." Then in a wonderful phrase which shows that his sense of irony was rather under-developed, Palairet adds "We do not want Schuschnigg to be accused of getting rid of Schmidt as a result of Anglo-French intrigues."[321]

It is not unheard of for ambassadors to find the foreign minister of the country to which they are accredited disagreeable, but to countenance mobilising that country's diplomatic service against the minister is a spectacular rarity. But Palairet was nothing if not dogged. Continuing, he proceeded to make another rather unconventional suggestion, "it seems to me that a warning is really called for. If Franckenstein cannot visit Austria again so soon after his return to London without arousing comment could he not find a means of sending a letter or a message direct to the Chancellor in person… we need only suggest to Franckenstein that he should commu-nicate his own views to the Chancellor." Palairet then ends this remarkable letter with an admission of total ignorance concerning the Chancellor's own views: "I have no idea whether the latter mistrusts Schmidt already: it would be practically impossible to find this out here."

The British envoy's self-confessed ignorance of Schuschnigg's views did not inhibit his wishing to move most unusual channels to discredit and dismiss Schmidt, but this breach of diplomatic etiquette proved too much even for London. Here was the final proof, if it were needed, that Palairet was completely out of touch with the Austrian leadership and even with the mandarins in Whitehall. Mr Noble, head of the Central Department, ponderously and loyally supported the letter: "we thoroughly distrust Dr Schmidt and that as long as he is Minister for Foreign Affairs we cannot to our great regret continue to deal with the Austrian government on the same terms as before." But Noble's superiors were more sceptical. Wigram, normally indulgent towards Palairet, felt compelled to minute: "I don't think we can fall in with this proposal." Sargent was even more dismissive and sagely agreed: "Of course not. Besides Schuschnigg knows his Schmidt all right."[322]

---

321 In this case Palairet is resorting to a normal diplomatic technique to refute an entirely accurate speculation.

322 FO 371/22320 1843/191/3 (R1843).

Undeterred by London's failure to fall in with his extraordinary suggestions, Palairet, rather than question his own views, quickly shored up his position to align further with his French colleague. Puaux, playing on Palairet's sentimental affection for France, manipulated the Englishman into tacit hostility and then active distrust of Schmidt. The records suggest that several documents were removed from the Foreign Office files with regard to Palairet's instructions. It is hard to ignore a suspicion that Palairet, the great Francophile, subordinated his outlook entirely to that of his French colleague in a way which must have raised some eyebrows in London. He reported a little defensively that "I have been careful to keep in constant touch with him [the French ambassador]" and that he wanted to put on record "my very great indebtedness to my French colleague."

This was perhaps understandable given Palairet's lack of experience of Austrian affairs, but French and British views on Austria were diverging fast in theory if not ultimately in practice. A French memorandum on Austria, post-Berchtesgaden had been given to the Foreign Office by the French ambassador, Corbin, in London on 18th February. [323]

It had attempted to put an optimistic gloss on events at Berchtesgaden, noting that *La situation n'est donc point définitivement perdue encore* (the situation is not definitively lost yet), but it had been greeted with some scepticism by the mandarins, one of whom had annotated it with the words "a typical French production." It was in danger of "misleading Schuschnigg" by promising rather "more than could be delivered." The British caution was understandable. The French memorandum contrasted sharply with a British one drawn up the following day by Alexander Cadogan, the recently appointed permanent Head of the Foreign Office. This began more bluntly: "We must assume Austria is doomed as an independent state."[324] Cadogan, unlike his predecessor Van, now Chief Diplomatic Adviser, was always more dispassionate about Austria, but he was also more honest.

Cadogan continued: "I have little doubt that the growing conviction since Lord Halifax's visit [to Berlin in November 1937] that we could be

---

323 FO 371/22312 17 Corbin, 18 Feb. 1938.
324 Cadogan memorandum, 19 Feb. 1938, FO 371/22312 12.

counted upon not to interfere with the peaceful penetration of Austria has been one of the facts which has encouraged Hitler to go ahead and present us with a *fait accompli* before the Anglo-German conversations on the basis of the Halifax visit had begun." [325]

Given this divergence one cannot help wondering whether Palairet's complete subordination of his activity to Monsieur Puaux was considered *salonfähig* (socially acceptable) at the Foreign Office. Nevertheless, whether or not London harboured reservations about the Palairet–Puaux entente, their envoy continued to pour poison into their ears with regard to Schmidt.

Already in a dispatch dated 16th February Palairet noted that Hornbostel, the anti-Nazi director of political affairs in the Austrian Foreign Ministry, had been opposed to the Berchtesgaden meeting (implying he had been overruled erroneously by Schmidt). Three days later, he wrote that the 1936 agreement which had provided the basis for the 1938 meeting and was thought usually to have been the work of the "dubious" Schmidt, had been in fact, according to Hornbostel, "two thirds my work." [326] But this admission by Hornbostel did not lead Palairet to ease up on Schmidt. The next day he reported that his French colleague considered that the "minister for foreign affairs has played a very sorry role in the recent events." There was even worse to come. A telegram from the British embassy in Berlin reported a conversation on Austria between the British ambassador Henderson and Ribbentrop, who had roundly abused Henderson for his government's policy "with regard to the Austrian Chancellor *after Berchtesgaden*." Palairet felt obliged to write: "after reading Berlin telegram Nr 40, I can only suppose the Austrian Minister for Foreign Affairs must have informed the Germans of my conversations with the Austrian Chancellor and misrepresented it." [327] This solecism, regrettable but hardly unheard of in diplomatic life assumed the proportion in Palairet's eyes of a capital offence.

Again, the documentation is tantalisingly incomplete and Palairet does not mention the substance of the German complaint or the grounds

---

325 Ibid. The talks ostensibly about the restitution of former German colonies were another indication of the growing Anglo-German dialogue.
326 FO 371/22312 240.
327 *DBFP* 2 530–531, p. 902.

for his suspicions, but another dispatch revealed obliquely what the German *démarche* was about. According to this, Palairet indicated that he was instructed to advise Schuschnigg to *withhold his signature* from the final Berchtesgaden agreement. Dr Schuschnigg demurred (he had after all signed the final draft in Berchtesgaden). Palairet reported that the Austrian Chancellor "was unable to accept your suggestion." Here was the source of the British minister's distrust: "I have little doubt," Palairet wrote, "Dr Schmidt leaked my conversation to von Papen."[328]

Palairet felt compelled to note that whatever the effects of these instructions on Schuschnigg, they had at least been well received by his French colleague: "In any case the French minister thinks that the step which you instructed me to make was of considerable value in encouraging Dr Schuschnigg to stand out against further demands."[329] This dispatch is revealing not just because of what it says about the substance of Palairet's instructions with regard to stiffening the Austrian Chancellor's position, but also because it implies that the British had a direct line to the Chancellor in addition to the usual communication via the Austrian Foreign Minister and his office. The British were not just passive observers of the unfolding crisis. The telegram strongly implies that the Chancellor was in such regular touch with London that he was more and more reliant on their advice as the crisis unfolded. Palairet's instructions to which he refers are not included in the standard documentation and archives. It is tempting to think that on the most important topics of discussion between HMG and the Austrian Chancellor a certain sensitivity prevailed which later archivists have striven to preserve.

As the February/March crisis gathered momentum, the British role assumed increasing importance, hence the hypersensitivity towards any "leakage." By 24th February, a terse note from the Legation to London notes: "undesirable danger of leakage makes it impossible for us to have any confidential communication with the Austrian government." Although Schmidt is not named, it is clear from Palairet's other telegrams where he sees the gravest threat of leakage. It is of course not to be excluded that Schmidt did indeed tell von Papen (though Papen may have

---

328 FO 371/22312 222.
329 20 Feb., FO 371/22312 222.

had other sources). It would have suited the Austrians to let the Germans know that they had "resisted British pressure." For Schmidt, Austria was fighting for her survival and no weapon could be left untouched even if it offended against the conventional norms including the niceties of diplomatic behaviour. If the information gave Berlin the impression that Austria was prepared to behave honourably towards Germany, it might help to reduce the momentum towards extreme measures.

This breach of trust, if indeed Schmidt rather than another source was behind it, finally closed the British minister's mind towards Schmidt. His comments on the Austrian Foreign Minister became even more increasingly hostile, growing in venom as Foreign Office policy towards Austria became ever more inconsistent as Cadogan and Van clearly differed on the best approach to be taken.[330]

Schmidt's promotion, meaningless to all intents and purposes and played down by Schmidt himself, was quickly seized upon as evidence of ambition and skulduggery. Again, Palairet sharpened his diplomatic cutlery: "Guido Schmidt... Papen's willing accomplice (I use the words deliberately) who by dangling before his ambitious gaze the post of Austrian Minister for Foreign Affairs." As the Ides of March approached, Palairet became almost obsessive about Schmidt's character failings, giving vent to sentiments and highly personal criticism rarely encountered, even in the diplomatic correspondence of those years: "From the flattery he has bestowed upon me I think it possible he realises my lack of confidence in him... he is a person of whom I have the profoundest distrust both by instinct and by reason."[331]

Yet in no telegram does Palairet detail the substance of these accusations other than the leakage referred to above. When Schmidt was asked about his views on Palairet after the war, he was the soul of discretion even though he must have sensed the Englishman's disdain for him. "Palairet was new to his posting and the situation in Austria... but I

---

330 Van clearly was spurring Schuschnigg and Schmidt on while Cadogan favoured explicit acknowledgment that Britain would not lift a finger to help Austria. See *Cadogan Diaries*. p. 69 and p. 62 (13 March): "All this is disjointed and unintelligible. It is the result of Van's policy. We are helpless as regards Austria—that is finished."

331 FO 371/22312 169.

have happy memories of him and our meetings" was Schmidt's skilfully neutral, disarming, diplomatic judgement on the man who perhaps did more than anyone to blacken his name in the corridors of Whitehall.[332]

Meanwhile, as Schmidt fought across the diplomatic front against this formidable range of enemies, the internal situation in Austria began to deteriorate dramatically. The newly appointed minister of the Interior, Seyss-Inquart, immediately went to Berlin for instructions. On his return he issued a routine press release to the police forces which began: "To the German police in Austria." This was typical of Seyss's ambivalence. In private he was all moderation and loyalty but his public utterances, closely monitored by Berlin, contained different sentiments. Although Seyss had gone to Berlin with the Chancellor's approval, the language he used on his return jarred. Palairet simply reported that Seyss's visit had been with the full permission and knowledge of the Austrian Chancellor.[333]

On 20th February, Hitler gave his long-awaited speech in the Reichstag which Schmidt and Schuschnigg hoped would put a favourable gloss on the Berchtesgaden talks and reaffirm Germany's commitment to Austrian independence. But while it noted that the Austrian Chancellor had shown insight and a "satisfactory agreement had been reached with Austria" not by a single syllable did Hitler hint at any support for the idea of Austrian independence.

About the same time, a personal message reached Schuschnigg from Mussolini saying that Italy's protective role with regard to Austria had not changed and that Austria appeared to have conducted herself very skilfully at Berchtesgaden. Neither Mussolini nor Ciano had a good word to say about Schmidt but if anything had been retrieved at Berchtesgaden it had been achieved by Schmidt. Had events turned out differently, Schmidt might have been depicted by the diplomatic corps as the hero of the hour rather than the villain. Certainly, notwithstanding a few Austrian Nazis being shocked by Hitler "treating" with their arch-persecutors Schmidt and Schuschnigg, whom they detested, the majority of Austrians heaved a sigh of relief at the thought of the chancellors' summit. Its immediate effects also appeared a harbinger of a brief respite. Leopold, the Austrian

---

332 GSN: *Meine Verantwortung*, p. 139.
333 Ibid.

Nazi trouble-maker, had been summoned to Germany and Seyss seemed to be such a decent and moderate figure by comparison. Far from being the "great error" and "ritual humiliation" with which the word Berchtesgaden became associated shortly afterwards, in mid-February 1938 it enjoyed a more positive interpretation.

Seyss moved swiftly to ban all demonstrations other than those for the *Vaterländische* Front for a period of four weeks but the new instructions to the police to tolerate Nazi salutes (if given silently) and not arrest people with swastika buttonholes *etc.* unsettled a force, already demoralised by having to incorporate their Nazi colleagues who had been granted amnesties the previous week. Seyss continued to work on the integration of the Austrian Nazi structures into the Fatherland Front. The SS would be integrated as "members of an Order," the Hitler *Jugend* (HJ) was to be incorporated as *Jungvolk* and the SA would be brought in as a *Kameradschaft* (veterans association). Given time and stability, these arrangements might have worked to create the "evolutionary" solution to the problem of incorporating Austria into the Nazi system and then into Nazi Germany but neither Seyss nor Schuschnigg nor indeed Schmidt reckoned with Styria and the process of *Volkserhebung* (popular upheaval) which now began to set the pace in Austria.

Styria, still rather remote today, even in the *Neue Mitte* which has emerged in Central Europe since the end of the Cold War, has form when it comes to being responsible for major historical trends. In 1598, the Archduke Ferdinand arrived in Graz on Easter Day and invited the local population to join him at mass. None turned up, largely because the Reformation had done its work so well in the Styrian alps that the population was entirely Protestant. Ferdinand, soon to become Ferdinand II was unamused, and he vowed to turn his lands into a wasteland rather than tolerate heresy for a moment longer. Within five years, Graz and the rest of Styria were completely Catholic. Well might Seton-Watson observe that Europe knows no more dramatic upheaval than the recovery of Austria for the Church which began one Easter Sunday in Graz.[334]

334 R. W. Seton-Watson, *A History of the Czechs and Slovaks* (London, 1943), p. 99. Some keen observers of the city might find it significant that in October 2021 it elected Europe's first (since the end of the Cold War) communist mayor.

In 1938, another explosion was being prepared. The "People's Political Representative" (*Volkspolitische Referent*), Professor Armin Dadieu, had visited Berlin in January and been told that as soon as the first shots were fired in Styria, Germany would march in. "Styria would perhaps have to sacrifice herself." Dadieu needed no further encouragement. On 18th February, the Graz hostelries were buzzing with talk of the "Nationalists" taking control. The demand for red and black material to make swastika emblems spread like wildfire through the town. By the following afternoon more than ten thousand people with Nazi insignia had gathered in the inner city. Even the German consul was impressed: "On the way to the Hauptplatz I noticed that no-one greeted anyone any more other than with *Heil Hitler!*"[335] These demonstrations soon spread to other Styrian towns. By the 24th, the swastika flew from the neo-gothic town hall in Graz. Three days later, with units of the Austrian army rushed from Vienna to Styria and roads blocked to prevent a Nazi "March on Graz," the tension was palpable, but fortunately there had been no incidents. Even when Seyss arrived on the first of March and witnessed a huge torch procession in his honour, the Nazi demonstrators remained peaceful. For Seyss it was a shock to see how powerful the "illegal" Nazi party was in the provinces. Peaceful integration as foreseen by the agreement in Berchtesgaden seemed very doubtful, Seyss reported to Schuschnigg on his return.

Other parts of Austria showed signs of developing in a Styrian direction albeit with less drama. In Salzburg and Tyrol, tens of thousands prepared to demonstrate in favour of the Nazis. Only Vorarlberg, the home province of Guido Schmidt, remained relatively peaceful until the second week in March.

Back in Vienna, the initial euphoria over Berchtesgaden winning for Austria some time dissipated rapidly, as at Munich a few months later. Schuschnigg decided to "clear the air" with a speech to the briefly convened federal Diet on 24th February. This was enthusiastically welcomed by all his followers and would later be seen as his last great moment. It repeated all the tenets of the Chancellor's policy: Austria would never

---

335 See Schmidl, *März 1938*, p. 113.

accept subordination or *Gleichschaltung* with the German Reich. Austria was German—its history, culture and character were German—but its traditions, mentality and outlook were very different and while the Austrians had chosen an authoritarian system they had no desire to be incorporated into a totalitarian structure based around absolute leadership. The 24th February address was not only a triumph in the eyes of his followers, for Schuschnigg personally it was a turning point. It seemed to clear within his own mind the fact that even if Austria was abandoned by the western democracies and Italy, she still had to make a stand. But the demonstrations in Styria emboldened the Nazis. Keppler, Papen's assistant, arrived with a host of complaints about Austrian infringements of the Berchtesgaden protocols and a demand for the officer exchange programme to be stepped up immediately. Schuschnigg gave him short shrift: "I told him in rather plain language that the Berchtesgaden agreement was but three weeks old and that I had no interest whatsoever in continuing the conversation."[336]

Schuschnigg now felt a certain confidence. Letters of support had poured in from the workers and the monarchists. Perhaps there was, after all, a way of organising a patriotic Austrian front against the Nazis. The news from the embassies and legations was less encouraging. When Schmidt asked the Austrian Legation in London earlier that month whether Schuschnigg could come to give a talk in in London, the response had been distinctly frosty. As Leo Amery, perhaps Austria's staunchest supporter in Westminster recorded in his diary of February. "Saw Mr Kunz of the Austrian Legation who had had a telephone message from Kitzbühel from Franckenstein suggesting that Schuschnigg might like an opportunity of addressing an audience over here some time soon. We agreed I ought to sound Eden about it and I saw him after Questions and found him generally sympathetic but just a little uncertain as to its effect on negotiations with Germany."[337] This was a characteristically revealing entry. The Eden brush off was immediately apparent to Amery but he waited a few days before confirming to the Austrian legation that "I had now heard from Eden that a visit from Schuschnigg at this moment would give rise to every kind of speculation and would be *definitely embarrassing*

336 Schuschnigg, *Austrian Requiem*, p. 39.
337 *Empire at Bay*, pp. 444–445.

to the government" [my italics].[338] If this was the best Austria's "greatest friend" in London could do, it was hardly surprising that Schmidt gave up on the British and the French whom he had always regarded as incapable of providing any unilateral support for Austria. To a man of Schmidt's intelligence it was becoming increasingly obvious that despite the positive words emanating from such philo-Austrian mandarins as Vansittart, Austria would be left to her own devices. But what devices were left? In the *Bundesländer*, deprived of any strong central direction from Vienna, local Nazis began to be incorporated into provincial governments.

The illegal left was one option, Schuschnigg released many of their number along with the Nazis after Berchtesgaden, but a planned meeting between their representatives and the official trade unions was cancelled on 22nd February while a similarly scheduled encounter between them and the Chancellor also had to postponed. It was only on the first of March that the preliminary contacts took place and two days later Schuschnigg received a largely communist "workers committee." This committee made four principal demands:

1 A similar political freedom for socialists to that now extended in the wake of Berchtesgaden to the National Socialists.

2 Integration of the workers into the Fatherland Front.

3 The establishment of a free working-class press.

4 Social reform.

Schuschnigg expressed himself willing to accept most of these demands but expressed a certain scepticism about establishing a worker's newspaper. The illustrious *Arbeiter-Zeitung*, founded by Otto Bauer in the late nineteenth century had been closed in 1934. The polarisation of the "civil war" of 1934 had left both sides in completely different worlds, even after the passing of four years. Only time could heal this rift but, by the beginning of March, time was beginning to run out.

Perhaps it was the talks with the representatives of the working classes which persuaded Schuschnigg to attempt his last "device": a plebiscite.

338 Ibid.

Certainly, the conventional narratives of the *Anschluss* suggest this but the idea did not quite come out of a blue sky. The plebiscite idea long predated his meetings with the workers' council. Documents embargoed until as late as 1989 reveal that the British role in Schuschnigg's decision was not quite as tangential as later historians have sought to indicate. The idea of a plebiscite which could secure Austrian independence because Germany, so the Chancellor believed, could never invade a country the majority of whose population had voted for independence, was first bruited by the Chancellor less than a week after the Berchtesgaden summit. However, long before it received support from Schuschnigg's colleagues or was even discussed by them the Austrian Chancellor had been keen to have London's views on the subject. Given Schmidt's and Schuschnigg's reservations as to the effectiveness of French policy on Austria, the dependency on British perspectives became more marked. This was particularly the case regarding the plebiscite question, an issue which the British *chargé* Mack had already raised in a telegram as early as the previous December.[339]

A letter from Palairet to Eden, dated 20th February, refers to a conversation with the Austrian Chancellor two days previously in which, according to the British diplomat: "The Chancellor feels in fact that if it were practicable to hold a plebiscite at the present moment in Austria, free from outside interference, he would be sure of a large majority."[340] Palairet then appears to be daunted by some unspecified practical problems and adds "but of course such an idea is impossible to carry out." This formulation is interesting. Palairet has clearly been asked by Schuschnigg to "float" the idea—why else would he have mentioned it?

That the potential plebiscite was freely discussed at the highest level in the Foreign Office over the ensuing days was apparent from the paperwork which followed, although it is again tantalisingly incomplete. Palairet might well not have intended to "fly a kite" but the paper trail points to a discussion which suggests the effects were precisely as if he had wanted to do just that. A dispatch two days later received heavy

339 See Mack's dispatch 6 December 1937 R8213; "If it were possible to hold a free plebiscite... the Austrians would reject an *Anschluss*." See also R2695/439/3.
340 FO 371/22312 224.

annotation. A junior official in the southern department, Nichols, noted that the Germans would not "permit the plebiscite to be held if they could help it" and Cadogan minuted with some finality and brevity "I fear we cannot entertain the idea of a plebiscite."[341] But in a textbook illustration of the collegiate nature of the institution of the Foreign Office, there are some important comments to the contrary. First came Ralph Stevenson who noted that "nevertheless the idea of a plebiscite remains attractive. Herr Hitler himself invoked the principle of self-determination on 20th February. Therefore, it would be difficult for him to object in principle."

Then in a telling addition, Stevenson continued: "In these circumstances perhaps the only action which the French and British governments could take in support of Austrian independence would be to lend their good offices to the idea that a plebiscite be held under neutral supervision." This sentence is revealing. It shows that already a degree of debate had occurred in the Foreign Office concerning the plebiscite and that it was being proposed that the envoys in Vienna get behind Schuschnigg's idea with some urgency. As Stevenson concluded: "A plebiscite of this kind does provide perhaps the only method by which the absorption of Austria can be postponed for a considerable period." With classic Foreign Office understatement, Stevenson ended: "it seems to merit examination."

Stevenson's words alone would not have swayed the direction of policy so effectively. Beneath his marginalia is the flowing hand of someone altogether more forceful and more important: "A successful plebiscite is about the *only* remaining way in which the Austrian government can strengthen its position. If the Austrians reject it as impracticable there is no more to be said. I should like however to know in more detail the reasons for spontaneous rejection." The initials on this annotation are instantly recognisable as those of still the most powerful diplomat in Whitehall, Sir Robert Vansittart. Even if he was no longer the Permanent Under-Secretary. To the already wildly incoherent and dysfunctional quality of British policy towards Austria at this moment of crisis there was introduced another powerful element of fracture, the machinations

---

341 FO 371/22312 111.

of Van, taking here predictably a diametrically opposed position from that of his successor, Cadogan.

Van may have been replaced a few weeks earlier as Permanent Under-Secretary by Alexander Cadogan, a man he regarded as his intellectual inferior, but Van was still the spider at the centre of an enormously influential web. Moreover, Cadogan was only beginning to feel his way into the job and Austria clearly was going to be his first great test. Van on the other hand, even though his position as Chief Diplomatic Adviser with time was to become less powerful than he had hoped, still commanded at this stage with the ink barely dry on his "elevation" the respect and loyalty of the office he had held for the previous eight years. In addition, he still had his own highly effective "intelligence service" with regard to Germany and Austria. Austrian politicians might have counselled caution but they were not consulted. Vansittart's views on the other hand were a powerful incentive, translating into Foreign Office "moral support" for the plebiscite. This without doubt was a significant factor in the Chancellor's decision to press ahead.

Van's desire "to know the reasons" why the Austrians might reject such a course of action suggest more than just an academic or passing interest in the issue. Thus, by 24th February, Palairet was given the discreet green light to reverse his previous spontaneous rejection and get behind the idea of the Chancellor's vote. "The sooner the plebiscite could be held the more votes would be recorded in favour of independence of Austria" became the Foreign Office view.[342] But given that the Head of the Foreign Office, Cadogan, had already written Austria off, there could be no hint that London was openly pushing for a plebiscite. At this critical moment the Foreign Office entered a phase of extreme contradiction. It knew full well that in the event of German pressure causing the entire plebiscite plan to backfire, there should be no paper trail suggesting that it was London's idea. Even so, from that moment onwards, Palairet adopted the plebiscite as if it was his own and, when eventually it was called off, it was he, more than his French colleague, who was most indignant that the Austrian Chancellor had not gone through with it.[343]

342 FO 371 22312 111.
343 See Puaux,. *Mort*, p. 112.

No doubt Palairet coordinated his support for the plebiscite idea with his French colleague and the two men would have worked hand in glove to support Schuschnigg in promoting it. Holding a plebiscite did not gain approval from Schmidt who knew how fragile the relationship with Germany post-Berchtesgaden had become.[344] Schmidt's reaction was similar to the sceptical mandarins in London.[345] "Under no circumstances and at no time would Germany permit the Austrian population to vote freely" had been their verdict. Schmidt's old school friend Hans Jung recalled Schmidt criticising Schuschnigg for calling the plebiscite "without consulting his cabinet."[346]

In these febrile times, Vienna continued, inevitably, to remain Vienna. January and February were traditionally the time to celebrate *Fasching*, a period of gaiety, frivolity and entertainment before the onset of the austerities and self-sacrifice of Lent. The annual ball season which had lost little of its glamour since imperial times was in full swing. While the question of a plebiscite was the subject of animated debate in London, the diplomats in Vienna waltzed their way through February. The ball on the 14th, straight after the Berchtesgaden meeting, has already been alluded to. A week later, on 20th February, Palairet felt sufficiently "unbuttoned" by the festivities to compose a "meditation" on the future of central Europe in which he proposed a "return of the dynasty within the framework of the German Reich."[347] This fantastical idea which again betrayed Palairet's complete ignorance of Austrian conditions, in particular, the dynamic between the former ruling dynasty, the Habsburgs, and the Nazis received short shrift in London: "at all practicable?" was Cadogan's pithy comment, while Orme Sargent no doubt expressed the views of many who saw the document when he wrote with equal brevity

---

344 Papen in his memoirs puts the idea firmly down to an initiative of Puaux, which Puaux stringently denied in his own memoir although he is strangely silent on his British colleague's involvement, simply (and ambivalently) stating that he was informed of the plebiscite by Schmidt on 9 March. See Puaux, *Mort*, p. 110. Puaux, however, notes that his colleague from England, unlike his predecessor (Selby), was a man capable of "taking the initiative," an intriguing observation in this context.
345 FO 371/ 22312 /111–115.
346 GSN: Hans Jung memorandum (undated).
347 FO 371/22312 240 *et seq.*

"not practical solutions." The memo once again reveals the British minister's lack of grasp of the realities of the problems with which he was dealing. The receptions and balls continued in a curious counterpoint to these "meditations" emanating from the British Legation in the Metternichgasse.

On 28th February, it was the turn of the French embassy to hold a gala ball. Puaux was convinced that the occasion would be the last of its kind for the foreseeable future and had laid down no less than 200 cases of Cordon Rouge for the occasion.[348] After a thoughtful discussion with Louis de Rothschild, the head of the Austrian branch of the banking dynasty, Puaux engaged Schuschnigg who was standing with Schmidt in a corner of the ballroom. "I could not resist" the temptation, Puaux later recalled "to ask Schmidt within earshot of Schuschnigg whether he had ever advised by a single word or deed anything which was contrary to the interests of a Germany which totally refused to respect the independence of Austria."[349] That Puaux does not confide to print Schmidt's no doubt bored and languid reply perhaps suggests that once again the Austrian probably got the better of him. In any event Schuschnigg was well aware that his Foreign Minister was hated by many of the diplomatic corps but as he had said famously to Starhemberg, Schmidt was "misunderstood" and was "totally loyal" to the Chancellor and Austria.[350]

It would be nearly another week before Schuschnigg shared "his" idea with his other close colleagues including the mayor of Vienna Richard Schmitz, and Guido Zernatto, the head of the Fatherland Front. The Finance Minister, Dr Rudolf Neumayer, only heard on 7th March when he was requested to allocate five million schillings for the implementation of the referendum. On the same day, the Austrian military *attaché* in Rome, Colonel Emil Liebitzky, was instructed to inform the Duce of the imminent vote. Mussolini was quick to point out to the officer that the vote would only be successful if Schuschnigg got 90 percent. At that time, the

---

348 178 cases were dispatched that evening, a new (and still unbroken) record for the French embassy in Vienna. Puaux, *Mort*, p. 106. The author's conversation with Georges Tzounis , 14 Park Place London, 9 Oct. 2017.

349 Puaux, *Mort*, p. 107.

350 See Chapter 4.

Chancellor reckoned on about 60 percent. But in words which were prescient, the Italian fascist leader warned that Schuschnigg's *coup de main* was *un errore*, a time bomb ready to go off in his hand.[351] Notwithstanding this negative reaction, Mussolini assured the Austrian that he would shortly make a speech publicly supporting Austria's independence.

Not all the news from Rome with regard to the "plebiscite bomb" was bad. Schuschnigg received strong support from the papal nuncio and the Cardinal Secretary of State Pacelli (later Pope Pius XII). At a meeting on 3rd March with the British minister D'Arcy Osborne, Pacelli pointed out that "were a free plebiscite to be held he had been recently told on excellent authority that the Nazis would only secure 30% of the vote."[352] The very fact that the point was discussed reinforces the idea that the plebiscite concept had diplomatic traction. Osborne had clearly been asked to sound out the Vatican on their views. Once again, the Vatican intelligence service demonstrated its unrivalled capacity for relevant insights into the thinking of the European chancelleries.[353]

Meanwhile the Foreign Office view of Schmidt began to improve, partly as a result of the arrival of the obviously more egregious Seyss onto the political stage. Seyss's speech in Linz on 5th March had shown that he was dedicated to integrating as much of the Austrian Nazi structure into the local provincial governments. As the new head of the Central department, Cresswell noted on the dispatch: "This Judas has now given complete proof of his treachery... in the event Schmidt seems to have been less of a traitor."[354]

The day after, and therefore more than two weeks after London had discussed the plebiscite idea, Schmidt was permitted to inform the President, Miklas. The President was anything but amused by this latest *démarche*. He counselled the greatest of caution and hinted that he might not support the idea. (The same day, Palairet would report to London

---

351 For *Oberst* Emil Liebitzky see Jedlicka, *Vom alten zum neuen Österreich*, pp. 337 *et seq.* Also a view shared by Ciano. See *Ciano's Diary*, pp. 67–68.

352 FO 371 22312 173 *et seq.*

353 For Churchill's respect for the Vatican's intelligence machine see Bassett, *Hitler's Spy Chief*, pp. 165–166 (quoting the author's conversation with Julian Amery, 6 May 1993, 112 Eaton Square).

354 FO 371/22314 136.

that the plebiscite was largely the idea of President Miklas, who had thought it "a risk worth taking.")

But Schuschnigg had anticipated the President's resistance to the idea of a vote. Drawing on the technical legalities of the 1934 constitution in Austria, Schuschnigg had called the vote a *Volksbefragung* (a people's survey), not a *Volksabstimmung* (a people's vote) so as to cut the head of state, Miklas, entirely out of the process. A *Volksbefragung* technically meant it could be organised at the Chancellor's behest rather than require the permission of other parts of the state including the President and the Minister of the Interior, Seyss.

Meanwhile, despite this dramatic quickening of the pace of events, Palairet appears to have lost himself again in irrelevancy. In a no doubt well-meant exposition of Austria's value to the British empire, he dwelt at length on the reasons why Austria's independence was a British interest. This long rambling essay was dated 5th March but only reached London on 11th March. As Orme Sargent acidly observed on the cover: "as this reached us on the day Germany invaded Austria it was already out of date when it arrived and does not bear minuting now."[355]

On 9th March Palairet suddenly did bestir himself to warn Guido Schmidt of German pressure and that the plebiscite "was not just an internal Austrian affair," a piece of advice Schmidt feigned mock surprise at hearing before saying rather forcefully that "the matter was not the concern of Herr Hitler." Doubling up on his unhelpful comments, Palairet noted "that was not how Germany viewed it" as if Schmidt needed to be told of this glaringly obvious fact.[356]

Schmidt was sceptical as anyone of the plebiscite, but he was determined to support the Chancellor in his decision in every way he could. Nothing demonstrates better his loyalty to Schuschnigg than how Schmidt now defended the decision for a vote against pressures from every side, not least from Berlin. Meanwhile, in a telephone call the same day to London, Palairet appears to have revisited the question of the origins of the plebiscite, noting that Schuschnigg had originally planned to announce it on 24th February at his speech to the Federal Diet but

355 FO 22314 9 *et seq.*
356 FO 371 22314 2.

had not "wished to appear under German pressure." Palairet's obsession with the genesis of the plebiscite betrays a strange gnawing sense of conscience over an event even he could see was likely to end in tears. But at no point did London instruct him to counsel caution. Thus, did good intentions, incompetence, fantasy and deviousness coalesce to form a peculiarly Austrian tragedy.

While support was pledged from the illegal left, and even Austrian communities close to the Bohemian frontier (notably Zwickau) asked where they could vote, the Nazis were predictably less enthusiastic. They only knew of the impending vote on 8th March through an illegal Nazi, who was Zernatto's secretary. She had heard her chief discuss the vote and telephoned Seyss's office immediately.

On the next day, 9th March, the leading Austrian Nazis gathered in Seyss's office and agreed to inform Hitler straight away. Globocnik flew to Berlin that afternoon and was received by Hitler around six o' clock the same evening. While the Austrian Nazis again took advantage of air travel, the Austrian Chancellor took the train from Vienna to Innsbruck to give the speech of his career. Broadcast on Austrian radio, it sounded convincingly patriotic. Schuschnigg had been fired up by the warm reception he had received from the Tyroleans in Innsbruck. They gave Schuschnigg the welcome that they had previously reserved for Dollfuss. The cross of Jerusalem, the emblem of the Fatherland Front, flew from every rooftop along with the banners of the towns ceded to Italy in 1918. Well might Mussolini and Ciano have observed cynically, if truthfully, that in any war between Italy and Germany over Austria, the "Austrians would all be on the side of the Germans."[357]

Seyss did not have long to await instructions. By the following morning, 10th March, he had drafted a letter to Schuschnigg demanding a postponement of the plebiscite. On his return from Innsbruck the Chancellor refused to receive Seyss. Schmidt unfortunately could not avoid receiving the German counsellor and *chargé d'affaires*, Otto von Stein. This bullying German met his match in Schmidt. Echoing Palairet, Stein insisted that the vote could not be seen as a "purely Austrian affair." The Austrian

---

357 Jedlicka, *Vom alten zum neuen* Österreich, p. 364 *et seq.* See also *Ciano's Diary*, p. 62.

exploded when Stein demanded that it be cancelled. Schmidt asked the German if he needed to be reacquainted with the terms of the 1936 agreement; the vote was an internal matter for Austria. Had Stein not read the terms of the Berchtesgaden agreement? Stein retreated under the onslaught and begged von Papen, who had suddenly popped up in Vienna, to take the matter up with Schmidt. Even von Papen, who was in Vienna to collect his last possessions, made no impression on Schmidt. When he rang Schmidt, desperately demanding that at the very least the Austrians added a supplementary question about Austria's "German mission" so that the participation of the Nazis could be assured, Schmidt said the decision was set in stone and nothing could be changed. In this grave moment of crisis, Schmidt whatever his own personal reservations about the vote, was completely loyal to his chief. Like von Stein before him, von Papen could make no headway with his arguments. Von Papen would leave Vienna the next morning and follow events from Berlin.

It is surely to Schmidt's credit that he unquestioningly supported the vote in the teeth of such strong opposition and in the face of his own powerful reservations. Had he been the stooge of von Papen, as Palairet and Puaux accused him of being, he would surely have folded at this moment. Instead he followed his instructions to the letter. Schmidt must have realised he was playing for the highest stakes in his career and risking something which could backfire all too easily, yet he defended Schuschnigg's decision to the hilt.

On the evening of 10th March, Schuschnigg finally received Seyss, probably on Schmidt's advice. Although Schmidt had supported Schushnigg's plebiscite, he must have always hoped that Austria could win time simply by developing some kind of *modus vivendi* with Germany, as in 1936. The Nazi activities in Austria and the external diplomatic situation had made this increasingly unlikely. Even so, Schmidt reckoned that negotiating with the Nazis would be playing for time and therefore not a wasted effort. There can be no doubt that Schmidt's fertile mind hoped to avoid what was gradually seen as inevitable elsewhere. The crisis was evolving its own relentless dynamic. Increasingly, there was little Schmidt or Schuschnigg could do to arrest events. Seyss later met the other Nazis in the Hotel Regina near the Votivkirche to report his conversation with the Chancellor but, to his surprise and disappointment, no-one was interested in what Schuschnigg thought. The demonstrations in Graz had emboldened the Austrian Nazis in Vienna and the Austrian SA in particular. These, the real Nazi hoodlums, were about to take matters into their own hands.

The next day began early for Seyss. He attended mass at the Dornbacher Pfarrkirche intoning the prayer *dass kein Blut fliesst* (that no blood should flow). Such piety would not deter him from calling on Schuschnigg to resign and surrender Austria's freedom within a few hours. An hour later, after picking up Glaise-Horstenau from Vienna airport the two men had collected Hitler's instructions from the German Legation. These were brief and to the point: Seyss was to issue an ultimatum to Schuschnigg demanding a postponement of the vote. If Schuschnigg demurred Seyss would resign from Schuschnigg's cabinet and form an alternative Nazi government. In order to "maintain order" this new "provisional government" would invite German troops to enter Austria.

When at 10.00 a.m. Seyss and Glaise-Horstenau were ushered into the Chancellor's office, there began three hours of hard negotiations during which Schuschnigg refused to concede. While he played for time, Schmidt and the Foreign Ministry attempted to galvanise support but, in his heart of hearts, Schmidt must have known that it was pointless. A *démarche* here or there would have no effect on Berlin. The Austrian position grew externally weaker throughout the day. Schuschnigg knew he could count on the army but he did not wish to repeat Königgrätz and shed "German blood." Moreover, his security advisers had told him that without external support resistance was futile and could barely last a few hours. The police chief, Skubl, whom a few days earlier had met the writer Joseph Roth who had brought a personal message from Crown Prince Otto, reported that while he considered his forces reliable, any deployment would be "a two-front affair."[358]

The time limit on the ultimatum was set to expire at 2.00 p.m. but Seyss negotiated an extension of an hour, later extended to 7.30 p.m. It was during this period that Schuschnigg met with the French and British

---

358 See Schmidl, *März 1938*, pp.100–101.

ministers to ask for their advice. In France the government had just fallen and there was no executive authority. Puaux could view all his work of encouragement and support for Austria going up in smoke, not because of Schmidt, as he had always so bitterly complained, but because of his own government, or rather lack of it.

Palairet, however, was part of a system which functioned smoothly irrespective of political vagaries. He telephoned London for "immediate advice" which arrived at 4.30 p.m., almost too late for Schuschnigg to read ahead of his resignation. The Chancellor found it next to useless anyway. Like so much of London's Austrian policy formulated by Van it had been based on words, deceptions and ill-founded hopes, not deeds. As Cadogan had argued rather forcefully with Van that very day, "it seems a most cowardly thing to do to urge a small man to fight a big if you won't help the former."[359]

The "advice" for Schuschnigg from London came in two parts. The first, *en clair*, stated: "We have spoken strongly to von Ribbentrop about the effect that would be produced in this country by such direct interference in Austrian affairs as demanding the resignation of the Chancellor. Ribbentrop was not encouraging but has gone off to phone Berlin."

This was hardly calculated to inspire, but there was worse to follow in an enciphered second part. Because there was no instruction to deliver the second part, Palairet did not see any point in showing it to Schuschnigg. He later recalled: "It would not have done any good."[360]

It is probably the most unhelpful codicil the Foreign Office penned in the whole sorry history of appeasement in the 1930s. It shows vividly to where appeasement could lead once the British bluff was called, as Cadogan said. There can be little doubt—and there certainly was none in Cadogan's mind, that Van bore a heavy responsibility for raising Austrian hopes. That very day, Cadogan wrote in his diary: "Van has been like a cat on hot bricks... I had it out with Van. I said: 'it's easy to be brave in speech: will you fight?' He answered 'No'."[361]

It would be of little solace to the Austrians to learn that on the very

---

359 *Cadogan Diaries*, p.60.
360 FO 371 22314 92.
361 *Cadogan Diaries*, p. 60.

day when Austria "died," Cadogan had entered into his diary the telling sentence: "it would have been criminal to encourage Schuschnigg when we could not help him."[362] This recognition of reality on the part of the Foreign Office, if a little overdue in its candour, was at least intellectually and morally defensible.

The second part of Palairet's message to Schuschnigg, however, was lacking even in that quality. In August 1914, Serbia, expecting at any moment to be wiped off the map of Europe by Austria, asked Sir Edward Grey, the British Foreign Secretary for advice. He had countered that Belgrade "should act in accordance with its own calculation of where its interests lay." When, in March 1938, another small defenceless nation faced extinction from its larger neighbour, diplomats with even relatively short memories knew what to expect from London in these circumstances.

Nonetheless, the enciphered part of Palairet's message still reads, nearly ninety years later, as a shameful masterpiece of British diplomatic callowness, the baleful climax of all the posturing and bluff of Vansittart, the indifference of Eden and the inconsistency of others in the Foreign Office all reduced to a few callous words: "His Majesty's Government cannot take the responsibility of advising the Chancellor to take any course of action which might expose his country to dangers against which His Majesty's Government cannot guarantee protection."

For once in his brief but inglorious period as minister in Vienna, Palairet had got the measure of this *démarche* right: showing this to Schuschnigg "would not have done any good."

---

362 *Cadogan Diaries*, p. 60.

CHAPTER 13

The Austrian Nazi takeover

DESPITE THE SEEMINGLY inexorable drift towards a Nazi takeover, barriers were thrown up across the Austrian political system. Schuschnigg's resignation was at first rejected by President Miklas. Moreover, Seyss was told by Schmidt in no uncertain terms that he should be content with serving as vice-Chancellor in a cabinet headed by Schuschnigg. But by now Seyss had no room for independent manoeuvre. He was just "history's telephonist" for Berlin, where Göring was angrily demanding he facilitate the immediate appointment of a Nazi government. Waiting outside the chancellery, Glaise saw Miklas arrive and Schuschnigg appear looking "already like a corpse (*scho a Leich*)."[363] The Chancellor had just read the first part of London's note to Palairet.

Illusions and fantasies abounded as the full implications of what was happening only gradually dawned on the protagonists of Austria's final drama. At this stage Seyss confided in Glaise that he would ask Hitler to agree that Austria have a "five-year transition period"(!) before being incorporated into the German Reich. His Nazi SS colleague, Odilo Globocnik, even went so far as to demand that Berlin prevent the "Austrian Legion" (SA) from marching into Austria from their Bavarian exile. The Legion were hell bent on revenge for their years of enforced exile. All manner of brutal excesses were to be expected should they cross the border but the rivalries between different parts of the Nazi machine

---

363 Mühlmann testimony, *HVPGGS*, p. 252.

began to open up sharply in the new situation. The Austrian Nazis were rapidly losing their *locus standi* in any negotiations as the equation of power moved remorselessly in Berlin's direction. Berlin ordered the German Legation secretary, Keppler, to intervene directly with the Austrian President to demand Seyss's immediate appointment as Chancellor. As Professor Erwin Schmidl has pointed out, this move was significant. It transformed a secret Austrian Nazi ultimatum, delivered earlier that day by Seyss, into a public German ultimatum delivered openly by the official representatives not of the Austrian Nazis but of the German Reich. The crisis was no longer an internal affair of the Austrian state.

The dynamic was moving inexorably in a very different direction from that envisaged by Seyss and Globocnik. Despite the German military timetable to march into Austria being put into action, there was still doubt as to whether the move was a bluff or, if not a bluff, whether the incursion of the German *Wehrmacht* into Austrian territory could still be avoided. Newly arrived in Berlin, Papen immediately called on Hitler and urged him to avoid military intervention. "I hoped that the whole business was just a show designed to exert pressure on Vienna," he later testified at Schmidt's trial.[364]

Hitler meanwhile had ordered Prince Philip of Hessen, a high-ranking SS officer, the great-grandson of Queen Victoria and a son-in-law of the King of Italy, to deliver a personal message to Mussolini assuring him that whatever happened the Italian frontier on the Brenner would remain inviolate. The Prince was shown into the Duce's study shortly after 9.30 p.m. on 12th March.[365] The following day Hitler would observe that "200,000 South Tyroleans could not be allowed to interfere with the destiny of 80 million Germans."[366] Despite his promises to Colonel Liebitzky to speak "in support of Austrian independence" made a week earlier, Mussolini had long ago written Austria off and could not have asked for more from Berlin. Probably informed, via the security breach at the British embassy, he would have seen no grounds for doing anything other than comply fully with Hitler's plans. As Prince Hessen reported to

---

364 Papen testimony HVPGGS, p. 371.
365 *Ciano's Diary*, p. 69.
366 Schmidl, *März 1938*, p. 105.

Hitler the following day, the Duce regarded Austria as an already "settled affair" (*eine abgetane Angelegenheit*).[367]

Meanwhile in Vienna, on 11th March, the German timetable had proved relentless. Göring had told Seyss on the telephone that after 19:30 it would be impossible to alter the German invasion plans, the so called "Fall Otto," named after the Habsburg Crown Prince whose restoration hitherto had been considered the only *casus foederis* capable of provoking German military intervention in Austria. This deadline had been conveyed to Schuschnigg and Miklas. At 7.00 p.m., Austrian radio announced Schuschnigg's resignation. Schuschnigg had been determined to avoid a German *Einmarsch* and he had again played for time in the desperate hope of diplomatic support from London but, when Palairet delivered London's *démarche*, Schuschnigg realised it was finally all over and the only thing worth saving was Austrian lives. Forty-five minutes later, Schuschnigg delivered his farewell speech. Gone were the calls for "Red-White-Red until you are dead!." Instead he announced that the army had been ordered to offer no resistance to any incursion and to withdraw if confronted with violence. The speech dwelt on the need to avoid shedding "German blood" and ended with the famous words: *Gott schütze Österreich* (God protect Austria).

It would be another hour before Miklas swore in Seyss's new government. Conspicuously absent from the cabinet was the name of Guido Schmidt, another sign that those who had thought him in the pocket of the Nazis had miscalculated. Seyss asked Schmidt to remain as foreign minister but Schmidt refused, explaining that his loyalty to the former Chancellor Schuschnigg precluded his serving in a government which was dedicated to undoing everything the two Stella Matutina graduates had attempted to achieve over the previous years. His successor, appointed on Schmidt's advice, was Wilhelm Wolf, who had worked closely with Schmidt, and was a close family friend. Having been born in Schmidt's hometown, the two families had known each other for generations. Wolf was another Nazi who was a practising Catholic; although sympathetic to pan-Germanism he only joined the Nazi party on 11th March. Hitherto

---

367 See Jedlicka, *Vom alten zum neuen Österreich*, pp. 337

he had worked to reorganise the federal press department "especially to ensure the preservation of press peace between Austria and Germany" following the Berchtesgaden meeting. He was considered hard working and "efficient" and, as a convinced Catholic, someone who might not be absorbed by the pagan Nazis entirely.[368] Above all from Schmidt's point of view, he was an ally in his difficult relationship with the architect of the Federal Press service, Eduard Ludwig, a bitter personal opponent of Schmidt's.[369] Wolf's appointment would be largely irrelevant in the great scheme of things as they were unfolding. The government he served was gone within days.

Schmidt's last duty discharged, he was escorted shortly before one o'clock in the morning into an SS car under the command of the soon to be notorious Austrian Nazi special operations pioneer, Otto Skorzeny. Together with the Chancellor and two senior officials of the Foreign Ministry, Hornbostel and Löwenthal they were driven to their flats.[370] Schmidt wanted to accompany Schuschnigg up to his flat but Austrian Nazi guards posted outside prevented his entering. The two men would not see each other again although they would speak on the telephone over the coming days before that line of communication was also broken. The following day, the 12th, Himmler and Heydrich would land in Vienna to set up their own security surveillance structure directed from the Hotel Metropole to which Schuschnigg would soon be confined. Schmidt would not be allowed to return to his office to collect his personal possessions from his desk. When he attempted to retrieve some personal objects, the German minister Stein, with whom Schmidt had clashed so often in the recent past, brusquely ordered him to be escorted off the premises.[371]

---

368 Another illusion. See GSN: Correspondence G.S. and Wilhelm Loos (undated) and G.S. to Wilhelm Wolf (Doc. 17) Wolf had to Schmidt's chagrin inserted into a draft speech of Schmidt's the words: *eines Volkes* (one people), *Unsere beiden Staaten* (our two states) and *unseliger Trennung* (unhappy separation) concerning Germany and Austria.

369 See below Chapter 15.

370 According to Schmidt's testimony at Nuremberg they did not continue to escort them once they had left the Chancellery. See 13 June Schmidt testimony, IMT 1946.

371 GSN: *Meine Verantwortung*, p. 70.

Returning to his own flat on the Prinz Eugen Strasse, past the Rothschild *palais*, Schmidt noticed that his quarters were also watched. The night before, Max Löwenthal had been allowed to accompany Schmidt to the front of his apartment block. As Löwenthal later recalled: "I was just about to say goodbye when Schmidt suddenly burst into tears. He recovered his composure and said: 'this is the end of everything that made our lives worth living and our work worth doing.' He then predicted the imminent outbreak of war and indeed how it would end." (i.e. with Germany's defeat).[372]

These insights were denied to the new leadership taking over in Austria. Seyss was about to learn the hard way what his German masters in Berlin really wanted out of Austria. At 9.10 p.m., a telegram in Seyss's name, but according to his later comments to Glaise, without his knowledge, was composed by Keppler of the German Legation in Vienna requesting formally the assistance of the German *Wehrmacht* "in keeping order" in Austria.[373] Schuschnigg's gesture of compliance had been in vain. The *Einmarsch* was going to happen whatever occurred in the chancery. "Seyss's" telegram would be an invaluable diplomatic prop to be used to defend Germany's policies over the coming days in the teeth of western diplomatic criticism. Göring had already assured Nevile Henderson that German troops would not remain in Austria longer than necessary and would be withdrawn as "soon as the situation stabilised."[374] The telegram arrived in Berlin causing huge sighs of relief: there was now no danger of "Austria becoming a second Spain." The occupation by the *Wehrmacht* would crush any opposition from the Marxists.

But this euphoria was not shared in Vienna. There now followed no fewer than four attempts by Seyss and others to reverse the German military timetable and stop the *Wehrmacht* entering Austria.

First Seyss, when he heard of what had been communicated to Berlin in his name, attempted to persuade Keppler to contradict the earlier telegram. When this failed, Seyss appears to have contacted General Muff and urged him to plead with Berlin not to allow German troops to

372 Löwenthal, *Doppeladler und Hakenkreuz*, p. 163.
373 Broucek, *Glaise*, p. 265.
374 Schmidl, *März 1938*, p. 106.

cross the Austrian frontier. Muff proceeded to do this, now supported by Keppler, finally getting hold of a junior official at the German Foreign Ministry at around two in the morning. An SS orderly was dispatched to wake Hitler who immediately dismissed the officer with the words that the mobilisation could not be arrested.[375]

A second attempt was then made via Hitler's deputy Herr Rudolf Hess who was told, according to one account: "Right Herr Hess: the news from Austria is as follows: there is absolutely no need for a mobilisation; everything has turned out without difficulties and the new government is in the saddle."[376] For the second time within a few minutes, Hitler was once again woken up. Once again, the hapless orderly was sent away with the insistence that the decision had been irrevocably taken. Even Keitel, the chief of the general staff, was enlisted in an attempt to prevent the *Einmarsch* but he too could make no impact on his Führer. Still the lines of communication between Vienna and Berlin continued to play out the text of this tragi-comedy. At 4 a.m., the German *chargé d'affaires* in Vienna, Herr von Stein, informed Berlin that "Herr Seyss-Inquart did not agree" to the dispatch of troops to Austria but was prepared to be "discreet" and not call openly to disavow the "request" dispatched earlier.

Weizsäcker minuted tersely: "The Führer an hour ago has already rejected Herr Seyss-Inquart's suggestion." Meanwhile, by the early morning of 12th March when Himmler and Heydrich appeared at Vienna airport with a token force of SS men, they were pleasantly surprised to find the airfield and indeed all other public spaces in Vienna already firmly under National Socialist control. As Glaise later commented, "there would be no glory of conquest for the Nazis to be had with this entry into Austria."[377] Himmler wasted no time on pleasantries. Globocnik and other Nazi stooges had assembled to meet the Reichsführer SS but Himmler and Heydrich, after a perfunctory greeting, had commandeered their cars and driven off to Vienna leaving Globocnik and his colleagues standing on the airfield like abandoned schoolchildren.

---

375 Altenburg and Weizsäcker former DDR archives quoted Schmidl, *März 1938*, p. 108.

376 Schmidl, *März 1938*, p. 108.

377 Quoted by Schmidl, *März 1938*, p. 109 based on Broucek, *Glaise*, p. 269.

The "smooth transition" in Vienna was not necessarily symptomatic of what was occurring throughout Austria. In Graz, demonstrations and attacks on Fatherland Front restaurants had already provoked the deployment of Austrian army units. Despite their having to clear the Graz bridges at the point of their bayonets, the officer commanding the troops reported that the manifestations remained largely peaceful, assisted by the fact that the local Styrian regiment rather than soldiers from other parts of Austria (especially Vienna) were deployed.[378]

With the appointment of the Seyss government, the SA proceeded to take over the police and Gendarmerie in Styria. They immediately placed the prince archbishop of Graz Seckau, Stanislaus Pawlikowski, under arrest and began settling accounts with their political enemies. If Graz was slightly ahead of the game, the local Nazis in Vienna were not slow in launching an orgy of revenge, directed in particular against the substantial Jewish population.[379] The Austrian and Viennese National Socialists were especially aggressive in their attacks on Jews, implementing anti-Jewish laws, directives and measures with great speed and developing new and efficient methods for disenfranchisement and expropriation and for driving Jews into emigration. Hans Keller, the brilliant musicologist recalled in his memoir, ironically named *The Time of My Life*, how Nazi thugs immediately began beating up Jews. Outside the British Consulate General in the Wallnergasse, Keller, an eighteen-year-old, queued up for a British visa. He and the others in the queue were set upon by the SA. After this had happened a few times, he summoned up the courage to ask the British official whether he and his companions might queue inside the Consulate to avoid future attacks. The British official was polite but insisted: "Absolutely out of the question: No."[380]

Hoping to acquire another vital document from an Austrian Jewish

---

378 "The Belgier" (former k. u. k. Infantry Regiment Nr 27), an elite unit and one of the most highly decorated regiments in the old Habsburg Army: See Bassett *For God and Kaiser*, p. 323.

379 At least 200,000 at the beginning of 1938. See Georg Gaugusch, *Wer einmal war: Das Jüdische Grossbürgertums Wien 1800–1938* (2 volumes: Wien, 2011 and 2016).

380 Hans Keller, *The Time of My Life* British Library deposition recording. Ref.1973/12/20. Keller recalled this was the only time he briefly felt his faith in England flagging.

agency, Keller found himself beaten up again by the SA and kept in a small classroom with a hundred other Jews for three days without food and two days without water. Whenever the "captives" tried to visit the bathroom along the corridor they would have to run a gauntlet of SA men who beat them black and blue with sticks. Keller noted how the orthodox Jews in his group did not even attempt to outwit or outrun their torturers but simply walked arm in arm in twos to the toilet or bathroom. "They returned unrecognisable, so badly had they been beaten, but their sense of humour never deserted them. When I asked how they could put up with such brutal treatment, one of them smilingly replied: 'Don't you think after two thousand years, we have had a little practice.'"

More distinguished and prosperous Jews were not spared. A few hours after Himmler and Heydrich arrived at Aspern airport, Louis de Rothschild was arrested as he tried to board a plane bound for Italy. Despite urgent advice to the contrary from relatives and friends, he had left it too late. He would spend the next fourteen months in the Hotel Metropole under arrest while Göring and Himmler attempted to steal as many of his family's assets as they could lay their hands on.

While Keller was experiencing the beginnings of the Austrian excesses against the Viennese Jewish population, and Louis de Rothschild languished under arrest, Count Max Thurn, a frequent dinner guest at the British Legation, was entering the House of Industry on the Schwarzenbergplatz for another day's work in the Austrian Chamber of Trade. A special emergency meeting had been called to discuss the resignation of the Austrian Chancellor for whom many members of the chamber had been collecting funds in support of his plebiscite only the day before.

At the *Versammlung*, the secretary of the Chamber, a committed Nazi, called on the assembled colleagues to "welcome" the latest developments by singing the *Deutschlandlied*. This they proceeded to do following the secretary's lead and raising their arms in the Hitler salute. Of the thirty or so men present only three refused to give the salute. One was the head of the legal department, a Dr Löwenstein, another was Dr Bauer, the head of the political department, both men of Jewish extraction, and the third was the 6'6" Oxford educated Max who decided then that his future lay outside the frontiers of the Reich. As he later recalled, compared to the Austrian Nazi takeover of Vienna, the German Nazi seizure of power in Germany in 1933 (which he had also witnessed as a student) was a walk in the park.

These cases were exceptions because the majority of Austrians greeted the news of the Nazi takeover with enthusiasm. Even in Salzburg when Goebbels addressed his attention to the plans for the next *Festspiele*, and announced that, "this festival just so recently in the hands of the Jews now ceases to be a so-called Austrian event and takes its rightful place in the German Reich," most of the locals cheered.[381]

Count Thurn may have been surprised by the numbers of Nazi sympathisers within his own organisation, but he always considered the events of those days as "an annexation" not an *Anschluss*.[382] For Schuschnigg and Schmidt, who had had to deal with this infiltration on the front line, it did not come as a total surprise, although the scale of the Nazi sentiments in their country was striking. As Schuschnigg would later write: "concerning the much talked about treason in the high offices of the Government staff I must say that there were unfortunately many cases of it—far more than we thought at the time."[383] Yet in Guido Schmidt's ministry, namely the *Auswärtiges Amt*, there were remarkably few compared to the ministry of the Interior and the Finance Ministry. It was entirely due to Schmidt that no less than seven of his closest colleagues were "non-Aryans." Despite considerable pressure from Papen and Nazi sympathisers, Schmidt had resisted repeated attempts to persuade him to sack his Jewish Head of personnel, Winterstein. Schmidt also proved resilient when Göring applied pressure to have the *Reichsmarschall's* brother-in-law, Hueber, appointed Austrian ambassador to Berlin.

Schmidt would later recall: "My colleagues in the Foreign Ministry were completely Austrian by conviction and anti-Nazis." Their fate after the *Anschluss* was indication enough of Schmidt's own refusal to fill the

381 See Goebbels speech rebroadcast extract in *Hundert Jahre Salzburger Festspiele* ORF 1, 19 July 2020.
382 See Max Thurn *Erinnerungen*, pp. 30–31.
383 Schuschnigg, *Austrian Requiem*, p. 168.

ministry with "traitors" and Nazis. "Hornbostel, the head of the political department, was condemned to five years in a concentration camp. Papen had always demanded his dismissal. Blaas, the head of protocol, was cashiered in 1938 and placed under house arrest. Schüller, adviser on trade issues at the ministry, was forced to emigrate. Wildner, the head of the trade political department, was sacked, as were Leitmeier, the head of international law, Winterstein, head of the personnel department, together with two other officials, Lennkh and Max von Löwenthal." Schmidt had resisted German pressure to change his envoys, nearly all of whom were "strongly anti-Nazi if not also anti-German: Berger-Waldenegg in Rome, for example, or Franckenstein in London and Vollgruber in Paris..." As Schmidt said, "One could not speak of parallel paths of Austrian and German foreign policy."[384] Moreover, although there had been an attempt to reduce the number of "Jewish" consuls in the Austrian service, to suggest that Schmidt implemented an "Aryanisation" of his ministry is laughable, as just a glimpse of the names of his colleagues above makes clear.[385]

In fact, Schmidt was in no less danger than his former colleagues in his ministry. The SS guard on his apartment was just the first sign of the pressures he was about to face. On the afternoon of the 12th, while walking to church with his old school friend, Hans Jung, he noticed the swastika flying from Vienna's oldest buildings. Excesses against Jews and political opponents were in full swing everywhere. His neighbour, Rudolf Knips, testified later that he found Schmidt at this time, "depressed and shattered over the events." Jung would also provide a vivid impression of Schmidt's mood and frankest thoughts on 12th March 1938.[386]

"At 4 p.m. I walked with Guido Schmidt to the Schwarzenbergplatz to see how many Nazi flags were flying. I thought there were rather few

384 GSN: *Aufzeichnungen*, p. 22. (Also in National Archives Washington DC, Record Group 226 XL 33359;).

385 This has not stopped some Austrian historians accusing Schmidt of this. See Oliver Rathkolb, "Liquidierung des Bundeskanzleramtes, Auswärtige Angelegenheiten durch die 'Dienststelle des Auswärtigenamtes in Wien' in März 38," in Kreissler, *Fünfzig Jahre danach*, p. 174–188.

386 HVPGGS, p. 214. Also GSN: *Aufzeichnungen* Hans Jung 30 Sept. 1946 (Jung did not testify at Schmidt's trial).

but got the impression from Guido that there were more than enough [*reichliche genug*]. Schmidt said: 'You know me from youth… you know also that from my parents I have a certain Germanophile position [*etwas germanophile Einstellung*], independent of the fact that as a *Realpolitiker* it had to be clear to me that Austria's commercial dependence on Germany required association and cooperation with the Reich [*Anlehnung bzw. Zusammenarbeit mit dem Reich bedarf*]. As a result, I have worked for a long time to find a means [*modus*] of coexistence which however had *nothing in common with what is happening today.* I imagined matters would develop rather differently [*Ich habe mir die Entwicklung der Dinge anders vorgestellt*]. Now Schuschnigg committed the mistake [*Fehler*] of holding his Innsbruck speech without consulting a single one of his cabinet members [*ohne irgendeinen der Kabinettsmitglieder sich darüber zu verständigen*] or even to say anything to them and that was not appreciated. Now there are foreign troops in our country. An armed resistance is as impossible as it is futile [*ebenso unmöglich wie aussichtslos*].'" Jung continued: "I asked him why did you resign? Would it not have been better if you cooperated? Schmidt replied: 'That is impossible. One must know in life when one must renounce prestige [*aufs Prestige verzichten*]. I shall never participate in a government which costs the blood of a single innocent person.'"[387]

The conversation then moved to Schmidt's successor at the Foreign Ministry. Jung asked how Schmidt could have permitted and even encouraged Wilhelm Wolf to succeed him. Schmidt replied: "It is today not a matter of indifference to me who liquidates my ministry (*Es ist mir keineswegs gleichgültig wer mein Ministerium liquidiert*) but he had no choice (*anderes hat er ja nicht zu tun*)."

Jung recalled that a "few days later" he saw Schmidt again.[388] "He looked miserable and completely broken. I said he should try to distance himself from these events but he replied simply 'one does not know from one moment to the next when they will come to take me away (*man weiss ja keine Stunde wenn sie einen wegholen*).'"

Jung now remembered asking: "What will happen next?" Schmidt replied with the air of someone who understood high affairs of state: "They will throw some billions of paper marks into the country, take

---

387 GSN: *Aufzeichnungen*. Hans Jung, 30 Sept.1946. This comment by Schmidt implies the plebiscite idea to be an Anglo-Schuschnigg project.

388 This must have been two days later on the 14th.

the little gold we have here and convince the population with bread and circuses. A couple of years will pass and we will have the greatest world war that has ever been seen (*den es je gegeben hat*)... I was frequently in the Reich. Do you think that all these armaments and canons manufactured are being made for exhibition in museums?"

Schmidt's comments can leave one in no doubt that he was horrified at the turn of events and took a very different view to what was happening from the majority of his fellow Austrians. Schmidt vented his frustration and fears with unusual candour.[389] "This is not how I imagined 'the *Anschluss*' would ever take place. What is happening in Vienna means only one thing my friend and that is war, war within a matter of months."

The French air *attaché*, Colonel Salland, noted with disgust the same day: "The Austrians are a nation of domestic servants who deserve everything that is coming to them. They have shown in these last days no backbone and have participated in the most depraved acts of brutality against their enemies and the Jews... Such a people do not merit independence."[390]

The German invasion, despite the rather improvised nature of the operation, worked surprisingly smoothly. Hitler flew from Berlin to Munich and then arrived in Linz to be greeted with a tumult and hysteria that banished at a stroke any thoughts he might have had of granting Austria the slightest sliver of autonomy. On the evening of the 12th, he examined a draft legal document which would incorporate Austria into the Reich with immediate effect. There would be, he told his subordinates, "No half measures" in settling the long overdue Austrian question. By the 14th, Vienna had witnessed the resignation of the Austrian President Miklas, his powers of resistance quenched forever. Hitler was so pleased that Miklas had finally given up his resistance, he granted the former Head of State a pension for life and a car with a chauffeur, two "luxuries" Miklas, with true Austrian *Anpassungsfähigkeit* (capability to blend in) accepted with alacrity. While Schmidt and all his colleagues may have been facing

---

389 GSN: *Brief eines Nachbarns*, 14 Mar. 1938.
390 SHA (Service Historique de L'Armee de terre Vincennes) E.M.A. 7 N 2718.

detention and the imminent threat of transportation to a concentration camp, the Austrian President, who had played a nugatory role throughout the crisis, was to have an SS bodyguard and a *Dienstauto* from now on. He was not alone. The conservative politician, Julius Raab, also escaped imprisonment thanks to the intervention of the Lower Austrian *gauleiter*, Hugo Jury.[391]

For Schmidt the outlook seemed rather grimmer. No Austrian Nazi would lift a finger to help him. Rather the reverse: Kaltenbrunner had already ordered his arrest.[392] Without exception he had offended all of the hardline Austrian Nazis and had been their most embittered opponent. Even Seyss could not help him. Schmidt was high on the list of the Gestapo's political enemies. He had been in regular touch with the highest levels of the French and British governments and had implacably opposed all who had sought to undermine Schuschnigg's policies. With the SA thugs taking control of Vienna, his days of liberty were certainly numbered. Hitler arrived in Vienna from Linz in the late afternoon of 14th March. The crowds around the Hotel Imperial where he was to be accommodated began to swell with thousands of onlookers.

One of them was the daughter of the Polish ambassador, Nella Gawrońska. Eighty years later she recalled the chanting outside the Hotel Imperial after Hitler entered the bombastic *palais* near the Schwarzenbergplatz. With a vigour and hysteria that left an overwhelming impression on the teenage girl, she heard the Austrians passionately chant:

> Lieber Führer, sei so nett, zeig dich doch am Fensterbrett!
> Lieber Führer, Österreichs Sohn, komm bitte aufs Balkon!
> Lieber Führer, komm und sprich! Eure Wiener bitten dich!
> Lieber Führer, doch kommens amal, am Balkon von Imperial![393]

---

391 I am indebted to Gerald Stourzh for this information.

392 See Löwenthal, *Doppeladler und Hakenkreuz*, p. 164. Also IMT: Kaltenbrunner testimony.

393 "Dear Führer, do be so kind and show yourself at the windowsill. Dear Führer, Austria's son, *etc.*" Information imparted by Signora Nella Gawrońska, 18 Oct. 2018 in Rome.

The next morning (15th March), preparing for immediate arrest, Schmidt was terrified to open the door when the bell to his apartment rang. A *Luftwaffe* officer politely saluted and said that on the order of *Reichsmarschall* Göring, Schmidt was to travel to Berlin immediately. A car would pick him up and take him to the airport shortly. There was no accompanying explanation. Nor was there any attempt to answer Schmidt's questions. He was completely dumbstruck. Was he being summoned to Berlin for incarceration or the firing squad? Three days earlier he had worked telephones and telegraphic machinery in one last desperate attempt to galvanise French and British support for his master. This would not have endeared him to the new forces taking over Austria. With his family in Moravia with his in-laws, he had little choice but to pack a bag and prepare for the trip. Who could guess when he would see Austria again. He would not witness the crowning triumph of the Führer, the parade and the hundreds of thousands of Austrians who gathered at the Heldenplatz to hear Hitler deliver his speech welcoming the *Ostmark* into the Reich and the land's "new mission" as the latest "bastion of the German people and the German Reich." Over the next two weeks there would be more than sixty thousand arrests and deportations in Vienna alone but Schmidt would not be among them.

In London meanwhile, *The Times* greeted the news of the annexation of Austria in characteristic terms. A leader in the paper read: "Alone, Austria could not be anything but a disturbing factor in European politics. She is removed as a source of friction and discord."[394] In the House of Lords, Lord Halifax, now Foreign Secretary, following Eden's resignation, gave a speech in which the mandarins avoided any hint of regret or criticism of the German Reich. The draft noted that "the Austrian state has now been abolished and is being completely absorbed into the German Reich, indeed without waiting for a plebiscite."[395] This pragmatic lowering of the diplomatic temperature did not prevent more concrete steps being taken by the Nazis with regards to certain British sensitivities. The SIS representative in the Vienna Legation, Captain Thomas Kendrick, would shortly be arrested and his network comprehensively rolled up by the

394 *The Times*, 17 March 1938.
395 FO/22318 29

Gestapo. Within less than a week of Hitler's entry into Vienna, on 21st March, a terse telegram from the Legation hinted at the tumult. It noted pithily: "All archives destroyed."[396]

---

396 Kendrick was eventually arrested in Freilassing in August 1938. He had it seemed devoted much of his activity to seeking ways of helping Viennese Jews escape their Nazi persecutors even if necessary by facilitating their travel to Palestine (at that time a policy which ran against the official British pro-Arab position following the publication of the White Paper on the Middle East of Spring 1938, but one finding favour with Eichmann's plans to expel Viennese Jewry). See Helen Fry, *Spymaster: The Secret Life of Kendrick* (London 2014).

CHAPTER 14

The *Reichsmarschall* to the rescue

THERE CAN BE little doubt that but for Hermann Göring, Schmidt would have faced imminent incarceration. When asked during his trial at Nuremberg to supply a witness statement as to why he had taken such a personal interest in Schmidt, the *Reichsmarschall* was subtly evasive. He said he had hosted Schmidt a "couple of times" and he was the only member of Schuschnigg's cabinet whom he knew. He had found Schmidt *sehr sympathisch* and knew his *Gewandtheit* (adroitness, skilfulness). "I enjoyed my conversations with Schmidt because he is adroit and educated company, someone with whom one could discuss everything."[397]

In fact, the unusual step of sending a plane on 15th March to rescue Schmidt may well have stemmed from a rather more hard-nosed calculation.[398] The full integration of the Austrian economy into the Reich was a priority. Göring had pushed for a military backed annexation precisely for this reason. The *Reichsmarschall* had discussed its implications with no Austrian who had grasped these essentials more intelligently than Guido Schmidt. We have seen how Schmidt had resisted Göring's proposals of a customs union during their substantial exchange of ideas in letter form.[399]

---

397 Göring's witness statement to Dr Sucher at Nuremberg, 6 July 1946, published in *HVPGGS*, p. 300–301

398 The actual date of Schmidt's "exfiltration" from Vienna was put at Nuremberg by Schmidt as "the 15th or 16th." See IMT Nuremberg Schmidt testimony, 13 June 1946. *HVPGGS* judicial summing up puts it as the 15th.

399 See above Chapter 6.

The correspondence highlighted how Göring had already discussed at length in his earlier meetings with Schmidt how to ensure both economies could be synchronised. The Four-Year Plans for the economy had long furnished an agenda for the *Reichsmarschall* in his talks with Schmidt. That this was uppermost in Göring's mind was shown a few days later when encountering Glaise-Horstenau, Göring boasted, pointing to his wallet, "*Das tut gut* (that feels good)."[400] The implication was clear: Germany was getting its hands on all of Austria's assets including its gold reserves. These were considerable, 1.4 billion compared to Germany's 76 million. The sums were transferred without hesitation on the authority of Montague Norman, the Governor of the Bank of England, where they were stored. Norman, who had once done so much to save Austria, moved, with the Chamberlain government's full support, swiftly to effect the transfer. Norman had developed a close friendship with Hjalmar Schacht, head of the Reichsbank. Norman's speed in effecting a similar transfer of Czechoslovak gold reserves to the Reich following Munich a few months later was seen by Churchill as a little "over-enthusiastic."[401]

Related to this practical need of Göring's was a more controversial desire to exploit Schmidt's "experience," a wish that the *Reichsmarschall* was keen not to draw attention to in his witness statement. The former Austrian empire's most important centre of iron and steel production had been the Witkowitz (Vitkowice) works in Ostrava in former Austrian Silesia. From 1918, the centre moved to Moravia, the province of Czechoslovakia where Guido Schmidt's wife's family also had their assets. The Witkowitz works had been jointly owned by the Gutmann and Rothschild families up to 1936 when the Austrian branch of the Rothschild family had taken over complete control. Given Göring's interest in strategic industries, especially those with an established munitions dimension, it is highly likely he thought Schmidt might even help to negotiate with the head of the Austrian Rothschild House, Louis Nathaniel de Rothschild, with whom Schmidt was fully acquainted in Vienna. Until a few weeks before, they had attended many official events

---

400 Broucek, *Glaise*, p. 291.
401 See *Financial Times*, 3 Nov. 2017, for account of Bank of England file disclosures.

together.⁴⁰² Moreover, Schmidt's flat was only a short distance from the Rothschild *palais* on the Prinz Eugenstrasse.

If Louis de Rothschild could be persuaded to part with Witkowitz, Göring's wallet would be even "fatter."

After Louis de Rothschild's arrest, there followed more than a year of solitary confinement in the Hotel Metropole while talks over his future were held by the Nazis with other members of the Rothschild family.⁴⁰³ On Göring's instructions Rothschild was held as a hostage for Witkowitz. However if Göring might have imagined Schmidt could play some role in persuading the head of the Austrian Rothschilds to cooperate, Schmidt would have no doubt disabused him and the reality of the ownership of Witkowitz would have excluded Schmidt from playing any role.

There is nothing in the surviving archives of the Austrian Rothschild family to suggest that Schmidt was connected with these tortuous negotiations in any way. Much of the Austrian Rothschild family archive was destroyed after the war, and the part seized by the Red Army was only restored to the Austrians and then to the family, heavily redacted, after the fall of the Berlin wall.⁴⁰⁴

However, one letter in the Schmidt *Nachlass* does suggest that Schmidt was involved in the discussions over the confiscation of the Witkowitz steel works. In a letter from one banker, Leonhard Wolzt, to another, Freiherr Peter von Holzing-Berstett, Wolzt was at pains to point out that: "Herr Dr Schmidt joined the negotiations (*hat an die Verhandlungen angeknüpft*) which we had with the Gutmann and Rothschild families with regard to affairs around Witkowitz."⁴⁰⁵

---

402 Most recently of course at the Ball at the French Legation on 28 February (see above p. 121).

403 The Hotel Metropole was Gestapo headquarters and also housed Schuschnigg until his move to another SS facility in Munich. See Schuschnigg, *Austrian Requiem*, p. 64.

404 See RA Files on Gutmann Rothschild holdings in Witkowitz. Ref RA "Moscow Papers" 637/1/253.

405 GSN: "Leonhard Wolzt, Vorstand der Länderbank Wien, an Peter Freiherr von Holzig Borstett," 14 February 1941. Although Rathkolb quotes part of a copy of this letter from the Washington archives, he ignores this reference to an obvious moral black mark. If the letter is inaccurate on this it must be considered potentially equally inaccurate on the "belastend" material Rathkolb does quote accusing Schmidt of being a key part of the German armaments complex on account of his views on

Other parts of a copy of this letter in US archives have been quoted, notably by Rathkolb, to accuse Schmidt of playing a significant role in the Nazi war industrial concern. Although Wolzt's bank, the Austrian Länderbank, played an important role in the financing of the Göring armaments industry and therefore he could be expected to be familiar with the detail of Witkowitz, the letter does not inspire on closer examination much confidence. First Wolzt misspells Holzing-Berstett's name, writing to him as Holzig-Borstett. Second, the Gutmann families had ceased to have any interest in the Witkowitz works in 1936 when the Rothschild family assumed complete control of the company. There were therefore no negotiations with the Gutmann family over Witkowitz. Third, fourteen months of "negotiations" between Schmidt and the Rothschilds would suggest that there should have been some paper trail pointing to Schmidt's involvement but there is none and the Rothschild archives are conspicuously silent on the entire affair.

Moreover, by the time Louis de Rothschild was arrested, the Witkowitz works had long ceased to be Austrian property, having been discreetly transferred through the London branch of the family to a holding of the Alliance Assurance Company some months earlier.[406] Apart from some archives, there was no longer any Austrian dimension to the company. Therefore, Schmidt's contribution or relevance to such a negotiation is hard to identify or even imagine. In this light the letter smacks rather of

---

consolidation of SE European heavy industrial companies. See Rathkolb, "Liquidierung," p. 174. It should be noted that Wolzt, although not a committed Nazi (he joined the Party only in 1940, following rumours of Freemasonry involvement), was a relatively important Austrian banker closely involved in structuring the financing of Göring's military industrial complex. He had also played a significant role in the aryanisation of the Mercurbank, an Austrian subsidiary of the Dresdner Bank. Wolzt was tasked with the "elimination" from the bank's board of Jacques Kahane who had been a board member since 1927. See Gerald D. Feldman, *Austrian Banking in the Period of National Socialism* (Cambridge, 2015), pp. 405–411 and pp. 530–543. Peter Holzing-Berstett does not also appear at first glance to have had much time for the NSDAP. He was the son of a Prussian Major General and his interests appear to have been mainly equestrian and he retired after the war to Gloucestershire where he died in 1974.

406 See Peter Melichar, *Neuordnung im Bankwesen* (Vienna, 2009). Also RA "Moscow Papers" 637/1/253.

a typical piece of Austrian *Schmäh* and *Schlamperei*, a deft attempt perhaps to puff up an old friend in the hope that the German banker might take him seriously and give the then underemployed Schmidt some meaningful role.

In light of approaching war and Germany's desperate need for currency, a shabby deal was eventually hatched whereby 21 million dollars was to be paid over to the Reich in return for Rothschild's safe passage to America. It was characteristic of this Austrian member of the Rothschilds that when he was informed of his release and freedom, Louis told the SS guard to come back in ten hours after he had had a good night's sleep. During the fourteen months of his solitary confinement he had had a number of "distinguished" visitors including Himmler but no evidence has come down to us that Guido Schmidt was ever among them. Schmidt was at this time unemployed and ostracised by all the new authorities in Vienna.

All this lay a few months ahead. On 16th March[407] at 7 a.m. an exhausted and cold Schmidt arrived at the apartment of the number two at the (former) Austrian Legation in Berlin and despite the early hour pressed the bell beneath the name "Schwarzenberg." Prince Johannes Schwarzenberg would become a highly popular Austrian ambassador to London after the war. At this stage he was but a junior diplomat on the first rung of the ladder. The Schwarzenbergs were scions of one of Austria's most illustrious aristocratic clans. One ancestor had defeated Napoleon at the Battle of Leipzig, and another had guided the young Emperor Franz-Josef onto the throne in 1848 and was generally reckoned to be the most powerful and impressive statesman of the Habsburg empire's declining phase.

After the war, the Prince refused at first to give testimony on behalf of Schmidt during his trial for treason in 1947. He claimed in a letter his

---

407 There is some discrepancy on dates here. Schmidl places Schmidt's trip the day after Schuschnigg's resignation (i.e. the 12th) while the *HVPGGS* puts it in the final summing up as 15 March. Göring himself says he sent the plane to pick Schmidt up at ten in the morning on the day of the German *Einmarsch*. See *HVPGGS* p. 302. Göring's Nuremberg statement 3 Oct. 1945, page 23. Schmidt at Nuremberg said "15th or 16th," IMT 13 June 1946, Schmidt witness testimony.

evidence would have no effect: "I would not hesitate for a second to be a witness if I was convinced it would help but following discussions in Vienna with people concerned with this affair I have come to the conclusion that the little I can contribute does not offer any relief. I can do what you ask only if your lawyer knows the situation." In the event the Prince did testify but some details of his testimony were altered slightly when his memoirs were published, offering in his words, an additional "gesture of saving one's honour (*Ehrenrettung*)."[408]

At Schmidt's trial, the Prince stated that Schmidt had appeared at eleven in the evening. The memoir however places the time at 7 a.m.[409] Both accounts agree, however, that Schmidt was in an appalling state on arrival, teeth chattering and suffering a high temperature. He more or less gasped that he had been summoned to see Göring at Carinhall later that morning but the Schwarzenbergs put him immediately to bed and called a doctor. A few hours later the two Austrians drove to the *Reichsmarschall* where Schmidt had had an hour-long meeting with Göring, after which they were offered lunch. As Schwarzenberg noted in his memoir: "Schmidt was much calmer after the meeting" and from his "much improved demeanour I assumed the discussions had gone well."[410]

We do not know the precise content of the conversation between Göring and Schmidt but Schwarzenberg noted that there had been much discussion as to how the "Austrian balance" might be preserved in the new Reich. Despite the fact that he was the architect of the *Einmarsch*, Göring was dismayed at some of the things happening in Vienna. The invasion had been a victory for his concept of full economic incorporation of Austria's industrial and mineral wealth into the Reich. His rival, Himmler, would have preferred building up the Austrian SS (which was loyal to him) to create a bastion of reliable SS acolytes before full incorporation into the Reich, but Himmler was at least in Vienna, having arrived at the Vienna airfield with Heydrich on the morning of the 12th.

---

408 This correspondence is in a part of the GSN: Schwarzenberg/Skrein/Schmidt Briefwechsel. See also J. E. Schwarzenberg, *Erinnerungen und Gedanken eines Diplomaten in Zeitenwandel 1903–1978* (Vienna, 2013), p. 135 *et seq.*

409 See *HVPGGS* p. 200, and Schwarzenberg, *Erinnerungen*, p. 135.

410 Schwarzenberg, *Erinnerungen*, p. 136

Göring knew that Schmidt would not only furnish him with a first hand account of the last hours of the Schuschnigg government but would also be able to give him a pretty shrewd idea of where the balance of power within the Austrian Nazis around Seyss really stood ahead of the full integration of Austria into the Reich. At the top of the agenda however would be the issues of economic coordination (including probably the future of the Austrian Rothschild holdings in Central Europe which at that time the *Reichsmarschall* still fondly imagined were in the hands of the Austrian branch of the family).

As Göring interrogated Schmidt about the latest developments in Austria, Schmidt began to relax. It did not seem from Göring's friendly and enquiring manner that he was going to be taken away to a concentration camp just yet. They were apparently just coming to the topic of where Schmidt saw his future when the telephone on Göring's desk rang. An orderly announced the British ambassador, Nevile Henderson, on the other end of the line. Henderson's relationship with Göring was certainly close. Like so many, he found the German the least uncouth (and most substantially pro-British) of Hitler's paladins.[411]

Henderson, who had two evenings before delivered a rather limp protest note over the German pressure on Vienna, asked Göring what the latest from Austria was. The German, knowing well how easily the highly strung Henderson could be needled, calmly retorted that he did not know everything that was going on but was hearing much interesting detail from the man sitting opposite him at that moment, Dr Guido Schmidt. Henderson was deflated with all the subtlety of a blade puncturing a balloon. When he recovered from the shock he asked what Schmidt

---

411   In this context it is worth reminding the reader that such was the strength of the relationship between Göring and the British political establishment that a few minutes after Neville Chamberlain's declaration of war in 1939, the *Reichsmarschall* was unhesitatingly put through to the Prime Minister by the Downing street switchboard with a request to "speak" to the Prime Minister. Frank Roberts, then a junior diplomat, was standing in Chamberlain's office and picked up the phone and took it upon himself, without any consultation, (as happens with civil servants) the political responsibility of telling the German that it "was too late now" for any conversation. Frank Roberts to author, 6 Oct. 1994 at Chatham House. See Frank Roberts, *Dealing with Dictators: The Destruction and Revival of Europe 1930–1970* (London, 1991).

might do next, to which Göring clearly relishing winding up the wrong-footed Henderson looked at Schmidt smilingly and said: "Who knows perhaps we shall make him a diplomat for the Reich?" Henderson's sense of outrage was a frequently exploited weakness by the Nazis who enjoyed provoking this most histrionic of British diplomats. For Henderson this was understandably confirmation of all the suspicions his colleagues had ever entertained about Schmidt. A day later Henderson wrote in scathing terms to Cadogan about the Austrian: "Talk of Judas. He has lost no time in coming for his thirty pieces of silver. He has long been the Nazi spy in Schuschnigg's camp all the time. It was undoubtedly from him that Göring got all his information about what was being said not only in Vienna but London."[412]

This was jumping to conclusions and unfair. Schmidt had been summoned; he had not asked to come to Berlin or for a post in the German diplomatic service which would not have been to his taste at all. He had not resigned his post in Austria simply to be "fitted into" some department of Ribbentrop's empire. In any case, Government service was out of the question on account of his staunch anti-Nazi conduct. A political role was also out of the question; Schmidt was a bureaucrat, not a party man. Indeed, he had never joined and would never join the Nazi party. As Göring said in his testimony, "it never came into my or Hitler's mind to have Schmidt in a cabinet led by Seyss because clearly such a cabinet was going to be of very limited duration."[413]

Nevertheless, being saved by Göring for whatever reason did mean, as Göring pointed out later in his testimony at Schmidt's trial, "being saved." "Whatever the reason for someone being under my personal protection, such protection had to be absolute in its validity… it was my responsibility."[414] If Göring had fobbed Henderson off with the line that Schmidt might be useful as "perhaps a diplomat," another "red herring" was to be planted a little later when Glaise-Horstenau dined with Göring and Hitler. Glaise, who had always found Schmidt "arch ambitious" and no great ally, expected to evoke some frostiness and criticism by mentioning

---

412 Henderson to Cadogan 16/3/38 FO 800/269,
413 *HVPGGS* p. 301.
414 *HVPGGS* p. 301.

Schmidt's name. Instead he was surprised to hear Göring say in cheerful tones: "Schmidt? We will take him into the Reichstag."[415] Here was Göring at his most playful; using Schmidt to rattle, provoke and amuse but, above all, exploiting him for his value as his own personal directly accessible authority on Austrian conditions.

This idea, even if it had been meant seriously, would have been implacably opposed by the Austrian Nazis whose hatred of Schmidt denied him any role in government service even had he desired one. "What to do with Schmidt?" might have become a refrain had not the commercial acuity of Schmidt not been recognised by Göring early on as the Austrian's "trump card."

There can be no doubt that Schmidt possessed a fine business brain. Similarly, there can be no doubt that he placed that brain at the service of a criminal state. The powerful ambition which so many of his contemporaries saw and often despised was now transposed into a strong desire to flourish, not merely survive. His vaulting ambition had not been entirely eradicated by the tragedy of the first two weeks of March 1938.

At first, no-one seemed to want this "funny little Austrian," even in a commercial capacity. In Austria, the Nazis refused to countenance his having any role, politically or commercially. Schmidt himself, according to his statements to the investigating judge Dr Sucher in December 1945, said that he had made it clear to Göring that he could not accept any post in the German state service but that he would be interested in something in business.[416]

A few days later, back in Vienna and clearly enjoying the protection of Göring (although still under surveillance), Schmidt met his old schoolfriend Hans Jung again. Jung recalled: "It was eight days after we had last seen each other, and he said Göring had invited him to the Hotel Imperial and offered him various chances. Schmidt had refused these, saying that he could not accept such possibilities but admitted that Göring had behaved in a very "generously correct (*sehr anständig*) way." Schmidt appears not to have mentioned to his friend that he had been in

415 Broucek, *Glaise*, p. 275.
416 GSN: Verhör, p. 26: "Meine Übernahme in den Aussendienst auf keinen Fall in Frage käme."

Berlin and that the possibilities mentioned by Göring included, if Glaise-Horstenau is to be believed, some political role.

Jung was surprised at Schmidt's attitude: "I had known his exceptional ambition from an early age," he wrote in 1946. He recalled that according to Schmidt, Göring had told the former foreign minister that he understood that he "could not from one day to the next change" and "find his way to National Socialism (*den Weg zum Nationalsozialismus finde*)." It might take a year but "Schmidt should calmly take his time."[417] In the event Schmidt would never "find his way" to National Socialism and embrace its ideology but this would not prevent his accommodating and tolerating its employment of him.

He no doubt attempted to find some way of earning a crust without being so dependent on the *Reichsmarschall*. Despite the rapport and Göring's *anständigkeit*, Schmidt would not have wished to be too dependent on one of Hitler's paladins. He owed his head and freedom to Göring; that was surely enough of a debt. "Finding his way towards National Socialism" was not a price he wished to pay.

As Schmidt later recalled: "I tried in the late Autumn of 1938 to find a commercial position in Vienna but this was not possible on account of the Nazi party's opposition to me so I approached Göring about a possible job in the German industry... He advised I should look for a position and he would support any concrete possibility which appeared."[418]

But Schmidt had no contacts on the German industrial scene who might point him in the right direction, so this also led to nothing. By the beginning of 1939, Schmidt was becoming increasingly depressed, so he decided to write to Göring asking for help. Together with the former cabinet director, Wilhelm Klastersky, Schmidt composed a letter.[419] This letter has not survived but it had the effect of reminding Göring that he had committed to help Schmidt. The German state secretary, Körner, summoned Schmidt to Berlin where he effected an introduction to the

---

417 GSN: *Aufzeichnungen* Jung, 30 Sept. 1946.
418 GSN: Verhör, p. 26.
419 Klastersky, Miklas's and then after the war Karl Renner's cabinet secretary was at this time in NS *Schutzhaft* (house arrest) but was clearly allowed visitors and enjoyed a senior position with the Vienna auction house Dorotheum.

Director General of Rheinmetall Borsig, an important manufacturer of locomotives and typewriters, being reorientated towards armaments. But as Schmidt recalled in terms familiar to every unemployed job applicant, "I received friendly words but my application was rejected."

Schmidt left Berlin empty handed. A month or so later in April 1939, he contacted Körner again. This time, Körner pointed Schmidt in the direction of the Hermann Göring Works (HGW) but, as the German made some disparaging remark about the "slack" Austrians, Schmidt became piqued and sharply commented that "in these conditions I should prefer to seek work selling cigarettes on the Ringstrasse in Vienna."[420]

This outburst of anger had the desired effect because "in Berlin they only respect the crude tit for tat (*grober Klotz auf den groben Keil in Berlin das einzige Mittel ist*)," as Schmidt recalled in a rare outburst of anti-*Piefke* prejudice.[421] A few weeks later, Schmidt was offered a very junior position. He had, by his own admission, no idea what the company was involved in at that stage and his job was "completely insignificant (*völlig bedeutungslos*)." He insisted that he was consistently anti-Nazi throughout his time there and always took their side in any dispute which permitted more than one opinion. Schmidt's former colleague from the Austrian Foreign Ministry, Dr Lennkh, accompanied him to the company, suggesting that however insignificant Schmidt may have sensed his job to be, it required an extra pair of hands (or at least another brain) implying that it was not that lowly or menial. But from this detailed account of Schmidt's time in the first half of 1939 it can be seen that the accusation, so often levelled against him, that he already had a sinecure waiting for him and that his career prospered as soon as the Nazis took over Austria, is far from the mark.

According to Göring, the decision to employ Schmidt in a commercial capacity came not from him but from no less a person than Adolf Hitler. "The incorporation of the Danube steam company and the Skoda works into the Hermann Göring Works had moved the centre of gravity of the business towards the Balkans... I spoke by chance about this with Hitler who said I should get an Austrian into the concern because the

---

420 GSN: Verhör p. 27.
421 *Piefke*: Austrian derogatory word to describe Prussians. GSN: Verhör, p. 27.

Austrians knew the Balkans better than 'our people (*unsere Leute*)'... to my enormous astonishment he suddenly suggested: 'Take the former Austrian Foreign Minister; he must know the situation there from his former days.'"[422] Even if this is an elaborate piece of embroidery around what really happened and the surprise Göring felt was not genuine—he recalled Hitler having hitherto expressed not the slightest interest in Schmidt—the very fact that the Austrian's future had been discussed at that level would have given Schmidt little choice in his pursuit of some commercial wartime career connected with Göring.

More plausibly, Göring testified that at first Schmidt was unwilling to accept a position. We know from Schmidt's own deposition that he was reluctant to work in just the *Sekretariat* but Göring, helpfully, insisted that Schmidt's reluctance was due to his Austrian patriotism. "I told him that he could not always be on the sidelines, looking on in a resigned way. For that he was far too young." Rather "as now also a German" he should contribute "I asked him to do this as a personal favour."[423] A "personal favour" at that time, from such a person, was not a request to be spurned lightly.

Schmidt's intellectual gifts had made undoubtedly a strong impression on Göring but most Germans with whom he came into contact were impressed. Glaise, who saw much of Schmidt in Berlin, noted that those businessmen who came into contact with Schmidt were hugely taken by him. He was dynamic and energetic, witty and sardonic with brilliant turns of phrase and use of language. Wilhelm Voss from the board of the Göring Works thought that Schmidt was wonderful. "He was *begeistert* (entranced) by Schmidt," Glaise confided to his diary.[424]

One area where Schmidt obviously fitted in was Bohemia and Moravia, the territory of his wife's family commercial interests. Schmidt was appointed the representative of the Hermann Göring Works on the Board of the Böhmische Union Bank (BUB). The BUB and its ambitious director, Walther Pohle, was keen to challenge the banking primacy of Vienna. Bohemia-Moravia had close connexions with Yugoslavia and the

---

422 *HVPGGS* Göring testimony, p. 301.
423 *HVPGGS* Göring testimony, p. 302.
424 Broucek, *Glaise*, p. 397.

BUB could cultivate industrial relations with Yugoslavia. The raw materials, especially bauxite, chromium and aluminium were a key economic interest of the German strategy for penetrating southeastern Europe. At this stage (November 1940), Berlin was confident of subordinating Yugoslavia peacefully, unaware that British and Soviet secret services were cooperating to stage a *coup d'etat* against the most anglophile monarch in the Balkans. Even here Schmidt's ambitions and ideas for industrial consolidation in South East Europe were doomed. In any event by the time Yugoslavia lay in ruins, Schmidt had lost his job at the HGW.[425]

Those who accused Schmidt of profiting from the German "war effort" may have mistaken his dynamic drive to do everything as best he could for partisanship. Nevertheless, although his commitment to the Nazi cause never grew, he undoubtedly served it even though he was fully aware of the price other people were having to pay for the Third Reich. There can be no doubt that Schmidt, like nearly everyone else in Nazi Germany, was aware that extremely unpleasant things were happening, right from the first moment of Austria's absorption into the Reich. This was especially the case after the *Wehrmacht* had invaded Poland. He met with Glaise in Berlin shortly after war broke out. The two men discussed reports of atrocities committed during the brief but bloody 1939 campaign. Two Austrian policemen had been murdered by a Polish resistance fighter. The reprisals by the SS had been harsh, setting the tone for much that was to come. Fifty Polish civilians had been rounded up and shot, their bodies falling into a mass grave. The fact that Glaise committed this news to his diary is an indication of the shock the reports had on this former exemplar of the old Austrian k. u. k. officer class. Schmidt may have been in Broucek's phrase a "military ignoramus" but he understood enough about what was happening to know that he was a part of an apparatus which was heading towards unique forms of bestiality.

This did not mean that Schmidt in his capacity at the *Reichswerke* somehow supported, in Rathkolb's memorable phrase "without the slightest doubt with great commitment (*mit grossem Engagement*) the armaments industry of the Third Reich." This accusation, articulated for the

---

425 See Gerald Feldman, *Austrian Banks in the Period of National Socialism* (Cambridge, 2015), p. 235.

first time by the *Arbeiter-Zeitung* in 1947 in the run-up to Schmidt's trial, is at the heart of most of the denunciations of Schmidt from respected historians of the left. Yet the only evidence Rathkolb advanced in support of this denunciation was to quote selectively from the unimpressive and inaccurate letter from Wolzt to Borstett (*sic*). We have already examined its misleading references to the Rothschild interests Schmidt is supposed to have "helped" with but the letter went on to note how Schmidt had also had time to outline his views that *"ein recht interessanter* (very interesting)" south-east mining conglomerate could be put together by "combining Skoda, Brunner Weapons, Brunner Machinery, Alpine, Resita and his new interests in Romania and Karabuk in Turkey into a single entity." Leaving aside the fact that Turkey was neutral as was Romania at this stage of the war, it is hard to see this idea as anything other than superficial brainstorming building on views Schmidt would have absorbed at the BUB. Yet Schmidt's accusers have elevated it into some Machiavellian knock-out strategy which could alter the course of the war. It is perhaps the most telling indictment on the seriousness of this letter that Wolzt urged "Borstett" if he met Schmidt not to tell him that Wolzt had told the German about these ideas.[426] In rather typical Austrian style, the representative of the Länderbank had let his imagination rip in this, as he certainly appears to have done in the story about Schmidt's "key" role in the Rothschild "negotiations."

The real discussion point between Schmidt and Wolzt in the Grand Hotel had not been either Witkowitz or the idea of a great South-Eastern European mining complex but rather the far more pedestrian details of business transactions between the Danube Steamship Company and the Länderbank. No doubt Schmidt threw him some throwaway ideas but Schmidt was in no position to influence anyone of importance in the Reich. His first positions in the Göring Works had been in the secretariat. He was not even an active member of the Executive Board (*Vorstand*). He was not even a *Frühstücksdirektor* (a director who just turns up for breakfast). It was only two years later, after a personality clash, that Schmidt was finally granted access to the Board of HGW, where he could play some

426 GSN: Wolzt letter, 14 Feb. 1941.

meaningful role with regard to shipping issues along the Danube. But this position was also a mirage because, overnight, Schmidt was told the job was no longer his because he had to make way for a relation of Göring's.

Schmidt had advanced through the power of nepotism and now through this same force he was cut down by it. He was now again out of work for over a year. He had certainly deployed all his energy into the business, often at considerable physical cost. Glaise recalled visiting him in hospital, the Krankenhaus der Kaufmannschaft in Berlin, after he had fallen down a mine in Serbia.[427] Glaise had been scathing about Schmidt when he had first met him calling him the *Ehrgeizling* (pushy one) and sarcastically committing to his diary an account of Schmidt's self-importance, "springing out of a car near the Chancellery with an air of grandeur saying: 'I've just come from Papen'."[428] But the two Austrians, at first so wary of each other, found they had much in common as they navigated their way through wartime Berlin.

Schmidt's career trajectory was neither smooth, easy nor especially successful. His passport reveals frequent journeys to eastern Europe, notably Slovakia.[429] There was little time for family life and, among his papers are indications that he fell foul of the Nazi German tax authorities with regard to his dividend and earnt consultancy income.[430] A prolonged correspondence with his brother-in-law, a Berlin tax accountant, details the worst predatory demands but the ensuing exchange shows how even in a totalitarian state such as Nazi Germany, the machinery of revenue collection worked with some scope for negotiation. According to papers in the Schmidt *Nachlass*, he was paid the "usual" deputy Board Director fee of 4,000 RM (Reichsmark) of which 55% was surrendered in tax, leaving him 1,800 RM of which 500 went to the cost of his flat. This remuneration lasted for a maximum of two years. Once deprived of this position, his income became much more precarious.[431]

427 Broucek, *Glaise*, p. 433.
428 Broucek, *Glaise*, p. 59.
429 GSN: Guido Schmidt's passports.
430 GSN: correspondence between G.S. and the Berlin Steuerbehörde 1941. The most interesting disputes appear to have been over Schmidt's freelance advisory activities and the high hourly rate he was charging.
431 GSN: *Meine Verantwortung*, p. 106.

His new freelance consultancy activity which aroused the scrutiny of the tax authorities concerned an export business which had a small working capital base of 25,000 RM and dealt exclusively with trade in non-military goods such as fridges and electric transformers. This was for two years Schmidt's exclusive "highly engaged contribution to the Nazi armaments industry." The company did no business with any Nazi occupied territories, on Schmidt's express instructions. "We did not work with France, Belgium, Holland *etc.* but with neutral states such as Sweden, Turkey and Finland." [432]

During his time in Berlin, Schmidt mixed almost exclusively with other Austrians including several who would be arrested in the wake of the attempted putsch against Hitler on 20th July 1944. Among them were the Wasmuth family, several of whose members were executed. When the family were bombed out of their house in Berlin, Schmidt arranged for them to be accommodated *en famille* in St Anton. In 1943, another dissident, Frau Rosen and her three children found temporary accommodation in Schmidt's apartment. They were only one of many families who benefitted from Schmidt's humanity and generosity. The Rosens' father was a Jew who had emigrated to America. Although Schmidt was told frequently by Nazi party officials in no uncertain terms that he should have nothing to do with the Rosens he ignored those "unpleasant encounters."[433]

His own time in St Anton was limited. Those who saw him regularly reported afterwards that they never once saw Schmidt give a Nazi greeting even when he was greeted with the words *Heil Hitler* by officials. He always "deliberately" said *Grüss Gott*, according to the villagers giving evidence after his arrest. Indeed, Schmidt's family were regularly denounced to the Gestapo for not giving the *Deutscher Grüss* and for insisting that their children went to church and were educated in the teachings of Christ. Fortunately, the simple peasant Catholicism of those parts at that time gave the Schmidt family a layer of support which became increasingly important as the war continued.[434]

---

432 GSN: Verhör, p. 31.
433 GSN: Verhör, p. 31.
434 See GSN: *Meine Verantwortung*: handwritten pencil note. Also HVPGGS.

In 1943, Guido Schmidt decided to take advantage of the etiquette which allowed Germans who were called Müller or Schmidt (two rather common surnames) to distinguish themselves by adding the surname of their spouse to their name, creating a double-barrelled soubriquet. Although the document approved by the Berlin authorities confirms that Guido Schmidt's children would be called Schmidt-Chiari, Guido himself remained plain Schmidt.

Schmidt's reasons for implementing this superficial change were largely academic. He was no doubt drowning in a sea of German Schmidts and perhaps desperately wanted to hang on to anything which could remind him that his family had a background in the old Austria.[435] In desperate times small status symbols perhaps mattered even more.

By 1945, it was increasingly clear that Guido Schmidt's business career was coming to an end. As the war progressed it became more and more difficult for him to export his fridges and machines to the neutral states. Germany's economy was tottering and Schmidt, whose blood sugar levels had been increasingly low, became ill with a high temperature. Somehow, he got himself to St Anton despite the huge disruption to rail travel following the allied bombing raids on German cities. The journey in early 1945, which before the war might have taken nine hours, took the best part of twenty-four. On arrival, he collapsed for a week to be nursed back to health gradually by his wife. During the years of their marriage, Maria Schmidt had loyally supported her mercurial husband at every turn. As the war came to a conclusion, she was under no illusions that her husband's difficulties were about to end.

The first allied troops reached Vorarlberg at the end of May 1945. The Reich was broken and unconditional surrender had been signed on the Lüneberg Heath. Schmidt witnessed the arrival of French troops with his brother. The French were firm but courteous, although the deployment of native units (Moroccan) caused quite a stir among the locals. However, they could be content that they were not hosting the Red Army whose atrocities and pillaging in the east and south of Austria were becoming rapidly-spreading horror stories. Although Austria was divided into zones

---

435 GSN: Namenveränderungsbillet, 14 March 1943.

it was, in contrast to occupied Germany, not partitioned. There was one interallied commission administering it and one single government.

As June progressed, the Austrian media began to publish wild articles about Schmidt, alleging he had met with American agents in a hotel in St Anton, but above all accusing him of complicity with the Nazi annexation of Austria.[436] To pre-empt a situation he could see was going to turn into a witch hunt Schmidt decided to surrender himself to the commandant of the French forces on 30th June 1945. They eventually handed him over to the Americans who took Schmidt to Bavaria for prolonged interrogation by the Nuremberg investigating Judge, Dr Friedrich Sucher, and his team of magistrates. He was then taken to Nuremberg as a witness against Seyss-Inquart, von Papen and Göring. His evidence was measured, articulate and above all forensic in its avoidance of loose formulations. To the frustration of the prosecuting judges, he would answer some questions with the unhelpful comment that it could be answered "with both a yes and a no." Overall, his evidence was not unsympathetic towards von Papen. He painted a picture of von Papen as a man who wished for a peaceful solution to the *modus vivendi* issue between Austria and Germany and did not intend there to be, in Schmidt's phrase, "a *modus vivendi male.*"

Schmidt's description of von Papen's behaviour at Berchtesgaden confirmed that Papen had been as surprised as Schmidt at the brutality of the threats deployed. Schmidt gave his view that Ribbentrop had been rather out of his depth at the meeting but had behaved with polite helpfulness when it had come to the detailed negotiations on the programme of German demands.

But if Schmidt was helpful to Papen his evidence was unhelpful from Seyss-Inquart's point of view. Schmidt stressed that he had told Seyss that he was unable to accept a position in his cabinet because he "still believed in honour and integrity." While Schmidt said he did not mean to imply that Seyss was a man without honour, and that he was "referring to himself," the condemnation was clear even to the unsophisticated.[437]

---

436 See GSN: *Meine Verantwortung*, pp. 51ff.

437 See IMT 13 June 1946, Schmidt Testimony: https://avalon.law.yale.edu/imt/06-13-46.asp. Papen would be acquitted at Nuremberg, while Ribbentrop, Seyss and

Seyss would be hanged for war crimes pertaining to his activities in Poland and the Netherlands where he held important executive authority as *Reichskommissar*, rather than for the part he played in the *Anschluss*. [438]

His duties discharged there, Schmidt was returned to Munich for further interrogation. His family received only the scantest of information concerning his whereabouts and were not told when he was moved from Bavaria to Salzburg towards the end of the year. His incarceration in the Festung of Salzburg where he was given an alias came to the family's notice in the most haphazard way. One day in the winter of 1946, Guido's sister, Schwester Borgia, a nun whose convent had received much moral and practical support from Schmidt during the war, set out to find her brother. Eventually she found her way into the office of the Salzburg City Commandant, an American whose office commanded a spectacular view across Salzburg from the *Festung*. She was about to ask tentatively whether he had any knowledge of her brother's whereabouts when she noticed on his desk a pencilwritten note on which the letters were scribbled in bold and strong lines sloping backwards. Guido Schmidt's handwriting was instantly recognisable. The letters are large, the lines bold and strong. An expert in handwriting analysis would instantly see it as betraying a determined and forceful character. Sister Borgia had no such training but she of course recognised her brother's distinctive script instantly and pointed it out to the American officer who had no choice but to admit that he knew all about the geographical whereabouts of Guido Schmidt.[439]

She was not allowed to see her brother but she was told she could write to him. There followed a series of letters which regularly (almost

---

Göring would be condemned to death (although Göring would cheat the hangman thanks to a cyanide pill smuggled to him with the complicity of his US guards in October 1946, but not before he had made a deposition concerning Schmidt which would be read out to the Austrian court in 1947).

438 Among the many tens of thousands of victims of Seyss' administration in the Netherlands was the discalced Carmelite nun Edith Stein, later canonised as a saint, who on Seyss's orders was rounded up along with other Jewish converts following the Dutch Bishops' Conference condemnation of Nazi racism, 20 July 1942.

439 Information from the Schmidt-Chiari family. Also GSN: Schwester Borgia/Guido Schmidt Briefwechsel.

every week) sought to boost Schmidt's morale. Each letter usually contained three important messages: first, that he must trust in God not to abandon him in this moment of physical and mental trial; second, that he could face the future with utter confidence because he had nothing to hide and nothing to be ashamed of in his conduct; and third, that he should continue to look after himself as well as possible and, above all, eat. This mixture of practical and spiritual advice was typical of the rustic Catholic ethos which remained one of the foundations of the Schmidt family's outlook through good times and bad.

Although it was decided by the Allies that there was no case against Schmidt worthy of bringing to Nuremberg, the Soviets, who at that time controlled almost a third of Austria, were determined to support any moves to put Guido Schmidt on trial. A show trial of Schmidt would expose the *Diktaturzeit* of the Schuschnigg regime as a "clerical fascist" system which had made Austria's incorporation into the Reich inevitable. Such a trial would strengthen the reputation of the Social democrats and even the Communists in Austria who had entered the government in May 1945. If the whole Schuschnigg system could be arraigned it might even help pave the way for a Marxist take over of the Austrian government. Thus Schmidt was going to return to the international stage, albeit in a quite different guise from his role before the *Anschluss*.[440]

---

440 In any event the Soviets did not need to push too hard to bring Schmidt before the Austrian People's Court. The numbers of Schmidt's enemies within the Austrian government were all too eager for a "scapegoat" to atone for Austria's sins of collaboration with a murderous regime.

CHAPTER 15

"Schmidt must hang!"

THE ALLIES HAD agreed in the Moscow declaration of 30th October 1943 that Austria had been the "first victim" of Hitler's aggression. This helpful view meant that Austria's status would reflect eventually the restoration of full sovereignty and independence from Germany. Quite what position the country would eventually hold in the quickly emerging Cold War politics remained to be seen but divided by the victorious allies into their respective zones suggested a political struggle for Austria's soul was imminent. Post-war power politics in Austria led to a Soviet backed Marxist political party and structure being established to ensure Austria would come firmly into the Soviet sphere of influence. Right-wing Christian parties backed by the West were built up with American help to block the Communist plans. Communism was a powerful force in 1945. One way of convincing Austrians that their future was brighter under Communism was to discredit everything to do with the Catholic Church and the pre-war Dollfuss/Schuschnigg *Ständestaat* (corporatist) regime. This was undoubtedly a factor underlying the decision of the People's Court to bring Schmidt back to Vienna and put him on trial for high treason.

There was also a widespread desire to accommodate the other segment of the Moscow Declaration of 1943 which had noted: "Austria is reminded that she has a responsibility which she cannot evade for participation in the war on the side of Hitlerite Germany" and that further, "in the final settlement account will be taken of her own contribution to her liberation."

By 1947, no "final settlement" had been agreed by the Allies over the future of Austria. Was she to remain divided indefinitely? Would she be allowed to become a fully-fledged western democracy? Would she come under the complete control of Moscow like Czechoslovakia, Hungary and Romania? A conversation between the American Secretary of State, Cordell Hull, and the British diplomat Ralph Stevenson, briefly reported in the *Guardian* in 1943, hinted that this had already been agreed.[441] According to this report, Hull had asked the British diplomat if it were true that "Britain had given an assurance to Moscow that after the war the Soviet system would extend to west of Vienna." Stevenson had replied: "Yes, we gave a half-promise to that effect." Austrians had they been acquainted with this exchange might well have asked themselves what happened to the other half of that promise?[442]

Within a couple of months, the Czechoslovaks would have voted for a Communist government and pro-Soviet forces would have taken over in Poland and Hungary. If Austria was to avoid this fate, her relatively nugatory "resistance" and "contribution to her liberation" would need reinforcing by some bold gesture.[443] A scapegoat in the form of the former Austrian Foreign Minister, a man who was universally disliked by nearly every European diplomat he came into contact with, communist, democratic or fascist, must have seemed a very safe bet. *Pravda*, in its editorial of 3rd April 1947, called for the trial of Schmidt to expose the shortcomings of the Austrian People's Party and the Austrian Socialists. They were just the post war "successors of the Austro-fascists, Dollfuss and Schuschnigg and the pan-Germans." The People's Party came in for particular criticism for "taking up Churchill's shabby idea of a United States of Europe." For good measure, Pravda threw in some criticism of the Catholic Church and the British and American authorities. "Why are there not other Austrian reactionaries in the dock with Schmidt?"[444]

As Max Löwenthal, a former colleague of Schmidt, noted in his memoir: People thought, "it did not matter whether Schmidt was guilty or not. It was about saving the country. Austria needed to be absolved

---

441 *The Guardian* 18 Jan.1943.
442 This question has not lost any of its relevance for Austria since the end of the Cold War.
443 Resistance in Austria was fragmentary but more widespread than is often thought. See Neugebauer, *Austrian Resistance* for a balanced overview of this rather emotive subject.
444 *Pravda*, 3 Apr. 1947. Article by M. Markov.

of its sins... extraordinary times required extraordinary ethics." Another view widely expressed was: "Just as the Viennese girls must make the Soviets happy in order to win their sympathy for Austria, so too would the condemnation of Schmidt wash the country clean... It is surely better that one man dies for the people."[445]

Thus was the last Foreign Minister of pre-war Austria held responsible for the German invasion and annexation of Austria in 1938. In this way, the fact that millions of Austrians had welcomed the *Anschluss* with cries of collective joy could be suppressed along with the other disturbing evidence that Austrians had not only greeted Hitler with unalloyed glee but had worked scrupulously on behalf of the Nazi regime to implement its appallingly inhuman policies. This was hypocrisy and spinelessness taken to dramatic new depths.[446]

Before Schmidt was brought to trial, there had already been a trial for high treason of Rudolf Neumayer, the Finance minister in Seyss-Inquart's short-lived government. Neumayer was found guilty and sentenced to life imprisonment.[447] This appeared to focus minds at the Foreign Office in London as no less a figure than Orme Sargent, Cadogan's successor as Permanent Under-Secretary, now took an interest in Schmidt's fate. "What is happening to Guido Schmidt, the Austrian Foreign Secretary at the time of the *Anschluss*?" Sargent asked.[448] A reply from the British political office in Vienna dated 12th February 1946 noted: "As regards Guido Schmidt, I understand he is due to be tried shortly on a charge of high treason by the People's Court. Considerable importance is being attached to this trial in Austria and Mr Nicholls also told me that Hornbostel, the most senior member of the former Austrian Foreign Service who was recently repatriated to Austria from Germany is delaying his return to the Austrian Foreign Office until he has completed his evidence for the prosecution at Schmidt's trial."[449]

---

445 See Löwenthal, *Doppeladler und Hakenkreuz*, pp. 119–120 .

446 The baneful legacy of this persisted well into the 1980s until the Waldheim debacle brought a more balanced narrative to a wider Austrian consciousness.

447 He was released in 1948 on health grounds. He died in in 1977.

448 Of course, Schmidt had already resigned by the time of the *Anschluss*. The error is characteristic of much British commentary on Austrian affairs before and after the war.

449 NA: C 1606/189/3.

A view by Mack whom, as we have already seen, had been in the Legation in Vienna before the war and was highly critical of Schmidt, was added to this report stating: "Mack told me that Hornbostel, curious as it may seem, had told him that his evidence would be in favour of Schmidt. Hornbostel realised that this would probably mean prejudicing his future career." The words "curious as it may seem" strongly imply that the British diplomatic service's distrust of Schmidt had not disappeared in the course of the war. Moreover, although the report indicated "considerable importance" being attached to the trial in Austria, "considerable importance" was also being attached to the trial in the British Foreign Office. Orme Sargent's request seems to have ensured a regular flow of highly detailed and exhaustive accounts of the trial from British personnel stationed in Vienna. No-one examining all this material could be in any doubt that there was a sensitivity to what Schmidt might reveal concerning British policy towards Austria in the run up to the *Anschluss*. The reports were dispatched with the utmost priority from Vienna. Distribution included the "War Crimes Section."

By 13th March, the British Political representative in Vienna was reporting: "I propose to send summaries of the trial which is expected to last some weeks. A formidable array of witnesses has been called including the Federal Chancellor, Figl, and many present and past members of the Ministry of Foreign Affairs. Among the latter it is anticipated that Dr Theodor Hornbostel, formerly Secretary-General of the Ministry will provide the most interesting evidence."[450]

As the trial opened, Schmidt stood already vilified by much of the Austrian media. "The Socialists, Communist and Soviet newspapers have already condemned Dr Schmidt 'as an active traitor'," the British political representative reported. The media had "taken the opportunity to indict the Dollfuss and Schuschnigg regimes and 'Austro-fascism' in general. Informed opinion is however disposed to regard him as no more than an ambitious intriguer who tried to keep a foot in both camps and who after the *Anschluss* compromised himself hopelessly by accepting a high

---

450 NA: POL/361/2/47 No 20. Another careless mistake on the part of the British observers of the trial: Hornbostel was never "secretary-general" of the Foreign Ministry but head of its Political Division.

industrial post from Göring." This seemed a fair if superficial summary of the case against Schmidt.

The actual indictment was rather more severe. The grounds for the trial, the charge sheet, were stated as follows:

1 That the accused had conspired with important personalities of the Third Reich and the Nazi party (von Papen, Göring, Kajetan Mühlmann, Seyss-Inquart, Wilhelm Wolf).

2 Without the knowledge of the Austrian government, in particular the Chancellor Schuschnigg, the accused had conspired to isolate the Chancellor from his government and advisers.

3 The accused had pursued a foreign policy which he had taken entirely into his own hands and followed "the German way" isolating in the process Austria.

4 The accused had worked hard to insult and alienate the representatives of foreign powers.

5 The accused was aware of the German aim to occupy Austria and deceived Schuschnigg about this.

6 The accused desired "the German way" despite the opposition of the Austrian people and the will of the Chancellor.

7 The accused advised the Chancellor to visit Hitler and concealed from the Chancellor that Mühlmann on the advice of Seyss-Inquart and Papen was travelling to Berchtesgaden first.

8 The accused only told the Chancellor that Mühlmann was in Berchtesgaden and negotiating with Hitler after they had arrived in Berchtesgaden

9 The accused concealed that he had known Mühlmann for years and that he was an avenue of communication with the Nazis who had been informed by Schmidt of the imminent talks in Berchtesgaden between the two chancellors.

10 The accused refused to give detailed information about Berchtesgaden to the envoys in Vienna and gave them only a brisk and superficial account of the meeting.

11 The accused persuaded President Miklas to accept the German

ultimatum so that he (Schmidt) could make a positive impression on his new masters.

12 The accused attempted after Berchtesgaden to promote the industrial plans of the Reich.

13 The accused while refusing the offer of Foreign Minister in the Nazi government nonetheless suggested his friend Dr Wolff who declared in his acceptance speech that he would exclusively follow the "German Way," a phrase which the accused had requested him to use.

14 The accused avoided incarceration in a concentration camp thanks to the protection of *Reichsmarschall* Göring

15 In pursuit of his own political ambitions he prepared the 1936 July treaty with Germany in opposition to the policy of Berger Waldenegg, declaring the treaty to be his own work whose future development was his own policy.

16 The accused followed "the German Way" despite the threatening danger it carried and warnings of the consequences of this policy.[451]

Such a charge sheet covered all the accusations against Schmidt and amounted to a weighty indictment of everything he had stood for before and indeed during the war. It suggested that it would be difficult to avoid some of the mud being thrown at him sticking. On the other hand, Schmidt was fortunate in securing the services of one of the best lawyers in Austria, Dr Rudolf Skrein.

Skrein, as a partly Jewish "non-Aryan" lawyer, had not been permitted to practise during the war. He had been ostracised and placed under house arrest on several occasions. He was well-known for his integrity and Schmidt's securing of his services was a strong card in his favour. No-one who knew Skrein would have thought for a moment that he would accept a brief if he did not "believe in his case a hundred per cent."[452]

The trial began on 26th February 1947. After hearing the charges,

---

451 The text here is taken from *HVPGGS* translated (with additional elementary errors of syntax and grammar included) by the British Political Representative, a good example of how the war had "opened the way for new talent" in civil service circles. See NA: C1606 *etc.*

452 GSN: Skrein/Schmidt correspondence, January 1947.

Schmidt said he would rest his defence on the fact that the accusations were a "crude distortion of the facts." The charge of high treason contained "no concrete political substance." The prosecution "speaks of a 'German Way' and speaks of 'satellite states' without explaining to what extent these terms form the basis of a punishable offence." It was clear to the state prosecutor, Dr Mayer-Maly, that the accused was unlikely, as a former Law student, to be cowed by the "Majesty of the Law." As Schmidt started complaining about the accusation that he had trivialised (*bagatellisiert*) the reports of one of his diplomats, Mayer-Maly attempted to gain the initiative, warning Schmidt to "stick to the point."

Schmidt obliged by delivering a long exposition of his Foreign Policy ideas, in particular that Austria could not as a country with so many frontiers engage in any combination or block. "These are eternal laws of Austria's foreign policy and in obeying them one consequence was the utterly uncompromising rejection of National Socialism which attacked us like a bacterium." At the same time our European foreign policy had, despite this, to deploy all substantial methods (*mit realen Mitteln alles zu tun*) to avoid a conflict with the German Reich which could only lead to violence. It was not a policy of appeasement and weakness which resulted in the pressure on us becoming ever stronger."[453]

Over the following days, Schmidt took the court on a detailed *exposé* of the foreign policy issues he had had to deal with from the Stresa Front, via Abyssinia to his rejection of joining the Anti-Comintern Pact. When asked why he had not allowed Austria to become part of this anti-Communist grouping, Schmidt rather than repeat his principles of Austrian Foreign Policy again, answered: "If I had accepted Ciano's and Berger Waldenegg's pressure for Austria to join the Anti-Comintern Pact, then the question as to whether Austria was a free country or not would already have been decided." There was no denying Schmidt's rapier-like mind. He was at the peak of his abilities despite his months of imprisonment and solitary confinement. [454]

Asked about his impression of Hitler, Schmidt simply said that, at that time, Hitler's position with regard to Austria and Czechoslovakia had

453 *HVPGGS*, pp.28–29.
454 *HVPGGS*, pp.28–29.

been "completely peaceful." Hitler had looked at Central Europe and all its problems in a *tour d'horizon* which was wide-ranging and practical. If he had been a member of the Czechoslovak government, he would have invited the representatives of the three and a half million Germans in the country to enter the government. Both Hitler and Göring were "well disposed" towards Austria.

When Schmidt was asked whether, as Austrian Foreign Minister, he had been ever asked to participate in the partition of Czechoslovakia. He answered: "Never: this assertion is completely unserious (*unseriös*)."

German demands on Austria included entry to the Anti-Comintern Pact, resignation from the League of Nations and recognition of fascist Spain. Only the last of these three did Austria accede to. Schmidt pointed out that even in that case Vienna never appointed a representative to Madrid but ran the Spanish representation out of the legation in Paris instead. By the fourth day of the trial, Schmidt had moved onto British foreign policy which he noted "was only understandable in the context of the structure of Britain being a 'world imperial power (*Weltreich*)'.[455] At every turn he demonstrated his wit, command of logic and fluency of expression.

Quoting Stefan Zweig who had had the opportunity to study the English disposition, Schmidt noted that the "men had decided to give way on Austria in order to preserve peace." Lord Salisbury had said to one of Schmidt's diplomats: "Why do you not make the *Anschluss*? What do you want to do all alone?" This was typical of the English ruling class's indifference to Austria. Göring had already testified at Nuremberg that at the time of the sanctions against Italy, the British had offered to give way on the *Anschlussfrage* if Germany had been prepared to join in the sanctions on Italy.[456]

Schmidt went on in some detail to explain his relations with Vansittart and the embarrassing leak of his memo to Eden quoting Schmidt's views on Mussolini. He noted that he had written a letter to the Foreign Office asking for an explanation but had been forced to drop the enquiry. "These matters should be seen in the correct light... these were matters of the

455 *HVPGGS*, p. 46.
456 *HVPGGS*, p. 48.

greatest secrecy." Schmidt was keen to point out that Vansittart had been Austria's "heartfelt friend (*Österreich von Herzen freundlich gesinnt*)." The Austrian's visit to London for the coronation of George VI in 1937 and his conversations with Vansittart had given Schmidt reason to believe that Britain might be prepared to support Austria and would inform Germany and Italy that the preservation of Austria's independence was after all a "British interest."[457] Schmidt and Hornbostel, had left England "convinced" that the British had a "direct interest in Austria." and that they would even "speak to General Blomberg" about this. If these statements confirmed the dysfunctionality of British policy, their formulation no doubt reassured London of Schmidt's discretion. He was not going to ventilate the inconsistency of British policy-making with regard to Austria in a public court.

The questioning moved on to Schmidt's relations with Göring and then on to his contacts with the diplomatic corps. Although Schmidt had given answers to questions about his relations with the British envoys, Selby and Palairet during his initial interrogation, he did not offer any thoughts about the British diplomats in the statement during the trial, another typically discreet omission.[458] Schmidt then gave a long and detailed account of the Berchtesgaden meeting, its preparation and agenda. He stressed the "brutality" of Hitler's behaviour but admitted that he had anticipated trouble and instructed Dr Fröhlichsthal to remain in Salzburg with instructions should neither Schmidt nor Schuschnigg return.

Schmidt was at pains to point out that, at that precise moment, the diplomatic situation was highly unfavourable towards Austria. "Germany

---

457 *HVPGGS*, p. 49. Also FO R3700 28 May 1937.

458 *HVPGGS*, p. 53, compared with GSN: Verhör, p. 132: "One should bear in mind that Palairet had only just arrived in Vienna so it was not long enough to form much of a personal relationship …" No doubt it had been made clear to the Austrians that no British official would participate in the trial even though Mack who had been number two in the Legation in1938 was now back in Vienna. It can only be left to the imagination as to how Palairet or Mack might have stood up to cross examination by Schmidt although had their dispatches been available to the court, they might well have provided the prosecution with more ammunition. They were embargoed until 1989 when no doubt it was considered they could do no more mischief.

knew that there was nothing to fear from the western powers. England was set on negotiations with Berlin and Austria was one of the bargaining chips."

On their return to Vienna, Schmidt recalled that they had had an urgent meeting with the Austrian President in which "remarkable ideas" were ventilated such as "the surrender of Braunau" (Hitler's birthplace) to Germany. The idea was dropped almost as soon as it was bruited. Schmidt vehemently denied that he had not informed the Austrian envoys abroad. He himself had been in touch with Eden through Franckenstein and the phrase "heavy pressure" was used in all the telegrams to the Legations. Schmidt then talked the court through the "catastrophe" of March 1938, noting that Schuschnigg himself had said that Schmidt was "at all times by his side." The Foreign Minister had repeatedly tried to persuade him to leave the country but the Chancellor had "refused to abandon his people."

"One can only doff one's hat to the way Schuschnigg conducted himself in those moments," was Schmidt's verdict on his former boss. This chimed with Palairet's view that the Chancellor had "risen magnificently to the challenge."[459]

By the sixth day of the trial, witnesses began to be called. As a dispatch from the British Political Mission in Vienna on 29th March noted: "With the outstanding exception of the former chief of the Austrian general staff Gansa [sic!] and the former head of the press department Eduard Ludwig, most of the witnesses had so far tended to exculpate Schmidt."

General Jansa had indeed always found Schmidt difficult to bear. For the regular soldier, Schmidt was altogether too much of a shooting star. Writing in his diaries twenty-three years later, Jansa asked what the point had been of investing so much of Austria's wealth in her armed forces if they were never to be deployed to defend the country. "How could one talk of 'Red White Red until we are dead (*Rot Weiss Rot bis in den Tod*)' while taking no steps to defend ourselves. Was this all a frivolous game. I

---

459 See PAL: Palairet private correspondence with C.B. Hurry, February 1938. These remarkable personal letters (Cambridge University Library GBR/0012/MS Add.7619) give a running commentary of Palairet's (mostly cultural) activities in Vienna during the crisis.

could have suspected Schmidt of such a thing but never Schuschnigg."[460]

Earlier he recalled his first meeting with Schmidt who had pointedly asked him whether there could be grounds for cooperation with the German military(!). Jansa had answered saying that he doubted German intentions in any such exercise in cooperation but thought they could cooperate on the military intelligence side.[461]

Jansa's testimony was delivered in a measured way, and he was certainly reluctant to criticise Schmidt directly. Rather, he noted that British rearmament could only begin sluggishly in 1937 and that it was far from making much progress by the spring of 1938. He also reiterated that in his view, faced with the threat from Nazi Germany, there were only two choices: total submission or war. Although Jansa conceded that there was little chance of the Austrians holding out against the Germans beyond two days, he argued that such a defence would have mobilised public opinion in the western democracies and elsewhere. He quoted the American diplomat Messersmith who said: "Whatever you do, don't go down without a fight." [462]

Schmidt was asked whether he concurred with Jansa's view that mobilisation could have supported the Austrian negotiating position at Berchtesgaden. Jansa had always argued *post factum* that Schuschnigg should have mobilised the Austrian forces as soon as he had departed for Berchtesgaden. Schmidt could not resist pointing out that such a step might have had an effect if it had been instigated by a great power but initiated by a small country it was "utterly pointless," unless the support of a larger country could be counted upon. It was abundantly clear to Schmidt by the end of the first week in March that such a military step would simply not be forthcoming from either France or Britain. To make the point even clearer, Schmidt felt compelled to add that the Czechoslovak government had informed Berlin on 11th March that

---

460 Broucek, *Jansa*, p. 676.

461 Broucek, *Jansa*, p. 650, which indeed they did, leading to a remarkably close relationship between Admiral Canaris and Colonel Lahousen-Vivremont, "the epitome of an old k. und k. officer." See Bassett, *Hitler's Spy Chief*, p. 115.

462 *HVPGGS*, p.216 *et seq*. For George Messersmith see obituary *Baltimore Sun*, 30 Jan. 1960.

their forces would not be mobilising in response to the German military advance on Austria. Finally, Schmidt recalled a conversation he had held with Lord Halifax who had stressed to him that "a war for Austria would not be popular... with that France also fell out of the equation because she would never march without British support." A similar fate had awaited Czechoslovakia a few months later and, as Schmidt observed, "it was hardly surprising that the western powers do not wish to be reminded of the unpleasant experiences of Munich."[463]

Another military witness who offered more accusatory comments was the Austrian military *attaché* in Berlin, Major General Anton Pohl. He claimed to have seen the accused at Göring's house in January 1938 and that the accused had visited Göring in secret, not even informing the Austrian Legation. Schmidt denied this simply claiming it must have been a "misunderstanding" as he had never visited Berlin without informing the Legation.

The next witness who had so impressed the British observers in the court was Eduard Ludwig, who proved to be less diplomatic than his former military colleague. Questioned in Munich by Dr Sucher during his original interrogation, Schmidt had made no secret of the bitter hostility he believed Ludwig felt towards him. "Ludwig's evidence is characterised by untruths, distortions, hatred and malice."[464] He added:

> "Ludwig was always my most bitter enemy. Not on account of political reasons but as a result of purely personal factors... Schuschnigg warned me repeatedly about Ludwig. His hostility towards me was based on the fundamental conviction that he believed that my sheer existence frustrated his great ambition to be Austrian Foreign Minister."

G.E.R. Gedye, the *Daily Telegraph*'s correspondent in Vienna in the 1930s, has left us with this evocative portrait of Ludwig who was in charge of handling the foreign press: "I called the first day at the Chancellery on the Ballhausplatz where Metternich had spun tangled webs of reaction, where Dollfuss later was to bleed to death in the hands of his Nazi captors and was enchanted by everything. The very address was an echo of spy thrillers by William Le Queux who had filled my boyhood with

463 *HVPGGS*, pp. 217–222.
464 GSN: Verhör, p. 57.

the romance of international intrigue. The head of the Press bureau, Gesandter Ludwig, a huge broad-shouldered man with all the guileless-ness of an educated son of the soil in his bucolic features received me with a display of affection which made me feel that he expected not the League of Nations but me to prove the saviour of Austria... Fulfilment of every wish was promised almost before I could formulate it and when we parted he did not brusquely bid me goodbye but 'he had the honour' (*Habe die Ehre*)." This of course said more about Gedye's naivity than the character of the man he was dealing with but the Englishman soon learnt the hard way what Ludwig's Viennese politesse really meant: "In later stages I entirely failed to suppress indignation at the complete non-ful-filment by Herr Ludwig of his ever flowing streams of promises... How often we of the Anglo-American Press community in Vienna, driven to frenzy by Ludwig's unfulfilled promises, indefinite postponements and buttery evasions said jokingly among ourselves: 'One compensation and one alone we'll enjoy if the Nazis triumph one day—they'll shoot Ludwig'."[465]

Given that we have seen Ludwig's name pop up in Palairet's dispatches as a trusted source (albeit of misleading information), it is hard to rule out the likelihood that Palairet's "informant" within the Chancellery who was pouring poison into his ear about Schmidt was none other than Ludwig or someone very close to him. Born in 1883, Ludwig was nearly twenty years older than Schmidt and clearly despised the younger man's ambition and ability. Ludwig had built up the federal press service into a coherent centralised body from the ruins of the disparate departments of the old pre-1918 imperial administration. This work had made him indispensa-ble to a series of Austrian chancellors and he understandably resented the way in which Schmidt's influence over the current Chancellor began to displace his own. "Ludwig was also of the opinion that I had moved the Chancellor to detach himself from Ludwig's influence," Schmidt related. Gedye's description of Ludwig certainly reveals a man equipped with all the weapons of an experienced *Beamtenintrigant* (bureaucrat-intriguer) who would bitterly oppose anyone who undermined his influence.

---

465 Gedye, *Fallen Bastions*, pp. 13–14.

While admitting the poor personal chemistry between himself and Ludwig, Schmidt maintained that he was also opposed to Ludwig for professional reasons on account of increasing criticism of Ludwig's handling of the media. "In foreign press circles (not Reichs-German) Ludwig was seen as an 'intrigant' rather than a press chief," Schmidt told the prosecutor, adding: "this was even the view of Dr Wasserbäck... I was certainly not [Ludwig's] only victim."[466]

Given this animosity, it was clear that the evidence of Ludwig would be of great interest and might well enliven the somewhat stiff proceedings of the People's Court. Those who attended the session of the court on 13th March 1947 were in for some fireworks.

They were not long in coming. Ludwig began his testimony with a *tour d'horizon* of his own encounters with the accused, questioning Schmidt and Schuschnigg's account of the events of 1938, noting that perhaps the former Chancellor's time in the concentration camp had deprived him of the memory of some "small events which produced greater events."[467] He went on to accuse both Schuschnigg and Schmidt of a "silent conspiracy (*stillschweigendes Arrangement*)" to remove him from his post before referring to Nazi journalists showering gifts on Schmidt including a presentation copy (*Prachtexemplar*) of *Mein Kampf*. One of these journalists, by name of Lohmann, had been so critical of Austria's independence that Ludwig had repeatedly asked for his expulsion only to have the Foreign Ministry refuse to take such a drastic step. This had clearly been Schmidt's doing, Ludwig insisted.

Moreover, when Göring had told Schmidt that Germany would have to take over the political and cultural leadership of Austria, Schmidt had, according to Ludwig, said nothing, a sign that he had agreed with Göring on this point. Finally, despite the fact that people "sang the praises (*Hohes Lied*)" of the closeness of the Foreign Minister and the Chancellor, he Ludwig well knew that there were substantial differences between the

---

466 GSN: Verhör, p. 57. Dr Wasserbäck was press *attaché* to the Austrian Legation in Berlin at the time of Dollfuss, described by the ever-urbane French ambassador, Francois-Poncet, as "faultless." See André François-Poncet, *Souvenirs d'une ambassade à Berlin, septembre 1931–octobre 1938* (Paris, 1946).

467 *HVPGGS*, p. 146.

two men. As Ludwig settled down to his theme this point was finally too much for Schmidt who exploded across the courtroom telling the witness that silence did not signify agreement. The accused was reminded by the Judges that he did not have the floor. But as Ludwig continued, it became clear that Schmidt was close to losing his temper.

When Ludwig began quoting an article which referred to differences between Schuschnigg and his State Secretary for Foreign Affairs, Schmidt finally erupted, shouting: "That is not a witness statement. That is a fantasy! This witness statement is nothing more than an accusation which he has made for ten years!"

The Court chairman swiftly called Schmidt to order, warning him that if he did not refrain from interrupting, the court would be forced to discipline him. With a certain satisfaction, Ludwig turned to Schmidt and addressing him directly. "Esteemed Herr Doctor; you will not put me under pressure! Your conduct is not that of an advocate!" Schmidt, ever the quickest of minds, immediately retorted: "The witness has insulted me and I insist on his being called to order and that he apologises. I propose an immediate Court decision." As the prosecutor accused Schmidt of "insulting" the witness, the Court adjourned amid scenes of mild uproar. The Judges returned after a brief consultation in private to announce that Schmidt would be disciplined for breach of court procedure and given a formal reprimand for interrupting the procedure of the court without permission despite frequent warnings. The Court brought to the accused's attention the consequences of any further interruptions under section 236 of the procedural regulations, noting that the Court was determined to conduct the trial in calm because "only then would the truth come to light."[468]

The Court went on to reprimand Ludwig as well, advising him to omit personal attacks on the accused as he could count on the Court defending him from similar attacks on the part of the witness. After that, Ludwig settled down to continuing his statement without interruptions. This now ran to accusing Schmidt of deliberately promoting Dr Wolf (his successor as Foreign Minister) on account of his Nazi sympathies and referring to a

---

468 *HVPGGS*, p. 148.

telephone call with Schuschnigg on 7th March in which the Chancellor, according to Ludwig, stated that he was not satisfied with the way Schmidt was conducting his office's policy (*Gestion des Angeklagten*).

Finally, referring to the "key" information he had to impart, he noted that Schmidt had testified under oath after the *Anschluss* that he had conducted "all his activities in conjunction with Seyss-Inquart and other men."[469] Moreover, a Romanian diplomat had overheard a long telephone call between Papen and the accused in which Papen had gone "into considerable detail" about the political situation.

Under questioning from the Judges, Ludwig stated that he had heard Schmidt frequently say that his ambition was for Austria to have the "closest connexion with Germany (*engste Verbindung mit dem Reich*)" and that he sought to eliminate "all points of difference" with the German Reich. As early as 1936, according to Ludwig, Schmidt had sought to promote a *Grossdeutsch Programm* and even organise then a meeting between Schuschnigg and Hitler.

Perhaps most damning of all was the accusation by the witness that Schmidt had said it was "impossible for the Austrian Legation in Berlin to have a half-Jewish (*Mischling*) press spokesman" in the shape of the Austrian press *attaché* Dr Schier.[470] Not only had Schmidt dismissed Schier from his position in Berlin but he had even promoted a policy of aryanisation during his time at the Austrian Foreign Ministry.

To this accusation Schmidt replied: "If I had had worries about the 'purity of blood' of Dr Schier, (a half-Jew) why would I appoint Dr Fuchs, a 'full' Jew (*Volljude*) to the post of press *attaché* in Paris?[471]My colleagues included only one or two complete 'Aryans' (*Vollarier*). In Geneva I appeared with the *Volljude* Schueller. Lennkh's wife was Jewish (*Volljüdin*). I have never espoused antisemitism and I certainly had more Jews and half-Jews as friends than non-Jews."[472]

---

469 *HVPGGS*, p. 150.

470 *HVPGGS*, p. 156.

471 Martin Fuchs was described by G. E. R. Gedye as having "a face like a whiskery spider... he was typical of the invaluable service which the Jews had performed for Austria for several centuries." Gedye, *Fallen Bastions*, p. 15.

472 *HVPGGS*, p. 161.

There then followed a number of accusations of venality, the most serious of which was one that the German embassy had provided a conduit for funds from Germany to Schmidt. To this Schmidt had replied in his pre-trial interrogation that it was true the German embassy in Vienna had arranged for funds belonging to his wife to be transferred from Moravia through Germany to Austria. Prince Erbach of the German embassy had been asked for help with the full knowledge of Chancellor Schuschnigg. Ludwig's testimony though full of venom ultimately lacked bite notwithstanding the deep animosity between the two men. Ludwig was at one stage reduced to claiming impropriety in that Schmidt alone of all Schuschnigg's advisers was the only man allowed to enter his office without prior notice. Torpedoing his own arguments that Schuschnigg had differences with Schmidt, Ludwig admitted that the two men were so close, "Schmidt would speak on the telephone with the Chancellor for hours during the night, sometimes until four in the morning."

To this Schmidt could only concur, observing with candour and detachment the following thoughts about Schuschnigg: "I gave the Chancellor much time from many of my best, most beautiful and young years. I was moreover at that time only recently married. We did not talk about politics at night. Over many weeks and months, the Chancellor (sometimes) simply sat and gazed into the distance in silence (*vor sich hinschaute und kein Wort von sich gab*)."[473]

Compared to Ludwig's emotional evidence, the sober testimony of Theodor Hornbostel carried greater weight. Although both men had been in concentration camps—Ludwig until 1939 (House arrest thereafter until 1942) and Hornbostel until 1943—Hornbostel was unequivocally an enemy of not just the Nazi system but the entire Berlin apparatus. In Schmidt's telling phrase, Hornbostel had been a *Preussenfresser* ("Prussian eater") since 1918. He was also the scion of a family with distinguished service to Austria over many generations. An ancestor had been Minister of Trade under Franz-Josef. Lean, spare and of distinguished appearance, Hornbostel personified the integrity and incorruptibility of the old imperial Austrian bureaucratic caste. As head of the Austrian Foreign Ministry's political department he was

473 *HVPGGS*, p. 162.

the senior civil servant responsible for Foreign Policy; a kind of Austrian equivalent of Vansittart, Orme Sargent and Cadogan rolled into one.

As we have seen from the British political observer's dispatches, Hornbostel was expected to support the accused, "surprising" though that sounded to the British.[474] Hornbostel was true to his word. After noting how under Dollfuss's various attempts to construct a *modus vivendi* with Germany had all failed and that Papen's proposals had already been presented without success to the then Austrian Foreign Minister, Berger-Waldenegg, in 1935, Hornbostel went on to note that the Austro-German agreement of 1936 removed a "millstone from the necks of all our legations abroad (*einen Stein der Belastung von allen ausländischen Gesandtschaften genommen*)."[475] Hornbostel added that "France and other countries congratulated the Chancellor on his courageous attempt." Only those who did not understand "our difficulties" and were exclusively self-serving (*Eigenbrötler*) opposed it.

"We were never frivolous or superficial" about the realities of the agreement. "We knew that one day it could become a scrap of paper (*Abkommen eines Tages zu einem Fetzen Papier werden könnte*) but the Chancellor and the accused strove hard to explain the agreement to the western powers and our neighbours."

Hornbostel recalled his visit with Schmidt to London at the time of the coronation of George VI. Eden and Vansittart had held positive discussions with the Austrians but Eden was "only prepared to go as far as saying he hoped to reach a joint recognition of Austria's independence with Italy and Germany."

Hornbostel then went on to dispute Ludwig's testimony concerning Schmidt's behaviour at the Paris embassy. Ludwig had accused Schmidt of alienating the French press by uttering pro-German sentiments during a visit with Hornbostel. Even more helpfully, he also admitted to working repeatedly on the drafting of Schmidt's letters to Göring. Above all he indicated that the Blomberg-Fritsch affair of 4 February in Germany had misled many into thinking some radical change was coming. With Papen's recall, a new direction in Germany's diplomacy was imminent. "Neither

474 NA: C 1606/189/3.
475 *HVPGGS*, p. 168.

I nor the Chancellor nor the accused were happy with these developments especially when Papen returned with a special mission, namely
Berchtesgaden... the accused and I were agreed that the Chancellor lacked
the agility and quick wittedness to match Hitler in a personal encounter."

Hornbostel went on to give a vivid description of the Berchtesgaden
preparations which were derailed by the late arrival of yet more German
demands. Although he did not travel to Berchtesgaden himself, he said
that when he saw Schmidt on his return, he knew immediately that
although Hitler's wish list had been softened "this was the beginning of
the end."

"The burning question was how and in what way should we inform
the foreign and domestic audiences about what had happened in
Berchtesgaden." Given that Schmidt was accused of not informing the
foreign missions in Vienna about Berchtesgaden what Hornbostel said
next was of some significance: "The briefing of the foreign representatives was exclusively my business and I took full responsibility for this,
even after the engagement of the accused in this activity."

Hornbostel noted that the enciphering of telegrams to the Austrian
missions abroad took time and it was vitally important not to inform
those representatives *en poste* in "hostile countries" in more detail than
they needed. This was especially relevant in the case of the Austrian minister in Belgrade "where we knew the government was entirely in favour
of the *Anschluss* and that our most important thoughts would be betrayed
to Germany almost instantly."[476]

Turning to the question of how Schmidt operated the Foreign
Ministry, Hornbostel was frank that his appointment at such a young
age was surprising and was greeted with dismay. When asked by many
how he could think of serving under such a young man, Hornbostel
asserted he was happy to do so. In a strikingly perceptive comment on
Schmidt's personality, Hornbostel observed, "the nervous temperament
of the accused made him appear much more blunt and harsh than in
reality he really was."[477] Hornbostel supported Schmidt's version of the
personnel changes in the Austrian Legation in Berlin observing that Dr

---

476 *HVPGGS*, p. 170.
477 *HVPGGS*, p. 171.

Schier was encountering considerable resistance from the German Nazi authorities on account of his non-Aryan origins and that it was becoming increasingly difficult for Schier to discharge his duties in any helpful way.

Hornbostel noted that his own release from Buchenwald concentration camp in May 1943 followed several written documents which Schmidt had composed pleading for his release including a letter to Himmler. (This act of charity by Schmidt only provided ammunition, however, for the prosecution to argue that this was proof of Schmidt's proximity to Himmler, an accusation the facts failed to support.)[478]

Above all, Hornbostel was able to reject the widespread view that Schuschnigg was weak and far too influenced by Schmidt. "From what I know of the Chancellor, I can only say my impression was that he was very difficult to influence. His views were personal, precise and principled." With that studied understatement so beloved of Austrian diplomats he added: "Unlike the accused, the Chancellor did not care to take advice from older people."[479] Hornbostel added that the reason why Schuschnigg had not travelled to the coronation festivities in England and the League of Nations in Geneva lay not in ambition of his state secretary but in the fact that he was not very sociable and was embarrassed by his weakness in foreign languages.

Asked by the judge about Palairet, Hornbostel limited himself to the terse, diplomatic statement that: "The Englishman Palairet was new in Vienna."

Schmidt asked the witness what Palairet and Puaux had said after being briefed on Berchtesgaden by him and Hornbostel. The diplomat stated: "The men gave an overall impression of dismay... I made no secret of my own horror. Both were very affected by the news but said: 'Perhaps it was after all the most sensible thing.'" The Chancellor was "lucky to have slipped out of it. It was embarrassing and the situation was delicate." This evidence showed beyond any doubt that Berchtesgaden, even if it was the beginning of the end, was perceived by the western envoys to have brought Austria a brief respite, despite all its unpleasantness.

---

478 Himmler's arrival in Vienna on the morning of 12 March is proof enough that Schmidt had not the slightest relevance to the SS chief. See above *HVPGGS*, p. 125 *et seq.*

479 *HVPGGS*, p. 173.

Undoubtedly, Hornbostel's evidence was largely in favour of Schmidt and was perhaps the most convincing argument the court heard to vindicate Schmidt's foreign policy decisions. During his time in the Austrian Foreign Ministry, Schmidt had relied enormously on Hornbostel's expertise and advice, often leaving much of the detailed work to him. Of course, had Hornbostel denounced Schmidt's policies, he would by implication have been denouncing himself. Yet Hornbostel's evidence was such a model of clarity and dispassionate analysis that it is hard not to be convinced by the sincerity of his arguments, not least because his few brief comments on the temperament of his chief seem both fair and accurate. The solidarity between the two men may have stemmed from their similar academic triumphs. Schmidt had come top of the Consular Academy exams in 1924,[480] and Hornbostel had come top of the Consular Academy's exams in the year 1912. Hornbostel knew from personal experience the depth of Schmidt's brilliance and the expectation and resentment such brilliance provoked in others.[481]

The charge of not wishing to condemn Schmidt because by doing so one condemns oneself might also be levelled at the second most important witness to offer evidence in Schmidt's defence. This was no less a figure than the former Chancellor, Schuschnigg himself. Aware that there were powerful forces in Austria prepared to blame the entire Dollfuss/Schuschnigg *Ständestaat* system on any high-ranking person they could find, Schuschnigg had been advised not to return to Austria to give evidence at Schmidt's trial. Instead he signed a statement in Rapallo on 21st May, which supplemented an earlier witness statement which was read out in court on 21st April.

This went into considerable detail concerning his personal relations with Schmidt. Noting that their "friendship lasted until 12th March 1938," Schuschnigg gave the impression of a sudden break possibly occasioned by Schuschnigg's incarceration while Schmidt was lunched by Göring.

Schuschnigg recalled their first meetings and stressed the reputation

---

480 GSN: in one document linked to his interrogation Schmidt claims he came top of these exams in 1918, but as he would have been barely 18 at that time this must be an error and really refer to his end of school exams, the Matura.

481 GSN: Commentary by Schmidt on the pressure of having come "top" in exams at a young age.

for loyalty and patriotism which Schmidt possessed and how their relationship was at first entirely personal rather than political or professional. "In the challenging moments of my private life, he offered me an extraordinary friendship, offering me considerable support."

Schuschnigg observed that it was "helpful" that in Germany Schmidt was perceived to be a "nationalist" but "he was not a nationalist certainly not a Nazi. He had no internal political support; he was a pure bureaucrat."[482] In other comments, the Chancellor painted a picture of Schmidt's personality bordering on the unstable and highly-strung. He was a man of "huge industry and application but also vast ambition and unusual irritability. Susceptible to outside impressions, his moods were unstable and mercurial (*labilen Gemütslage*)."

It did not surprise Schuschnigg that a "primitive spirit" such as Göring might interpret Schmidt's behaviour as agreement with his views but this was far from the truth. The former Chancellor went on to deny all of Ludwig's claims while at the same time recalling that his work with Ludwig had always been very successful and that he had always appreciated Ludwig's advice![483]

Schuschnigg's testimony was another *tour de force* of Jesuitical skill. He criticised Schmidt but not in the essentials which could lead to his being found guilty. Rather he attacked him on superficialities. "I think Schmidt was too strongly impressed by the Germans and allowed himself to be led to see the Austrian point of view through German spectacles." This chimed with Selby's comment that the Chancellor had felt his state secretary had "gone too far in Berlin."[484]

However, Schmidt's conduct at Berchtesgaden had been "exemplary and he had spoken very firmly with Papen about the 'surprise' sprung on the Austrians and he had negotiated hard with Ribbentrop to soften the Nazi demands." Moreover, after the meeting, "on leaving Berchtesgaden he was as depressed as I was."[485]

---

482 *HVPGGS*, p. 433

483 This is on a par with Schuschnigg's later comment to Jansa in the 1950s that he did not understand why the Chief of the General Staff had resigned.

484 SEL Registry summary.

485 *HVPGGS*, p. 437.

With regard to the crisis in the first days of March, Schuschnigg observed that he had no reason to suspect Schmidt was not carrying out his policy although a difference between the two men began to emerge as it became clearer to Schuschnigg that his Foreign Minister wanted to maintain a "compromise (*Ausgleich*)" with Germany at any cost. Schuschnigg denied the idea that the referendum was Schmidt's idea. "It was entirely my idea."[486]

"The 11th-12th March changed many people's views." In a comment subtly implying British input into the fateful decision while remaining diplomatically silent on the detail, he added ambivalently: before 11th March "we were not aware of any change in the British position."

Thus did Schuschnigg redeem Schmidt and at least make it clear that he saw no grounds until his resignation to suspect Schmidt's behaviour as anything but loyal and correct. Given that Schuschnigg always held overall responsibility for foreign policy, the argument that Schmidt could have had much room to pursue a policy course independently of the Chancellor beggars belief. Nevertheless, the almost throwaway sentence indicating the fact that their friendship had only lasted "until 12th March" was a far from oblique way of suggesting without saying it that Schmidt had disappointed Schuschnigg.

After these "big guns" had spoken in favour of Schmidt, the cast of supporting actors was just "grist to the mill." The former Chancellor Dr Ender noted how Schmidt had never been a Nazi while diplomats, Winterstein, Blaas, Lennkh and others including Schwarzenberg also testified to Schmidt's patriotism. Whether it was Schmidt's insistence a swastika be removed from the chemist's at Klosterneuburg or whether it was his refusal to sit down at a diplomatic table decorated with cornflowers, there were no shortage of eye-witness accounts testifying to his unambivalent anti-Nazi stance.

"The behaviour of the accused" the court summed up, "whether in Berchtesgaden in February 1938 or in the Ballhausplatz on 11th March, can be seen as expressly Austrian. Had the accused promoted the forceful takeover of Austria by the Nazis then on 11th March he would surely have revealed himself as a collaborator of some prominence. Yet this did

486 *HVPGGS*, p. 585.

not happen and he played no role in the new political authority which enveloped Austria…"[487]

The court noted that Schmidt's personal qualities left many people unhappy about him but observed that "it should not be forgotten that during the war he used what influence he had to help a large number of Austrians who were being persecuted by the Nazis or had as a result of their position with regard to the regime lost their jobs and income. In many cases this help had had a favourable effect on these people."

Yet the court could "not overlook that a number of witnesses were hostile to the accused and that this rejection of the accused whether from personal grounds or political opposition clearly coloured their evidence, just as an equal number of witnesses out of collegial ties or friendship brought their sympathy for the accused to expression. As a result of this tendency an obligation lay on the court to rigorously and precisely examine every witness statement in order to evaluate its worth and truthfulness."

Finally, the court noted that in defending his own honour, the last Foreign Minister of pre-war Austria was also "casting a light on the honour of Austria." Concluding, the judges continued: "We have examined completely objectively all the evidence, taking into consideration the position the accused embodied and the risk to Austria's reputation at that time. It is the conviction of the court to find the accused not guilty of high treason to the Austrian people and, aware of its responsibility, to free the accused with a good conscience."

But there was a sting in the tail. The court refused to grant any compensation to the accused for his imprisonment and interrogation between 2nd December 1945 and 12th June 1947 because "for such incarceration there were sufficient reasonable grounds which have not been fully removed by this trial." Moreover, the evidence that Schmidt met secretly with Göring in January 1938 behind the back of the Austrian Chancellor "remained sufficiently convincing that a complete invalidation of the suspicion cannot be countenanced."[488]

---

487 *HVPGGS*, p. 690.

488 This had been the view of the Austrian military *attaché* in Berlin, Colonel Pohl. See *HVPGGS*, pp. 126–127.

CHAPTER 16

"Honours and Praise"?

ALTHOUGH SCHMIDT WAS free, the verdict of the court did not alter the fact that alone of all the most prominent political and diplomatic figures of Austria, Schmidt had spent a large part of the war, not in a concentration camp but working as a well-paid director for the Hermann Göring Works. The trial had cast an uncomfortable spotlight on Austria and Guido Schmidt; it had also prompted questions concerning the former State Secretary's relationship with the *Reichsmarschall*.

Although we have already examined the dynamic between the two men, it is worth recalling that Schmidt was not the only beneficiary of his actions. Schuschnigg's brother, Dr Arthur Schuschnigg, was given a job at the Kaiser-Friedrich Museum in Berlin thanks to Göring's intervention. No doubt Göring had hard-nosed reasons in that case as well as his *Ritterlichkeit* (chivalry) to thank for this decision but, unlike Schmidt's case, Göring's intervention on behalf of Dr Schuschnigg did not result in the Austrian's reputation being deconstructed for many years afterwards. For Schmidt, his reputation continued to arouse controversy (as indeed it has continued to do to this day), despite the court verdict.

Schmidt was smuggled out of the court—there were wild rumours the Soviets would try to kidnap him—and eventually returned into the American zone of Austria where he began to look for work in the commercial sphere. As a man in his mid-forties, he felt far too young to retire, notwithstanding his ill-health.

But the controversy around his reputation and career before and during the war continued to pursue him. In particular, the Socialist and Communist parties continued to inveigh against Schmidt. On 13th June 1947, the Socialist-Marxist *Arbeiter-Zeitung* published a long article demanding that Schmidt be tried again, this time for aiding the German war effort and supporting the Nazi machinery of aggression.[489] The Interior Ministry ordered the official Complaints Commission (*Beschwerdekommission*) to open an investigation on 30th July 1947 and a document was prepared articulating a strong case against Schmidt.[490]

The document stated that the latest accusations "have been drawn up at the instigation of the Socialist Parties of Austria" and that the accused was "liable under section 7 of the *Verbotsgesetz* and guilty of working between 1939 and 1945 to secure the objectives of the NSADP (Nazi party) as a deputy board member and General Director of the Göring Works." By this action the accused had "damaged the interests of an independent and democratic Austria."

This was party political language rather than legal precision and at first Schmidt imagined he could thwart the charge by simply stating that an "independent and democratic Austria did not exist between 1939 and 1945." But the Austrian officials were not so easily put off and a more detailed defence had to be drawn up, once again with the help of lawyers.

The Commission accused Schmidt of working for an organisation, the Hermann Göring Works, which was "one of the most important instruments of achieving the domestic and foreign policy aims of the Nazis." The company also pursued a policy of making "Austria totally dependent on the German Reich" with the result that a large part of Austria's industrial capacity "was plundered." Guido Schmidt had been "committed to supporting and enlarging this work." Moreover, as a director of the *Binnenschiffahrt* (internal shipping division) he had been in charge of a company "hugely important" for the Nazi war effort. In the course of all these activities, Guido Schmidt had damaged extensively Austrian *Gedanken*. Moreover, he had worked to secure and oversee the merger of the DDSG shipping company with the Bavarian Lloyd.

---

489 A charge resurrected against him by Rathkolb and others fifty years later: See Kreissler, *Fünfzig Jahre danach*, p. 175.
490 GSN: *Bundesministerium für Inneres: Abschrift Dr Etz Geschäftszahl KO 1/47*

These were important accusations and Schmidt moved swiftly to respond through his lawyers. The exchange was exhaustive and demonstrates that the case against Schmidt for "collaboration" was substantial and plausible even if it ultimately failed in meeting the legal requirements to secure grounds for a second trial.

His lawyer, the indefatigable Dr Skrein, deployed a number of compelling arguments based on the reality of Schmidt's commercial career in the German Reich such as it was. First, he reiterated the point that after 13th March 1938, an independent and democratic Austria simply did not exist.

Second, it was pointed out that Schmidt's conduct at this time demonstrated that he was always "a good Austrian (*ein guter Österreicher*)."[491] At no time did he support the Nazis, remaining a "bitter opponent of the National Socialists (*ein erbitterter Gegner des NSDAP*)" as those who worked with him could testify.

Third, it could be shown that Schmidt was never connected with the armaments industry. His principal role was to negotiate the purchase of crude ore (*Roherz*) in Spain and Yugoslavia. As for the Binnenschiffahrt activity, the documents showed he had played no role in overseeing or negotiating the merger of the DDSG shipping company with the Bavarian Lloyd. Indeed, this charge was quickly dropped by the Commission. He had been almost exclusively concerned with supporting the former Austrian DDSG by ensuring its pension obligations were transferred to the Reich Finance Ministry so that they could be honoured. In the process, the pension fund's 4 million RM debt was cancelled after Schmidt's intervention. As a result, the finances of the DDSG were not only placed on a more stable footing, the entire commercial fleet of the company could be rationalised and restructured.[492]

Fourth, *Stahlring*, the small company Schmidt found himself involved with after his sudden dismissal from the HGW, was a purely civilian operation which exported non-military goods and was not concerned even indirectly with armaments.

---

491 GSN: Schmidt/Skrein paper, 30 July 1947.

492 The Donaudampfschiffgesellschaft (DDSG), as the name implied, operated commercial and passenger services along the Danube. None of its vessels bore arms.

Fifth, given that his pension from the Austrian Foreign Office was less than 600 RM a month, it was clear that he would have to find some work if he were to support a young family.

To sum up, Schmidt demonstrated that in 1941 the Hermann Göring Works was reorganised into three separate divisions: Mining, Armaments, and Shipping. In 1942, he had been suddenly replaced in the shipping division by Rudolf Diels who had married Göring's niece.

The Commission found that although Schmidt had been replaced by Göring's nephew-in-law Diels, in 1942, Schmidt returned to the shipping division of the HGW in 1944 when, in turn, Diels fell victim to Göring's capricious nepotism.

Given that by 1944, the full militarisation of the German war economy had been more or less completed, it was difficult for Schmidt to claim that his activities were unrelated to the Nazi war effort. The Commission thus found Guido Schmidt *belastet* (charged) in accordance with S4 Abs 1 lit e V.G. 1947. As HGW was one of the "main instruments preparing for war," even if it also produced non-military goods, it was necessary, the Commission argued, to examine whether Schmidt was directly responsible for activities which were working to "achieve the goals of National Socialism." But the Commission admitted "not everyone working for the HGW was guilty of supporting Nazi aims. For the case against Schmidt to succeed, it would be "necessary to show that the accused demonstrated a personal engagement for the objectives of National Socialism, going beyond the normal interests of a commercial entity." This criminal law demand for *mens rea* was of course impossible to fulfil because Schmidt could prove with countless witnesses that even though he wished "to help the company" he never supported the aims of the NSDAP, namely the creation of a Greater German Reich, and he clearly did not possess a certain *seelisches Verhalten* (mental behaviour) to that end.

Summing up, the Commission concluded: "Guido Schmidt is an unusually ambitious person who could not tolerate a subordinate position, but his appetite for prestige fell far short of furthering the political aims of the Nazis. He had enjoyed corporate rank and title but his executive power had been modest."[493] The case was dropped and Schmidt was able to send Skrein his final cheque.

Thus did Schmidt elude another long and costly trial which would have ruined his finances and exacted a heavy toll on his health. Vorarlberg beckoned, and in St Anton he was at least among family, friends and supporters. It was recognised locally that it had largely been his inspiration to establish in the 1930s the spectacular Galzig lift, which had opened the most dramatic scenery of the Arlberg pass to the visiting skier, revolutionising the tourist potential of the resort.[494]

The Americans having got to know Schmidt rather well since the end of the war, recognised Schmidt's qualities and language skills and promptly pushed him towards the Semperit tyre company, a US intelligence asset in post-war Austria. At Nuremberg, they had found him to be a useful witness with a quick and ready grasp of essentials. He was clearly not a communist and could be relied on to work with a capitalist agenda. Once again Schmidt, with his customary energy, threw himself into his work. In between commercial trips to Western Europe and the Middle East, there were reminders of the pre-war days. In 1947, the year of his trial and potential arraignment for collaborating with the Nazi war effort, Schuschnigg had published a slim volume on the dramatic days of 1938, entitled *Austrian Requiem*. It contained the following protective comments on his former closest colleague:

> "I would like to make a few remarks about Austria's last Foreign Minister, Dr Guido Schmidt. It has been said that Dr Schmidt had inspired the treaties with Germany of July 1936 and of February 1938 and had disloyally influenced my position. That is not true. Dr Schmidt was appointed to the post of State Secretary for Foreign Affairs in the spring of 1936 at my request, without the previous knowledge of any foreign power... I do not believe, nor have I ever heard that Dr Schmidt had been known to either German or Italian authorities."[495]

But after this supportive statement, Schuschnigg, even though he was

---

493 GSN: KO 1/47.

494 To this day the Galzig lift is one of the gateways to some of the most superior skiing anywhere in the Alps.

495 Schuschnigg, *Austrian Requiem*, p. 166.

aware that a trial of his colleague was probable, articulated the questions and doubts of all Schmidt's critics with brutal frankness:

> "I think it is important to state these facts because Dr Schmidt's behaviour after the *Anschluss* was objectively unclear and personally difficult to understand. It is not up to me to judge his conduct as future investigators of his case might shed new and so far unknown light on his motives. But I am equally far from trying to excuse behaviour which unfortunately had no plausible explanation. One cannot accept a position as director-general of the Hermann Göring Works when one's friends and colleagues are—at best—in prisons and concentration camps. Such actions cannot be explained and seem altogether unjustifiable."

Here was perhaps of all the statements by Schmidt's detractors, the cruellest of comments on his behaviour, argued with the familiar rigour and logic of an intellectual formation devoid of any sentimentality. Schuschnigg did not hesitate to assume his own moral responsibility for Schmidt's pre-*Anschluss* actions but did not shy away from accusing his closest political friend of what Jesuits would recognise as "equivocation" in his subsequent behaviour.[496] The bond between the two men had been so close and so intense that to read these words must have been a shock to Schmidt. In a letter to Professor Werbereitz, Schmidt voiced his reaction to Schuschnigg's censure:

> "It is so difficult to explain with clarity the whole affair of those times. It is all so tragic because I served Kurt with a loyalty and devotion (*Hingabe und Treue*) few friends could ever have offered each other."[497]

The post war correspondence between Schmidt and Schuschnigg conveys something of the frost which seemed to descend over these two men's relationship after 1947. While Schmidt constantly refers to mutual friends and acquaintances from the 1930s, Schuschnigg writes in a distant

---

496 Equivocation: A form of "mental reservation" well known to Jesuits on account of it being frequently deployed by their members during penal times in England when it was a capital offence for a Jesuit to enter the country. See Henry Garnet SJ and Robert Southwell SJ, *A Treatise of Equivocation: a Treatise against lying*, 1595 (most recently published Cambridge, 2016)

497 GSN: Letter from G.S. to Professor Werbereitz undated but (probably) early 1947. This comment of Schmidt's does not address the former Chancellor's point.

abstract way, never once following Schmidt's lead by referring to anyone with whom he was associated as Chancellor.[498] Even when Schmidt attempts to break the ice with some amusing anecdotes, it is as if he is communicating with a blank wall.[499] Schmidt asks when Schuschnigg might return and whether he has read Ludwig's book on the 1938 crisis but Schuschnigg refuses to be drawn on these subjects, simply observing somewhat laconically that "America is not so bad." Given the intensity of their friendship in the run-up to 1938, it is clear that for Schuschnigg, as he had indicated in his testimony during the Schmidt trial, their friendship had indeed "ended" on 12th March.

A more positive contribution to Schmidt's reputational rehabilitation internationally came in the form of the former British Minister to Vienna, Walford Selby. Selby, as Palairet's predecessor, had had more time to develop a far more realistic and better-informed grasp of what was going on in the country to which he was accredited. Unlike Palairet, he was never in the pocket of the French minister Puaux, and he had been a fierce defender of Schuschnigg and Schmidt's policy even when it came into conflict with Vansittart and others at the Foreign Office.

Writing in *The Times* on 26th August 1947, he first praised the court case against Schmidt for expressing an "Austrian sense of guilt." The trial and the verdict reached could be "regarded as a very high tribute indeed to the impartiality of Austrian justice and to the wise statesmanship which has been shown by Austria's present leaders."[500]

"At all costs we should desire to discourage anything in the nature of persecution in Austria and in this vital matter it is for the best interests of the people of Austria that statesmanship be shown." Turning directly to Guido Schmidt, Selby now made a remarkable comment exonerating Schmidt of any whiff of treason that might be lingering in the embargoed and secret Foreign Office files. "I can testify to the fact, *and no-one was*

498 GSN: Schuschnigg letter to G.S., 26 Mar. 1953. The lack of warmth is all the more marked when compared with for example Schuschnigg's correspondence with his erstwhile potential assassin, Reinhard Spitzy. See Reinhard Spitzy, *So haben wir das Reich verspielt* (Munich, 1986), appendix, 5 Dec. 1967 correspondence Schuschnigg to Spitzy.
499 GSN: Schmidt letter to Schuschnigg, 21 Apr. 1954.
500 Letter Selby to *The Times*, 26 Aug. 1947. See Selby, *Diplomatic Twilight*, pp. 30–40.

better aware than I of Dr Schmidt's behaviour at the time, [author's emphasis] that up to the time I left in October 1937 Dr Schmidt had not become a traitor to his country and had not abandoned the Rome protocols to which Austria looked to assist in protecting them from Hitler."

Although Selby was leaving open the possibility that Schmidt could have been corrupted in February or March of 1938, as his successor, Palairet, reported, his declaration was a broad offer of support for the former Foreign Minister and one which certainly suggested that Schmidt had been a "Good Austrian" as far as Selby was concerned. Selby could not resist having another swipe at Vansittart in the same letter. Despite the sensitivity of the subject, he recalled the famous Van memo to Eden which had so infuriated Mussolini. "In this respect," Selby continued, "I consider completely justified Dr Schuschnigg's repudiation of Sir Robert Vansittart's misrepresentation to Eden of Dr Schmidt's attitude towards Italy in September 1937."

Whether Selby consciously intended to or not, his linkage of Schmidt, Vansittart and the infamous memo hinted at a relationship between Van and Schmidt of greater complexity than commonly imagined. Selby had often implied that Van was encouraging the Austrians while at the same time obstructing efforts to secure British assistance. This argument had become increasingly heated as 1934 developed. Van had rapped Selby over the knuckles: "I frankly do not think any new initiative or contribution by His Majesty's Government is at the moment possible. I sympathise with your feeling of gloom and muddle but I still have a hope that if the Austrian government show a degree of statesmanship and courage they may be able to hold the pass long enough for the Nazi danger to subside."[501]

"Hold the pass" had been Schuschnigg and Schmidt's policy. Selby in a very diplomatic way implied in his letter that Van used Schmidt as a tool to advance a policy which would buy time for Britain rather than Austria. The implication is that when it suited Van, he was even prepared to sacrifice Austria in general and Schmidt in particular.

Certainly, Selby and Van clashed on many occasions over Austria in the 1930s. At one point, Van was driven to exclaim: "In regard to Austria,

---

501 See FO 371/18356 Walford Selby/Vansittart correspondence.

Selby is so ignorant that he has confused me with Nevile Henderson."[502]
Thus, while Selby appeared to be exonerating Schmidt in his letter, he
was also settling old scores with Van. This became especially obvious a few
years later in 1953 when Selby published his own memoirs, accusing Van
of having "single-handedly encouraged the Nazis to invade Austria."[503]
This explosive accusation set Vansittart into a rage which soon engulfed
his former colleagues in Whitehall.

While Warren Fisher, the Head of the Home Civil Service and
Permanent Secretary to the Treasury during Van's time, advised his
friend that "Selby was not worth the powder or shot," Vansittart felt so
strongly about Selby's criticism that he proceeded to waste considerable
amounts of "ammunition," financial and literary, in an attempt to destroy
Selby's reputation. He consulted several lawyers for written opinions on
the chances of success for a libel action against Selby. When they offered
only lukewarm advice, he orchestrated an establishment campaign,
involving Harold Nicolson, John Wheeler-Bennett, the future historians
Lord Blake and Hugh Trevor-Roper to dismiss the book in all the main
London papers. This substantial unedifying correspondence reveals
Vansittart's determination to crush Selby's reputation.[504]

Significantly, two men distanced themselves from this rather vicious
campaign by Van. First, William Strang, the senior relevant official at the
Foreign Office, noted that the typed manuscript had been submitted by
Selby "in accordance with standard procedure." Strang "could not determine whether the manuscript was different to the eventual published
book." To Van's intense annoyance, Strang refused to name the official in
his office who had approved Selby's manuscript.

Second, perhaps the most perceptive comment on Van's ill-tempered
campaign against Selby came from Sir Lewis Namier, then the doyen
of *emigré* historians. As an *emigré* from Central Europe, he enjoyed a

---

502 VNST II 1/50

503 See Walford Selby, *Diplomatic Twilight*.

504 It is revealing to compare Van's efforts in his private papers in Cambridge with Selby's own correspondence at the same time, with his supporters at court and in the
literary world. Both antagonists could call on significant establishment figures to
support them.

sceptical view of the British establishment, especially in full cry over some personal vendetta.[505]

He had been thanked by Selby in his acknowledgements. This was enough to invoke Van's ire. When Vansittart wrote to Namier complaining about the book and inviting the historian to dissociate himself from it, Namier commented that "all the pages in Selby's book which concern you deal with matters which happened within the Foreign Office, about which I certainly could not be consulted or express an opinion as they fall within a period of time for which British documents have not been published."[506] Thus did Namier place the tip of his unbuttoned intellectual foil on the former Chief Diplomatic Advisor while making a wider point about the sluggishness of Foreign Office archiving.

No doubt for Schmidt, such academic debates among British historians and in the letters columns of *The Times* must have seemed remote. A press argument about his actions much closer to home followed the publication of an article in *Die Furche*, the leading intellectual and Conservative Catholic weekly, by its editor, Friedrich Funder. Entitled "*Regnorum Fundamentum*," it attempted to clear Schmidt of any moral culpability for his behaviour.[507] The article led to a quite heated exchange between Funder and several correspondents who took issue with his line of reasoning. Copies of the correspondence were forwarded to Schmidt.[508]

One correspondent, Heinrich Wenninger, the former deputy leader of the *Heimwehr* in Upper Austria, who had been sent to Dachau for a year after the *Anschluss*, welcomed the article but criticised Schmidt for "going around basking in the glory of the innocent." Wenninger asked, "How could a man who had opposed the polices of Hitler so vigorously that he should have been the first to satisfy the Nazi thirst for revenge

---

505 Namier had written several studies highlighting the incoherence of the Foreign Office and British policy towards the dictators. For his critical indictment of British appeasement see *Diplomatic Prelude* (London, 1948) p. xi *et seq.*

506 For the surprisingly large volumes of correspondence generated by this subject see VNST II 1/40 Vansittart to Blake, Trevor-Roper, Wheeler-Bennett, Warren Fisher descendants, Namier, Kennedy, Harold Nicholson *etc.*

507 *Iustitia Regnorum Fundamentum* (Justice is the foundation of the state), the motto of Joseph I of Austria (reigned 1705–1711).

508 GSN: Funder file.

escape untouched?" This was particularly the case given that not only were his colleagues carted off to camps but some of them were murdered by the Gestapo or forced to commit suicide. Among them were Fey, the former vice Chancellor, Zehner, the State Secretary for Defence Affairs, and Neustädter, a former minister to Hungary. For Wenninger, Schmidt's relationship with Göring could not in itself explain this (*Bekanntschaft mit Göring erklären zu wollen ist doch kaum möglich*). Mentioning the fact that Schmidt was acquitted for "lack of evidence (*Mangel an Beweis*)," Wenninger concluded: "Only one thing should be said but with all clarity (*mit aller Deutlichkeit*): Schmidt is morally condemned! (*moralisch gerichtet!*)... each of us would have been ashamed to take a senior position in the life of the Third Reich while his closest colleagues were persecuted and eliminated. Surely each of us would have preferred to leave his gifts and talents unused and lead a quiet modest existence." Wenninger insisted that ambition and egotism alone could not excuse such conduct.[509] Here were Schuschnigg's arguments against Schmidt articulated with renewed vigour.

Funder replied that the phrase "lack of evidence" was misleading because the authorities had been unable to present "any evidence" of Schmidt's wrongdoing. Moreover, Funder continued: "the trial was less about Schmidt than an attempt to discredit the Austrian People's Party as the heir of the old system." Therefore, all who had served the Schuschnigg regime could be discredited including Figl, Austria's first post-war Chancellor who had been leader of the Lower Austrian *Sturmscharen*, a right wing Catholic conservative paramilitary group.

Funder noted that contrary to popular belief, Schmidt had not been the only member of Schuschnigg's government to escape the Nazis. "Neither Raab (another post-war Austrian Chancellor) nor Heindl (an important member of Schuschnigg's cabinet) had ended up in Buchenwald or Dachau. In addition, "a whole row of our people had ended up in good positions."[510]

Funder conceded that "it would have been more heroic had Schmidt

---

509 GSN: Funder file, correspondence Heinrich Wenninger to Friedrich Funder, 22 June 1947.

510 Funder might have added that Berger-Waldenegg had asked Mussolini for a job after the Anschluss and was helped by him and Ciano to survive financially in wartime Italy.

not accepted any position even though it was a time when no-one foresaw the destruction of the Reich." Funder then posed the question which is perhaps the most difficult for Schmidt's critics to answer: "How many of the prisoners of the Third Reich would have willingly exchanged their lot with that of Schmidt if they had had the chance? We should give up this exaggerated fantasy of heroism (*übertriebenen Heldenfabeln*).[511]

No doubt Schmidt followed these debates with interest, but he had already determined to move on. When he was not advancing the projects of the Semperit tyre company, demonstrating daily his business acumen, he was lavishing as much attention as he could on St Anton. The Galzigbahn, which he had been largely responsible for bringing to St Anton when he had visited the resort with Chancellor Schuschnigg in 1937, was up and running, a monument to Schmidt's determination and financial acumen. The resort's popularity, above all with the English, continued to flourish. Even today in the second decade of the twenty-first century, St Anton still has more English tourists each year than most other Austrian resorts combined.[512]

One of the first decisions the Nazis made after they had seized control of Vorarlberg in 1938 was to deprive Schmidt of his honorary citizenship (*Ehrenbürgerschaft*) of St Anton. This was now restored and the locals embraced a family which had held onto its Catholic faith and studiously avoided cultivating any prominent local Nazis.

The approbation of his neighbours could not conceal the fact that Schmidt's health was broken. Less than ten years later he died aged 56. He had expended more energy in his relatively short lifetime than many men in their eighties but his diabetes had weakened his health considerably. One day while out shooting he had forgotten to pack his medicine. He did not want to interrupt the sport by going back to fetch it and as a result he fell ill. His condition quickly deteriorated and he was taken to Vienna to be operated on. The surgery failed to remedy the soaring temperature and infection set in. Austria's most controversial Foreign Minister had finally exhausted even his formidable capacity for survival and he died within hours of the operation.

511 GSN: Funder file, p. 2.
512 Information from Guido Schmidt (grandson), 30 Mar. 2019.

The funeral of Dr Guido Schmidt was held in deep snow in St Anton. Most of the village was present and the mayor read out an appreciation which did not try to make sense of the controversies and historical episodes which had marked Guido Schmidt's life and Austria's greatest dramas but rather focussed on his human qualities. "He was a good Austrian." Above all it was to his Vorarlberg roots that reference was made repeatedly as well as to his brilliance and sense of service. "Of the many flags which hang over this grave is the flag of Vorarlberg, and the Vorarlberg hymn *Du Ländle: meine teurer Heimat, ich singe Dir zu Ehr' und Preis* (You my country, my dear homeland, I sing your praises and honour)," the mayor began.[513]

He had served not only his family and his village but also his homeland of Vorarlberg. The greater his career and academic achievements, the greater the spotlight on Vorarlberg. "Now Vorarlberg has lost this great son and thanked him for all he had done for the "honour and praise of this land". The mayor remarked on his "sudden death" and his great gifts of language and worldly, practical skills and went on to say that Guido Schmidt had also brought Vorarlberg immense commercial advantage. Starting with the J. Schmidt business at Montafon, and then onto the Arlberger Bergbahn, the Bergbahn St Anton, the Tyrol Raw metal works and the Austro-American Semperit rubber company, Guido Schmidt always demonstrated his agility and energy. With these skills, he personified the other words of the Vorarlberg hymn which praised an "industrious people" (*rührige Völklein*).

The mayor had characterised his subject's native gifts well. It is perhaps no coincidence that the most accurate epitaph to Guido Schmidt came not from statesmen or diplomats but from the simple, modest unacademic voice of a local neighbour.

---

513 GSN: Funeral oration: *Sehr geehrte Trauergemeinde...*

CHAPTER 17

Conclusion

WHILE MANY WHO had openly embraced the Nazis had gone free and even been given important government posts, Schmidt, who had never joined the Nazi party and had been on the Gestapo watch list, was imprisoned and put on trial. Yet to convince any court which accepted the rule of Law that he had been a Nazi was always going to be a tall order. As an infamous Austrian Nazi, Friedrich Rainer, stated at Nuremberg: "There was never any question of our working with him, he never even belonged to us (*gehörte nicht einmal zu uns*)". He was absolutely loyal to his head of government and fought for Austrian independence. "He belonged to the opposing camp."[514]

Schmidt's fate was that of the brilliant maverick whose genius was too raw to be acceptable to many, especially those whose minds were less swift and less able to keep up with the verbal pyrotechnics which were Schmidt's "house style." As his secretary Max Löwenthal recalled: "He could say nothing colourless. He talked in fireworks. He loved irony and hit his enemies with the light thrusts of the fencing foil. Who enjoys being on the receiving end of that? Thus, did he make many enemies." Those who cannot suffer fools are often condemned to be tied down by them as they exact their revenge. Löwenthal offered a few vivid examples

---

514 GSN: *Aufzeichnungen*, Rainer evidence Nuremberg IMT: Volume 16 12th/13th June 1946 *et seq*. Rainer, SS officer and *gauleiter* of Salzburg and then later Carinthia. Executed in Yugoslavia 1947 for war crimes.

of Schmidt's "house style": "One day, ringing late, Schmidt demanded to speak to an official who simply could not be found. In a tone of rising anger, he told me: "You must find him. Don't ask ME how! FIND HIM!" On another occasion when Löwenthal boldly asserted that he was not to blame for some breakdown in communication Schmidt had exploded: "I don't give a damn who is to blame! Why do you think that matters? Someone is to blame; and at this moment YOU are the one standing in front of me!"[515]

Schmidt's capacity for making enemies was truly *sans pareil*. There was probably not a single member of the Diplomatic Corps *en poste* in Vienna (with the notable, if ironic, exceptions of Walford Selby and von Papen) he had not wilfully offended and converted from friend or at least neutral observer to embittered foe. Nor were these enemies limited to the western democracies and other interested parties such as Poland and Italy. On 17th February 1938 even Otto von Habsburg had written to Schuschnigg begging him "not to rely on Guido Schmidt."[516]

As a report in the German diplomatic archives reveals, Schmidt was also completely distrusted by the German Foreign Ministry, (despite all the accusations of pro-Nazi bias). After Berchtesgaden, a report from the German legation in Vienna to Berlin complained bitterly that "Schmidt was working very hard to prevent Nazi personalities gaining any influence over state affairs."[517] The German *chargé*, Stein, did not even allow Schmidt to clear his desk the day before the *Wehrmacht* arrived in Vienna.

The mantra so often quoted by Jesuits "to be meek as doves and cunning as serpents"[518] may have encouraged Schmidt to combine a powerful intellect with a manner which disarmed and alienated. Even by the standards of twenty-first century politics it is hard to imagine the layers of sophisticated deception required to navigate Austria's Foreign Policy between 1936 and 1938. Schmidt was a master of all the techniques of "creative ambiguity," long before the phrase was coined by hapless British

---

515 Löwenthal op cit. p. 129
516 See Brooke-Shepherd, *Uncrowned Prince*, Chapter 12.
517 ADAP Ser. D BD I Nr 313, 18 Feb. 1938, Lagesbericht über Österreich.
518 Matthew 10:6.

cvil servants in the 2020s trying to reconcile the irreconcilable. Schmidt well knew that the Nazis were pathological liars and that only the coldest of calculation could withstand the enormous pressure building up from Berlin. For four years Austria waged a defensive campaign against the most powerful of enemies. Schmidt was convinced that his exceptional brilliance could somehow find a way through such hostile territory. In the end his rearguard action from 1936-8 showed that little Austria managed to resist longer than most expected.

It is hardly surprising therefore that Schmidt made enemies. Starhemberg could accuse him of having isolated Austria but it was not Schmidt who drove Italy into the arms of Germany or made France completely dependent on London for her foreign policy. It was not Schmidt who gave Lord Halifax the confidence to give Hitler "the green light" for the *Anschluss* in November 1937. It was not Schmidt who had persuaded Belgrade, Prague and Budapest that their relationship with Nazi Germany was far more important than any support they could offer for their smaller, beleaguered neighbour. A more likeable or "pliable" figure in charge of Austria's Foreign Policy could not have changed by a jot the reaction of Italy, France and Britain to Austria's absorption by the Nazis. Nothing Schmidt could have done differently could have moved them from their position of studied inactivity on Austria's behalf. When Schmidt finally did (privately) deviate from Schuschnigg's policy and question vigorously Schuschnigg's call for a referendum, he was overruled by his chief. The charge of unduly influencing the Austrian Chancellor was as inappropriate as the charge of high treason. Rather, Schmidt should perhaps be seen as embodying an opposition to Hitler's plans which Austria, alone of any state in Europe, practised with great skill and tenacity during two difficult years.

Monarchists and Legitimists still question whether Schmidt's opposition to a restoration prevented Crown Prince Otto's return to Vienna in early March and thus stifled the emergence of a unifying force which might have led to a general mobilisation of Austrian patriotism capable of checking German military planning. There can be little doubt that a serious Austrian military reaction to any German military incursion, however short-lived, would have had a powerful effect on public opinion throughout Europe. It also would have raised some morale issues for a German military force more than happy to indulge in a *Blumenauftritt* (flower parade) but at that stage untested in battle and probably rather reluctant to fire on their "German brothers." When Schuschnigg had invoked the spirit of Andreas Hofer the great Tyrolean freedom fighter of 1809 in his Innsbruck speech on 9th March, (*Man der ischt Zeit!*) he was clearly not entirely ruling out a defensive armed response.

Certainly, FML Jansa, the chief of the general staff who was a thorn in the Nazis' side and whose pensioning off was one of the concessions Schmidt felt he could offer the Nazis at Berchtesgaden, believed, as we have seen, that armed resistance could have been possible and would have had a decisive effect on world opinion. But by 12th March it was too late. "The mobilisation (of the Austrian army) should have begun the moment Schuschnigg returned from Berchtesgaden (13th February)" he wrote in his memoirs.

As mentioned earlier, writing 23 years after the events of 1938, he insisted that Schuschnigg should have stuck to his line about "Red-White-Red until dead" (*Rot-Weiss-Rot bis in den Tod*). Otherwise the millions of schillings spent on armaments were utterly wasted. "How can one speak about Red-White-Red *bis in den Tod* if one is not prepared to fight?" Jansa questioned[519]

Jansa was especially embittered by Schuschnigg saying to him in 1958 that he did not understand why Jansa had retired. "Something does not make sense about this!" (*Da stimmt doch etwas nicht!*). Jansa believed that Dollfuss would reacted very differently: "he would have mobilised the entire Austrian nation and even if Hitler had still marched into Austria, Austria would have gone down in history with its head held higher than it was through Schuschnigg's professional indecisiveness."[520]

The Austrians, however enriched with Slavic blood, are not Poles or Serbs. Martyrdom is not in their historical narrative. Faced with the choice of war or co-existence with Germany, Polish and Serbian officers chose the former. As one of them explained to a young British officer in Belgrade: "The right course for the Serbs was to stand up to the Germans even if this meant war. Though a military defeat might follow they would have a place

---

519 Broucek, *Jansa*, p. 676.
520 Broucek: *Jansa*, p. 677.

of honour at the conference table. A people's honour was more precious than material possessions and more crucial to their future greatness."[521]

Such a view was unlikely to appeal to Schuschnigg or Schmidt because both men knew the temper of their people well. They understood that Austrians were pragmatic and that Nazism in Austria was not an alien imposition. As even Jansa observed with astonishment when walking down the Mariahilferstrasse the day after the *Einmarsch*: "I saw only happy smiling faces and garlands being erected on the street-lights to greet the Führer who was expected that afternoon. Where now were the convinced Austrians?"[522]

Schuschnigg, however enthusiastic his support in Innsbruck had been a few days earlier quickly realised the implications of any armed response and understandably flinched from the prospect. Reality and responsibility had taken the lead in his thinking. In a letter to Otto von Habsburg in those days, he stated that "to lead one's country into a futile, hopeless war is irresponsible. I know what war is and what civil war means. I know also that it is our utmost duty to save Austria from such situations."[523]

In addition to these rather noble sentiments, there were also practical grounds for not ordering an armed defence of the country. Mobilising the Austrian forces in Salzburg and Upper Austria to resist German incursions would have risked reducing those towns of those two provinces of Austria to rubble and would have certainly resulted in Austrian Nazi uprisings in both Salzburg and Linz, making any Austrian military action chaotic and expensive. Salzburg, the city which the great Prince Archbishops Markus Sitticus, Wolf Dietrich and Paris Lodron had done so much to preserve from the destruction of the Thirty Years War, might even have risked the fate of Warsaw, Rotterdam or Belgrade; it could have been significantly damaged. Moreover, with the first roar of the guns, Austria's neighbours, as Schmidt had long predicted, would have seized the opportunity to annex contiguous territories with their minorities. Yugoslavia would have marched into Carinthia and Hungary would have been tempted to recover Burgenland. These considerations render the idea fanciful that Schmidt

---

521 Bassett, *Last Imperialist*, p. 64.
522 Broucek, *Jansa*, p. 677.
523 Schmidl, *März 1938*, pp. 253–254

somehow thwarted the rescue of Austria by "neutralising" the monarchist overtures to Schuschnigg in February 1938, and "sacked" Jansa at the critical moment of a potential Austrian military response.

Schmidt may not have been a hero in the run-up to the *Anschluss* but his dogged support for his chief, and his brave fight for whatever Austrian sovereignty could be rescued at Berchtesgaden was undoubtedly heroic. However depressed and anxious he was, he never while still in office "fell to pieces," and a certain spiritual strength, combined with his brilliant intellect and ego, kept him going at a time when weaker men would almost certainly have succumbed to the pressure of events and suffered a total breakdown. This was certainly impressive and if the German saying "many enemies much honour" (*Viele Feinde, viel Ehr*) is to be taken seriously, then Schmidt was in every sense an honourable man doing his duty to the very utmost of his ability. The charge of "passive acceptance" of Austria's incorporation into the German orbit levelled at Schmidt and the entire Austrian diplomatic effort in the run-up to the *Anschluss* by some Austrian historians can be easily shown in these pages to be highly speculative if not wildly inaccurate.[524]

It is when we come to Guido Schmidt's post-*Anschluss* behaviour that the more difficult questions arise. They are the same questions that Schuschnigg asked in 1947 in his book *Austrian Requiem*. To repeat them again here: "Dr Schmidt's behaviour after the *Anschluss* was objectively unclear and personally difficult to understand... I am far from excusing behaviour which unfortunately has no plausible explanation. One cannot accept a position as director-general of the Herman Göring Works when one's friends and colleagues are—at best—in prisons and concentration camps. Such action cannot be explained and seems altogether unjustifiable." It is clear from this that Schuschnigg expected the faithful lieutenant who had played the loyal Count Terzky in the Stella production of *Wallenstein's Death* in 1915 to have shared the same fate as his master in real life, not just in Schiller's drama.

Unlike Count Terzky who was murdered with Wallenstein, the younger boy had not faced the trials of the camps or worse which his

---

524 See for example Rathkolb: *The Austrian Foreign Service and the Anschluss* (German Studies Review Vol. 13)

leader and colleagues had endured. Whatever the relevance or not of Schmidt's work to the Nazi war effort, whatever the emptiness of the title *Generaldirektor* at the Hermann Göring Works, it was as if he had accepted promotion in the enemy's camp.

For Schuschnigg, the idea that a man might seek to survive and preserve what he can from a criminal regime appears to have been a base motive, unworthy of a product of the Stella Matutina. In this sense, Schuschnigg was right. Stella Matutina, like every Jesuit institution at that time, prided itself on producing men who, when faced with the choice of their faith or the scaffold, would choose the latter with unhesitating obedience. Rupert Mayer SJ in Munich was just one of several Jesuits who risked that thorny path.[525]

To accept Göring's protection (even if he was behaving like a gentleman); to be paid as a manager in the Göring industrial complex (even if it was in a role remote from armaments); these were judgement "faults" which the Jesuit formation should have been quick to identify during the thrice daily examination of conscience.

Moral courage is a grace not given to everyone. Pride and ambition are more common. Moreover, "highly gifted or fortunate people are sometime truly to be pitied." As a later English Jesuit once commented: "The odd and perverse fact is that it is often harder to have more rather than less entrusted to one. For the more we have the more will be demanded of us. Better in some ways to be a mediocrity: God bless mediocrities everywhere as poor Salieri says at the end of Peter Shaffer's play *Amadeus*."[526]

Schmidt could never have taken refuge in the defence of mediocrity. Thanks to his outstanding gifts of intellect, hard work and energy he was, paradoxically indeed, to be pitied. Difficult enough to have such faculties

---

525 Rupert Mayer SJ had served as an army chaplain in the First World War winning the iron cross for his bravery. Arrested by the Nazis following his public denunciations from the pulpit of their anti-Catholic policies, he was sent to Sachsenhausen concentration camp from where he was liberated by the Americans in 1945. He died a few months later while celebrating mass. His funeral was attended by over twenty-five thousand mourners and he remains a figure of considerable veneration even today in Munich.

526 Anthony Meredith SJ, *Faith and Fidelity* (London, 2002), p. 158.

married to overweening ambition in a time of great crisis between 1936 and 1938 but to have them when their only deployment can be through the vehicles of a criminal regime is an even greater challenge. How many of us, with a fraction of his gifts and faced with such choices, could place a hand on our hearts and say we would have acted differently? How many of us would have been prepared to sacrifice ourselves and our families to martyrdom? In an age when we have become accustomed no longer to expect high moral standards from figures in public life some may find it almost ludicrous that the question is even posed. Yet Schuschnigg was surely correct in imagining that the Stella might have been disappointed that their most dazzling and gifted pupil, having navigated his way so ably through the many formidable challenges he faced during Austria's final agony, had failed to acquit himself with his customary brilliance in the subsequent even greater personal challenge.

Select Bibliography

PRIVATE PAPERS

Amery papers (Julian and Leo) Churchill College Cambridge.

Avon (Eden) papers NA FO 800.

GSN (Guido Schmidt *Nachlass*) Guido Schmidt private papers, Vienna & St Anton.

Halifax NA FO 800/309-28.

Henderson (Sir Nevile) papers NA FO 800/267-71.

Rothschild Papers (RA),

Sir Michael Palairet correspondence with C. B. Hurry, Cambridge University Library, GBR/0012/MS Add. 7619.

Sir Orme Sargent correspondence NA FO 800/272-9.

Sir Walford Selby papers, Oxford, Bodleian Libraries, MS Eng. c. 6587–6589.

Vansittart papers, Churchill College Cambridge.

OFFICIAL PAPERS

Documents on British Foreign Policy 1919-1929, 3rd Series, Volumes I-VII (London, 1949-1961).

Documents on German Foreign Policy 1938-1939, Series D, Volumes I-VII (London, 1949-1964).

Documents diplomatiques français 1936-1939, Serie 2 (Paris, 1963-1986).

DöW (Dokumentionsarchiv des österreichischen Widerstandes) Vienna.

HHStA (Österreichisches Staatsarchiv: Haus- Hof- und Staatsarchiv) Vienna.

SHA (Service Historique de l'Armée de Terre) Vincennes.

HVPGGS: Der Hochverrats Prozess gegen Dr Guido Schmidt vor dem Wiener Volksgericht: Die gerichtlichen Protokolle mit den Zeugenaussagen, unveröffentlichten Dokumenten, sämtlichen Geheimbriefen und Geheimakten (Vienna, 1947) (Proceedings of the trial for high treason of the Vienna People's Court against Dr Guido Schmidt).

DIARIES

Amery, Leo, *The Empire at Bay: The Leo Amery Diaries 1929-1945*, ed. John Barnes and David Nicholson (London, 1988).

Cadogan, Alexander: *The Diaries of Sir Alexander Cadogan*, ed. David Dilks (London, 1971).

Ciano, Galeazzo: *Ciano's Diary 1937-43* (London, 1947).

Hassell, Ulrich von, *The von Hassell Diaries The story of the forces against Hitler inside Germany…*, ed. Hugh Gibson (New York, 1946).

Maisky, Ivan, *The Maisky Diaries: Wartime revelations of Stalin's Ambassador* (London, 2016).

SECONDARY SOURCES

Ardelt, Rudolf G. *Zwischen Demokratie und Faschismus: Deutschnationales Gedankengut in Österreich 1919-30* (Salzburg, 1972).

Bassett, Richard *Hitler's Spy Chief* (London, 2005).

Bassett, Richard *For God and Kaiser* (New Haven: Yale UP, 2015).

Bassett, Richard, *Last Imperialist: A Portrait of Julian Amery* (Settrington:

Stone Trough, 2015).

Beneš, Eduard, *Memoirs of Eduard Beneš* (London, 1954).

Bullock, Alan, *The Ribbentrop Memoirs* (London, 1954).

Bärnthaler, Irmgard, *Die Vaterländische Front: Geschichte und Organisation* (Vienna, 1971).

Barth, Werner, "Germany and the Anschluss", unpublished PhD thesis, University of Texas, Austin, 1954.

Bartz, Karl, *Grossdeutschlands Wiedergeburt: Weltgeschichtliche Stunden an der Donau* (Vienna, 1938).

Bernbaum, John, *The New Elite: Nazi Leadership in Austria 1938-1945* Austrian History Yearbook 1978.

Black, Peter, *Ernst Kaltenbrunner: Ideological soldier of the Third Reich* (Princeton 1984).

Brauntal, Julius, *The Tragedy of Austria* (New York, 1948).

Brooke-Shepherd, Gordon, *The Austrian Odyssey* (London, 1957).

Brooke-Shepherd, Gordon, *The Uncrowned Prince* (London, 2004).

Broucek, Peter (ed.), *Ein General in Zwielicht: Die Erinnerungen Edmund Glaises von Horstenau* Volume 2 (Vienna, 1983).

Broucek, Peter (ed.), *Ein österreichischer General gegen Hitler: Feldmarschalleutnant Alfred Jansa Erinnerungen* (Vienna, 2009).

Chadwick, Owen, *Britain and the Vatican in the Second World War* (Cambridge, 1986).

Charles-Roux, F., *Huit ans au Vatican* (Paris, 1947).

Charmley, J., *Chamberlain and the Lost Peace* (London, 1989).

Colville, J., *The Fringes of Power* (London, 1985).

Colvin, Ian, *Vansittart in Office: The origins of World War II* (London, 1965)

Craster, H. H. (ed.), *Lord Halifax's speeches on Foreign Policy* (New York, 1940).

Danimann, Franz, *War Österreichs Untergang 1938 unvermeidlich?* (Vienna, 1963).

Dilks David (ed.) *Appeasement and Intelligence in Retreat from Power: Studies in British Foreign Policy of the 20th century* Volume I (London, 1981)

Dilks, David (ed.), *The Diaries of Sir Alexander Cadogan O.M. 1938-1945* (London, 1971).

Diakow, J., *Generaloberst Löhr: Ein Lebensbild* (Freiburg im Breisgau, 1964).

Dollinger, Georg, "Ungarns Aussenpolitik 1933-1938 und der Anschluss Österreichs", unpublished PhD thesis, University of Vienna, 1982.

Drax, Reginald Ranfurly Plunkett Ernle-Erle-, *Mission to Moscow* (Wareham, 1966).

Eichstädt, Ulrich, *Von Dollfuss zu Hitler: Geschichte des Anschlusses Österreichs 1933-1938*, Veröffentlichungen des Instituts für Europäische Geschichte, Volume 10 (Wiesbaden, 1955).

Feldman, Gerald D., *Austrian Banking in the Period of National Socialism* (Cambridge, 2015).

Franckenstein, Sir George, *Facts and Features of my Life* (London, 1939).

Franckenstein, Sir George, *Diplomat of Destiny* (London, 1940).

Franckenstein, Sir George, *Zwischen Wien und London* (Graz, 2005).

François-Poncet, André, *Souvenirs d'une Ambassade à Berlin* (Paris, 1946).

Funder, Friedrich, *Als Österreich den Sturm bestand: Aus der ersten in die zweiten Republik* (Vienna, 1957).

Garnet SJ, Henry (with Robert Southwell SJ), *A Treatise on Equivocation 1595* (Cambridge, 2015).

Gaugusch, Georg, *Wer einmal war: das jüdische Grossbürgertum Wien 1800-1938* (2 volumes) (Vienna, 2011 and 2016).

Gawroński, Jan, *Moja misja w Wiedniu* (Warsaw, 1954).

Gedye G.E.R., *Fallen Bastions* (London, 1939).

Gedye G.E.R. *Introducing Austria* (London, 1955)

Gehl, Jürgen, *Austria, Germany and the Anschluss* (Oxford, 1963).

Gromyko, Andrei, *Memories* (London, 1989).

Groscurth, Helmuth, *Tagebücher eines Abwehroffiziers* (Stuttgart, 1970).

Hartlieb, Wladimir von, *Parole: das Reich: Eine historische Darstellung der politischen Entwicklung in Österreich von März 1933 bis März 1938.* (Vienna, 1939).

Hayter, William, *A Double Life* (London, 1974).

Henderson, Nevile, *Failure of a Mission* (London, 1940).

Hobsbawn, Eric, *Interesting Times* (London, 2002).

Hochmann, Erin, *Imagining a Greater Germany* (Cornell, 2016).

Hull, Cordell, *The Memoirs of Cordell Hull* (London, 1948).

Irving, David, *Göring: a biography* (London, 1986).

Jedlicka, Ludwig, *Vom alten zum neuen Österreich: Fallstudien zur österreichischen Zeitgeschichte 1900-1975* (St Pölten, 1975).

Kelly, David, *The Ruling Few* (London, 1952).

Kirkpatrick, Ivone, *The Inner Circle* (London, 1959).

Kreissler, F. (ed.), *Fünfzig Jahre danach: Der "Anschluss" von Innen und Aussen gesehen* (Vienna, 1985).

Lamb, Richard, *Mussolini and the British* (London, 1997).

Lamb, Richard, *The Drift to War* (London, 1989).

Lassner, Alexander, "Peace at Hitler's Price: Austria, the Great Powers and the Anschluss 1932-1938" unpublished PhD thesis, Ohio State University, 2001.

Löwenthal, Max, *Doppeladler und Hakenkreuz: Erlebnisse eines österreichischen Diplomaten* (Vienna, 1985).

Maisky, Ivan, *Who helped Hitler?* (London, 1964).

Maisky, Ivan, *Memoirs of a Soviet Ambassador* (London, 1967).

Meredith SJ, Anthony, *Faith and Fidelity* (London, 2002).

Namier, Lewis, *Diplomatic Prelude* (London, 1949).

Namier, Lewis, *Europe in Decay: A Study in Disintegration* (London, 1950).

Namier, Lewis, *In the Nazi Era* (London, 1952).

Nevile, Peter, *Appeasing Hitler* (Basingstoke, 2000).

Oliphant, Lancelot, *Ambassador in Chains* (London, 1944).

O'Malley, O., *The Phantom Caravan* (London, 1954).

Pribram, A. F., *Austria-Hungary and Great Britain 1908-1914* (Oxford, 1951).

Puaux, Gabriel, *Mort et transfiguration de l'Autriche* (Paris: Plon, 1966).

Rathkolb Oliver: *The Austrian Foreign Service and the Anschluss 1938* (German Studies Review 1990).

Roberts, Frank, *Dealing with Dictators: The Destruction and the Revival of Europe* (London, 1991).

Rosar, Wolfgang, *Deutsche Gemeinschaft: Seyss-Inquart und der Anschluss* (Vienna, 1971).

Schmidl, Erwin, *März 1938: Der deutsche Einmarsch in Österreich* (Vienna, 1987).

Schmidt, Paul, *Statist auf Diplomatischer Bühne 1923-1945* (Bonn, 1949).

Schuschnigg, Kurt von, *Austrian Requiem* (London, 1947).

Schuschnigg, Kurt von, *Im Kampf gegen Hitler: Die Überwindung der Anschlussidee* (Vienna, 1969).

Selby, Walford, *Diplomatic Twilight* (London, 1953).

Sheridan, R.K., *Kurt von Schuschnigg* (London, 1942).

Spitzy, Reinhard, *So haben wir das Reich verspielt* (Munich, 1986). *How we squandered the Reich* (Norwich 1997).

Starhemberg, Ernst Rüdiger, *Between Hitler and Mussolini* (London, 1942).

Strang, William, *The Foreign Office* (London, 1955).

Strang, William, *Home and Abroad* (London, 1956).

Strang, William, *Britain in World Affairs* (London, 1961).

Vansittart, Robert, *Lessons of my Life* (London, 1943).

Vansittart, Robert, *The Mist Procession* (London, 1958).

Weinzierl, Erika, Österreich 1918-1938 Geschichte der Ersten Republik (Graz, 1983).

Wheeler-Bennett, John, *The Nemesis of Power* (London, 1964).

Zernatto, Guido, *Die Wahrheit über Österreich* (New York, 1938).

Index